THE OTHER GENERATION GAP

THE
OTHER
GENERATION GAP

*The Middle-aged
and Their Aging
Parents*

by Dr. Stephen Z. Cohen
and Bruce Michael Gans

Dodd, Mead & Company
New York

Copyright © 1978, 1988 by Stephen Z. Cohen and Bruce Michael Gans

A GAMUT BOOK

1 2 3 4 5 6 7 8 9 10

Library of Congress Cataloging-in-Publication Data

Cohen, Stephen Z.

The other generation gap: the middle-aged and their aging parents/
by Stephen Z. Cohen and Bruce Michael Gans.
    p.   cm.
Includes index.

1. Parents, Aged—Care—United States.   2. Middle age—United
States.   3. Parents, Aged—United States—Family relationships.
4. Adult children—United States.   I. Gans, Bruce Michael, 1951–.
II. Title.
HQ1063.6.C63   1988
306.8'74—dc19   87-36592
ISBN 0-396-09246-2 (pbk.)

For
Hi and Celia Cohen
(of Blessed Memory)
and
Benjamin and Dorothy Gans

Acknowledgments

We wish to express our gratitude to a number of people who have helped us in the preparation of this book.

Elaine Goldberg of Follett Publishing Company guided us throughout and made important contributions in all aspects of our work.

Bob Cunningham provided significant editorial revisions.

Helen Harris Perlman and Florence Goldwasser read the initial manuscript and offered valuable observations and advice.

The clients and staff of the Council for Jewish Elderly, Chicago, Illinois; the Drexel Home for the Aged; and agencies of the Illinois Department of Mental Health, through their day-to-day life and work experience, gave us innumerable insights and understandings in developing materials and illustrations.

To all of them, we offer our sincere thanks.

Stephen Z. Cohen
Bruce Michael Gans

Contents

THE OTHER GENERATION GAP

I

The Overlooked Relationship

1

Do You Think Your Situation Is Unique?

We want to say plainly at the start that our first concern is for a beleaguered, overlooked group—the middle-aged men and women for whom this book was written. You are the first generation in history to confront a situation that exists in our society on a scale unknown to other cultures. We are referring to a special sort of "population explosion"—the large numbers of Americans who survive today into their seventies and eighties and beyond. Our society has barely begun to cope with the physical, emotional, financial, and social problems these elderly people present. Furthermore, the traditional definitions of an adult's responsibilities toward an aging parent are now largely outmoded or inadequate.

And so, for perhaps the third time in twenty-five years, middle-aged people are called upon to create a new, fresh set of personal standards and ways of dealing with members of their families.

The first experience many of you had in coping with this bewildering and often painful position came about when you were young mothers and fathers. Yours was the generation that pioneered the modern approach to parenthood. You were the first parents with the courage and the determination to reject traditional formulas. Instead you were guided by the theories of early childhood development proposed by Sigmund Freud, and you sought advice from such authorities on child rearing as Dr. Benjamin Spock. As a result you learned and came to grips with an entirely new way of interpreting your children's needs and shaping their characters.

For some of you, your children were members of the post–World War II baby boom and reached adolescence in the late 1960s and early 1970s. Adolescence is normally a time of rebellion against authority, and guiding a son or daughter through that stage of life is usually an exasperating responsibility.

It is in the nature of adolescents to question and challenge many of the values and the conduct which their parents subscribe to. Often, the challenge is drawn along sexual, political, and moral lines. Parents of adolescents often have to cope with children who experiment with drugs, premarital sex, radical political activity, and outrageous dress. The difficulties facing parents of children going through such stages has, of course, been described as *the generation gap.*

In response to this turmoil between the generations, books and movies appeared that attempted to explain to adults the attitudes and the conflicts of the younger generation. One of the purposes of these publications and films was to assist parents to achieve a broader understanding of their children. This material may not have provided answers to specific questions, but it probably did help you as parents to feel that, if your child behaved in ways that confused and distressed you, he or she was not necessarily deranged or even abnormal.

You may not have found at the time solutions for all your problems. But you probably benefited from the discovery that you were not alone. You often found that the burdens placed upon you by your sons and daughters lessened if you were able to achieve an enlightened, well-informed perspective. This, then, represented a second adjustment on family matters. Thus middle-aged men and women probably have more practice in and more skills at dealing with family relationships than they realize.

This experience may stand you in good stead as you begin to face the *other* generation gap—the one that has arisen between many adult children and their aging parents. The specific set of problems related to this new generation gap is in many ways quite different from the demands and difficulties your children posed just a few years ago. Let's take up a typical situation.

Marcia Pratt wished her eighty-two-year-old father-in-law, Max, the best of health. She knew how difficult it had been for him to get out of his house ever since he broke his hip. But her husband, Ken, could not bring himself to say no to his father's demands for company and attention.

After the last of Marcia's children left for college, she had looked forward to a kind of second honeymoon. She and her husband would now be free to take the vacations they had always postponed, free to enjoy more time with their friends, and free, most of all, to spend quiet evenings alone together.

Instead Marcia found that at every turn her father-in-law's needs were ruining her longed-for new start in life. Three evenings a week Ken had to skip dinner at home in order to drive across town to prepare his father's supper. Every other Saturday evening Marcia found herself at her father-in-law's house, listening to him reminisce about his old job, which bored her, and complain about his infirmities, which seemed endless. Even the small but precious pleasure of a full night's sleep or of an extra couple of hours' rest on a Sunday morning was denied her. Her father-in-law had begun to make a series of late-night and early-morning phone calls about his physical difficulties, which invariably turned out in the end to be nothing at all.

Ken did not enjoy his new responsibilities. His own plans for the future had been identical with Marcia's and had certainly not included this unexpected round of activities. What was worse, his father was a querulous, critical old man who never seemed satisfied with Ken's efforts on his behalf. Although the two had never been particularly close, it pained Ken to see Max confronted with so many problems. Suspecting that the old man would not be around much longer, Ken wanted to do all he could to make his father's last years (or months) of life as comfortable as possible.

On the other hand, the emotional strain of attending to his father was becoming intolerable. Ken knew that Max had not intentionally set out to rob him of the pleasures to which he was entitled now that he was in the prime of life. But he found himself wishing that the whole responsibility would just go away, even if it meant the old man's quick, painless death. Quite naturally, that last thought made Ken feel guilty and uncomfortable. He wanted to be a sensitive, dutiful son. But he did not see how, for example, he could possibly listen again to the same old stories about his father's successes as a real estate agent. The late-night phone calls and the trips across town to Max's house left Ken in a continuous state of irritability and exhaustion.

Worse still, Ken realized that the situation was beginning to hurt his marriage. He was bringing a great deal of his frustration and bitterness home to his wife. At first Marcia had been a paragon of understanding and empathy. But gradually she became frustrated and dissatisfied with the arrangement and made no bones about saying so. She no longer had the patience to listen to Ken's complaints. The result was that Ken felt caught in the middle. Was it his fault that there didn't seem to be anyone else to care for his father? His brother and sister lived in different parts of the country. Did Marcia really expect him to place his father in a nursing home just so the two of them could enjoy Sunday brunches with their friends? Wasn't she being a bit cruel and insensitive to the pain, guilt, and responsibility he had to shoulder? Sure it made him angry and resentful that he could never seem to do enough to please his father. Of course the old man's attitude made him furious and miserable. But wasn't Ken obligated as a son to do all he could for his parent?

Marcia's answer was that she did not feel her husband's conflicts. After all, Max wasn't her father. If the roles were reversed, would she have expected him to feel any different than she? Besides, it surely was not unreasonable, selfish, or unhealthy for her to want her husband to spend more time at home than with a manipulative, grasping old man.

The position the Pratts found themselves in is not a universal one. There are some families who have had few, if any, difficulties with their own teenagers. So, too, are there middle-aged adults whose parents will not cause them any of the wide range of problems that often accompany old age.

To become a senior citizen does not automatically mean a life of sickness and dependency or a time of physical and emotional deterioration unrelieved by any pleasures or gratifications. Thanks to improved medical care and a higher standard of living, people in the United States today live longer and better than in the past. For example, the average life expectancy for Americans, which was forty-seven years in 1900, had risen to over seventy-four years by 1987. As the life expectancy has increased in the United States, professionals in the field of gerontology have found it useful to divide the elderly into two groups: the "young-old," or those from fifty-five years of age to seventy-five; and the "old-old," or those over seventy-five years of age. As you might suspect, most of the problems with aging parents are found among the "old-old" group.

Like the Pratts, more and more middle-aged people find them-selves quite unprepared for the real—and often destructive—feelings of anxiety, confusion, and guilt that they experience because of their parents' difficulties.

Much of this anguish can be alleviated, for during the past ten years a tremendous amount of research and study has been conducted about the process and problems of aging. As a result a fresh understanding of the subject has developed as well as a general set of approaches for coping more effectively with the problems that arise from the aging process.

As was true with the generation gap between parents and adolescents, there are no absolute answers or perfect solutions to the problems related to the generation gap between middle-aged children and their parents. But an enlightened perspective can be achieved, and a number of guidelines exist to help you effectively lessen the burden you may currently feel and to anticipate new problems that may emerge.

Both groups involved in the new generation gap, the elderly parents and their children, are in critical stages of their lives. Both have special and very different physical and emotional needs that are important and must be met.

We are attempting here to offer sons and daughters some assistance in protecting their own well-being from the demands, feelings of guilt, and other pressures that may arise as a result of this situation. The problems of an adult child-parent relationship can have many dimensions. Each of you exists in quite separate biological, economic, and emotional worlds. Conflicts come about for many reasons, and all too often solutions—even partial solutions—seem beyond your grasp. People on each side of the generation gap misunderstand the basis of the behavior and views of the other party; all too often they may not fully understand their own inner needs and feelings.

For example, perhaps your mother has become so involved with her physical infirmities that she refuses to leave the house for any reason. She may have exaggerated her physical limitations to the point that she has lost contact with many of her friends. In her boredom and loneliness she may begin to rely upon you as her only social outlet.

Or perhaps your father, who has always been a self-sufficient, independent soul, has gradually lost the ability to handle the house-cleaning and assorted chores of single life after your mother's death. He may now need assistance and yet angrily refuse to let you lift even a finger to help him out.

One of the reasons many of us find it hard to deal adequately with such parents is that we may feel that our problem is peculiar or unique. Often, however, our parents are simply struggling through a stage of human development that presents a set of relatively normal, predictable, and understandable difficulties.

Many of us have no clear, objective notion of the universal forces at work during old age. We rely a great deal on the informal advice of a friend, neighbor, or coworker who may have recently faced a similar situation. But there are real drawbacks to basing important family decisions on the casual advice of someone we know. Let's consider for a moment the case of a woman for whom such advice, innocently offered in all good faith, was not well suited at all.

> Carolyn Marcus was concerned about her father, who lived alone in an old neighborhood—a place that was now run-down and infested with street crime. She shared her anxieties one day with a next-door neighbor who told her that, since his father had taken care of him while he was growing up, he had been pleased to invite his aging dad to take up permanent residence with him in his home.
>
> Carolyn's father, however, had always been a distant, irascible man. She had neither a spare bedroom in her home nor a genuine desire to deal with him on a daily basis.
>
> After talking with her neighbor—who had acted in such a generous, admirable fashion—she began to feel guilty.
>
> She was torn between what she supposedly "ought" to do and what she felt she could do for her father.

In this instance Carolyn's neighbor did what was appropriate and comfortable for himself and his family. His advice came out of the context of an upbringing and general orientation quite different from Carolyn's. Small wonder that his solution—if Carolyn had followed it—would have been a disaster for her and her father.

If Carolyn had been concerned about the right time to wean her infant daughter, she would not have considered her neighbor's advice as the last word—or even an authoritative word—on the subject. But she did take seriously his advice about her father's difficulties because she knew no other authority to consult.

One of the main purposes of this book is to pull together, from a wide range of sources, materials and insights that will equip a middle-aged son or daughter to view a parent's physical, emotional, and social needs within the larger context of aging.

In a sense we have attempted to approach the problems of our parents' old age in much the same way that you once did the needs of your newborn child. Most of us referred to Dr. Benjamin Spock's *Baby and Child Care.* As with your infant, you should try to assimilate a general body of knowledge that will enable you to comprehend the needs of older people who cannot describe or articulate them for themselves.

Some kinds of background information have equipped you to anticipate your child's behavior. Your elderly parent, like your child, is a unique and individual human being. Nonetheless, he or she is a participant in the cycle of life—the process of growth—which you should be able to interpret and comprehend.

In this book we have sought to present psychological, medical, and sociological findings in a fashion that should prove useful to you in several ways. Some of the physical and emotional changes the elderly encounter, such as the loss of hearing or the shrinking of their circle of friends through deaths, can be distressing and frightening to them. As a result an aged parent's responses to such problems may appear mystifying and disturbing to you.

Old age often brings about a change in a person's life-style and preferences. It is a transition period analogous to the period of changes we go through between young adulthood and middle age. An elderly father, for example, may restrict his activities and begin to center his life for the first time around his immediate neighborhood. He may tell you quite frankly that now the most important person in his life is his physician.

The current generation of elderly people matured in a different era and share an ethos different from your own. Your father, for example, may insist upon eating at the most inexpensive restaurants whenever you invite him out for dinner. He may refuse to apply for first-rate senior citizen public housing to which he is entitled solely because he has "never taken a handout" in his life.

As you become familiar with the basic information on aging now available, you should be better equipped to reduce not only your own distress over a parent's problems but also the distress he or she may be experiencing. You may become better able to help him or her cope with and make up for his or her losses. In addition, the behavior of a parent may become less aggravating or seem less peculiar. All topics will be discussed within the context of the reactions and misinterpretations middle-aged people frequently make. This, we hope, will assist you in your efforts to prolong your parents' independent functioning and to strike an appropriate balance between your parents' needs and your own responsibilities toward them.

Many, if not most, people approach the problem of their responsibilities toward their parents by creating an ethical quandary for themselves. They do this, not always on a conscious level, by viewing every real or potential new responsibility in terms of the question, "How much do I owe my parents?"

It is a perfectly natural reflex. After all, a part of us feels, like Carolyn's neighbor, that our parents responded to our needs when we were young and dependent. So we feel that we should "act in kind" now that a parent has become old and dependent.

If life were a clear-cut affair, perhaps it would be possible to provide moral answers in mathematical terms. An expert in this area might be able to decide that you ought to devote an eighth or a third or a half of your time and energies to your mother, for example. The expert might even break the time down further, prescribing a phone call a day, two visits a month, and six Saturdays a year to be devoted to running errands for a mother who cannot do them herself.

The simple truth, however, is that there are no moral answers to these problems. It is a terrible mistake to think only in such terms. The overall answers you must struggle to find for yourself have to reflect a balance between the needs of your parents for care and attention and your own needs for living your life with minimal guilt and maximum peace of mind.

One aim of this work is to provide you with an overall philosophy or frame of reference for coping. Once you comprehend such a philosophy, you will be free to arrive at balanced decisions and pursue the alternatives that are the least painful or harmful for all concerned.

The emotional, physical, and social needs of elderly people exist quite apart from the fact that they happen to be someone's father or mother. As you begin to understand those needs and your own needs with greater objectivity, the moral stumbling block mentioned earlier should become manageable.

There is a fundamental difference between taking it upon yourself to solve a mother's or father's difficulties, no matter how unwillingly, and identifying their problems in order to explore the resources that might provide an adequate solution.

It may surprise some sons and daughters to hear that they are by no means the only ones—or, for that matter, the best ones—to become intimately involved with a parent's daily welfare. Often a parent will benefit *most* from any one of a wide number of substitutes that will be discussed at some length in this book.

In a sense a daughter who is willing to sacrifice her marriage, her relationship with her children, and her own emotional well-being for her elderly parent is no "better" than a son who refuses to become the least bit concerned about or involved with a mother who is overwhelmed by physical infirmities.

The most effective and responsible approach toward a parent comes about as certain key concepts become almost second nature to us. This is an essential step toward cultivating a conceptual framework within which most of the specific problems of aging you may run up against can be accurately assessed and dealt with.

The information presented in this book will help you accomplish that goal. There is no *one* way to resolve complex, personal situations. On the contrary, there is a great need to be flexible and to rely on resources that can supplement your efforts to achieve flexibility.

Unfortunately, many children of aging parents are faced with decisions that must be made on a day-to-day basis. "Would my father be better off if I moved him into a new home or into some kind of protected environment?" "Should I consult a physician about my mother's forgetfulness?" "Should I, or should I not, invest more time in my parents' welfare right now?"

The best way to find such answers is to become sufficiently at home with the overall concepts of aging so that the solutions most suitable for your situation begin to suggest themselves.

This approach is much like the ones psychiatrists take. They may have a patient who presents them with a sexual fantasy they have never encountered either in their private practice or during their training. Yet this does not mean that the therapists are unable to interpret their client's conflict or offer any assistance for it. Because psychiatrists have mastered the basic underlying concepts of human behavior, they are able to see the fantasy within a larger context and can, therefore, make an accurate assessment of its meaning.

In the chapters that follow, problems will be examined in an overall manner in order to achieve the widest possible perspective. Extended discussions will include illustrations that tell you how to apply basic principles in a fruitful way to the solution of specific problems—problems that are the most representative and common ones you might encounter.

Rules of thumb and guidelines appear several times in different contexts. This is not only unavoidable but important. The experience of repetition here can hopefully spare you the back-to-step-one syndrome when you have to meet real-life situations.

The general aims of this book are:

- to provide useful information on relevant topics for middle-aged people trying to cope with the most frequent physical, psychological, and social difficulties of their aging parents.
- to gather the guidelines, resources, and techniques amassed by professionals in the fields of medicine, psychology, sociology, social work, and geriatrics and to present these materials from a middle-aged person's point of view in a straightforward, understandable manner.
- to provide an understanding of the dynamics of aging and thus help our readers strike a better balance between their own needs and those of their parents. (In this connection we wish to help you prolong your parents' independent functioning and postpone the time when they become a burden to themselves, you, and our whole society.)
- to give, in an indirect fashion, to middle-aged readers a general understanding of aging so as to help them to plan for, and cope with, their own eventual old age.

In the past, elderly people doubtless did not receive their fair share of study and attention. Professionals have now reacted to their plight and are beginning to focus on the problems of old age. Just as the problems of the youth of our country were examined at the expense of their parents in the recent past, we once again discover that you—the middle-aged parents—are again being overlooked.

The plight of old people has not been shortchanged in this book. Their physical decline, social losses, and waning ability to function independently are dealt with in depth. In addition, the hazards of nursing homes are discussed, and a model social service program for the elderly is described.

As previously stated, there are sound reasons that the emergence of a parent's dependence may often be particularly hard and even destructive to a middle-aged son or daughter. It was stated at the outset that the needs of each generation are of equal importance. To emphasize this, the following chapter is primarily concerned with the physical, psychological, and social problems of middle age.

2

Why Are New Responsibilities Hazardous to Your Health?

Psychology has probably found nowhere else in the world so congenial a home as the United States. No other society has been so receptive to the explanations that the psychologists offer for the forces that shape our emotional needs, intimate relationships, and general conduct. We Americans have even used psychological principles, in some almost indiscernible ways, as a basis for our personal values.

One aspect of the psychoanalytic approach to life has had a tremendous impact on the way many of us have come to view ourselves as well as our family responsibilities. We are referring to the notion that our development during roughly the first five years of life determines the level of our emotional well-being once and for all. While you may not think so at first glance, this belief says a great deal about adulthood. It implies that for all of us there are no profound stages of human growth comparable to those we experience in infancy after our own adolescence is behind us. One result of this concept has been to heighten the demands we place upon ourselves to be the right kinds of parents. Surely a big reason for the intense scrutiny and concern we devote to our children during their childhood comes from a dark awareness that mistakes we make may have disastrous, even indelible, consequences for them in later life. Raising a family has always been a wearing responsibility. But as far as we know, this task has never taken on such dimensions in other societies that any of them could be labeled, as ours has been, child-centered.

15

Recently, however, the original scope of psychological thought on child rearing has been expanded and refined. In this connection the psychologist who may have done the most to expand our collective awareness and change our way of thinking was Erik Erikson. His contribution was to identify eight broad stages of personal development. He believed that as we near each stage, we must resolve a series of questions about ourselves. Erikson called each stage a crisis because the answers we must bring to these questions may lead us in vastly different directions. Each such experience or stage of growth can amount to an opportunity that results in a greater feeling of personal satisfaction, growth, and success.

Of course few, if any, of us resolve each of these eight stages in a totally happy way. But the degree to which we *do* resolve them shapes, for better or for worse, our ability to meet day-to-day problems as well as our approach to the next stage, or crisis. Although most of these crucial periods occur in childhood, they extend throughout our lifetime. In other words, we are all in an ongoing process of personal development. Our personalities are not fixed in stone before we encounter the world as adults. On the contrary, our vulnerabilities and frailties must be protected from unreasonable assaults as long as we live.

New responsibilities that you assume for an aging parent pose real and medically certified hazards to your health. Generally our culture underestimates the seriousness of the physical and emotional changes that overtake middle-aged people. As a result many of us are largely in the dark about the nature of the mid-life crisis we are undergoing. Unfortunately, this same lack of awareness is one main reason that so many of us are unequipped and unprepared to set appropriate limits to our involvement with an elderly parent. Nor do we understand how our particular conflict over the prospect of unexpected additional responsibilities is really only a single instance of a general problem of our society. This contributes to the creation of situations such as the one involving Marcia Pratt and her father-in-law that we examined in the opening chapter (pp. 4–6). Such problems are not only unnecessary but also unhealthy and destructive for each person involved.

One of the typical binds that adult sons and daughters find themselves in is the feeling of being "caught in the middle." A man in his late forties may find life with his teenage daughter a never-ending source of frustration. On the one hand, the girl is probably terribly troubled and in need of guidance and support. On the other, she may spend hours brooding in her room, or she may stay out somewhere at night with questionable companions. When she finally returns home, she may act visibly pained just to be in the presence of her family. She may treat every sentence addressed to her as idiotic, insulting, or vicious. However exasperated a father may become at such behavior, he will probably make an effort to temper his feelings because he knows his daughter is passing through what Erikson termed the fifth stage of human development—the identity crisis.

This middle-aged man may also find himself confronted with the problems and demands of his aged father. The elderly gentleman may have always been prudent about his health. But now he has become so worried that he never sets foot outside his home. He sees none of his old friends, and he has started to depend on his son for a sympathetic ear as well as for his social life.

Such a middle-aged man may conclude that the needs of his daughter in the younger generation and of his father in the older generation take precedence over his own needs. After all, isn't he the only individual competent enough to provide for each of them? Since he is supposed to be in the prime of life, isn't this a foregone conclusion? On what grounds can he reasonably refuse to help?

Frankly, though, the man's own emotional needs are struggling to assert themselves. This comes out in the form of an insistent question that keeps running through his mind—"What about me?"

That question would present itself forcefully whether or not we had a closetful of obligations. The mid-life crisis is not unlike the identity crisis of adolescence—one just as overwhelming and demanding. The question "What about me?" is an inescapable one. It is downright critical that we come up with some answers to it.

Why is this so? Many of us who are entering middle age have devoted the past few decades of our lives to the struggles we committed ourselves to upon marriage. Since we decided then what kinds of people we wanted to become and the things we wanted out of life, we have been about the arduous business of trying to achieve our goals.

For women this usually has meant trying to cope with the responsibilities of raising children and running a warm and efficient household. For men it most likely has meant earning a living at a job for which they felt themselves relatively suited. It involved establishing themselves socially, seeking advancement, and attaining recognition from associates in their professional circles.

Needless to say, our personal responsibilities have been considerable. The commitment to raise children required self-denial, which at times seemed grueling and endless. To build a successful marriage meant learning to adjust and sacrifice. The pressure of earning a living and supporting a family—either by starting a business or by working our way up the ladder of a company or institution—was no less nagging a burden. All this was undertaken without any guarantee that such investments of time and effort would turn out for the best. Often we had little choice but to live by trial and error, by grit and blind faith.

Above all, it meant that most of us conducted twenty or more years of our lives according to one of our society's first rules. That is, we postponed opportunities to indulge and fulfill our immediate pleasures. We could not, for example, buy the splendid modern furniture we wanted for our home because the children would have destroyed it. The money, we knew, would best be put aside for the children's college education. The extravagant and extended vacation, the sports car, and similar "flings" were all put off for the same reason.

Such gratifications had to be postponed indefinitely. Every parent knows that such a rule is utterly intolerable to young children, even though their emotional growth in some measure depends upon their ability to master it. Frankly, this rule asks a great deal of mature adults as well. To. live under constraints without feeling steady frustration is a quality that distinguishes the relatively happy from the discontented of this world.

But the future most of us have been working toward was not an indefinite one at all. The crisis of our middle age stems from many sources, all of which convey a strong message: *The future has now arrived.*

It does so in a number of ways. One of the first is a growing awareness of our own mortality. For the first time we begin to confront the inevitability of death. It may be thirty years away, but it no longer seems remote. It has now come unquestionably into sight. As one man put it, "One of the changes I've noticed over the years is the premature deaths of people I've been associated with. It's something younger people never give a thought to."

We also begin to notice physical changes within us. Our

once-young figure and good looks have faded. The sheer energy and stamina that could always be called upon at will have now gone the way of the United States's limitless supply of inexpensive fuel. We find we cannot work as long or play as hard as we once did. Reading glasses may have suddenly become necessary. Lower-back pain may have made its first appearance. Men may find that their sex drive has diminished, and women experience menopause. All these things inform us that we are not what we once were. Our bodies have declined, and we sense that we have begun to grow old. This change compels us to develop a new perspective on our lives and personal priorities. It has become unrealistic to live under the comfortable impression that our good health and our days on earth will continue forever. As Professor Bernice Neugarten of the University of Chicago notes, we stop seeing our lives in terms of "time-since-birth." Instead, for the first time, we base our plans for the future on "time-left-to-live."

We are called upon to cope with the loss of a precious illusion that we have had all our lives. To be sure, the awareness of death plays a considerably different role in your existence than it does in an elderly parent's. Even so, we should try to grasp it squarely within the separate contexts and different sets of problems that must be confronted in each stage of life. The significance it has for your own life has not been diminished by comparison with the significance it also has for your parent's life. It is the awareness of our own mortality that brings an urgency into our lives.

Painful as this sense of our future death is, attempting to deny it would amount to a dangerous self-deception. The sense of urgency serves several purposes for us. It inspires us to take stock of ourselves, it becomes a tool and a spur for greater self-understanding and maturity, it adds zest to our immediate circumstances, and it is the first step in the slow, gradual preparation we must make in the emotional adjustment to our own inevitable old age.

Middle age is the first time in our lives when we are in a position to evaluate comprehensively and critically who we have become and what our lives have turned out to be. At this stage it is natural to ask ourselves if our lives have been meaningful, if we have accomplished most of our goals, and if our closest relationships have been honest and rewarding.

A middle-aged husband and wife are no longer the young initiates of a community, who are working to raise a family and secure a place for themselves. They have become fully settled and established members. They have probably never had a wider range of friends, acquaintances, and contacts. They probably never will have such extensive contacts again. They are as accepted and well-thought-of as they are ever likely to be.

By this time a man has risen about as high as he is ever going to in his job. He is at the height of his authority and responsibility. His business or employment situation is about as prosperous as it will ever be. His earning capacity, for better or worse, is at its peak. Thus he has become as established, recognized, and esteemed as he can expect to be. He can reasonably assess how near he has come to the prestige and power he wanted as well as determine whether his present position has been worth the effort. Men ten or twenty years younger may still switch jobs—even their line of work—with relative ease. But this may well be the last time in his life a middle-aged man can do so.

A major change also is occurring within the home. Most, if not all, the children have grown up, left the house, and become more or less self-supporting. The direct, ongoing demands and responsibilities the children imposed have been lifted. The struggle to be proper parents and the difficulties adolescents imposed are now over. The energy and attention the children absorbed can now be freely devoted to other activities and people, one's spouse in particular, for now there is peace and quiet in the house.

A husband and wife can see the kind of job they have done in life as well as the kinds of people their offspring have turned out to be. The couple is now alone together for the first time in perhaps twenty-five years. At this time the quality of the relationship becomes quite clear and open to examination.

Then too, the major financial burdens children represented have been lifted, presumably at a time when a man's income is at its peak. There may no longer be any need to scrimp or budget. Now there is money to remodel the house, to indulge in a fresh wardrobe, to travel. All the struggles, risks, constraints, and sacrifices can be laid aside. The time has finally come to focus on the outcome, the payoff, and the rewards for past labor. A period of freedom and self-indulgence has finally arrived. Although some of us may secretly suspect that these impulses are wrong because they are selfish, the truth is that for us now *it is self-denial that can do the most physical and emotional harm.*

Ideally, middle age is a period when we cash in on the

investments we have made in our vocation, marriage, and family. It is a time to relax and enjoy our dividends. Of course things do not turn out so fortunately for all of us—perhaps not for most of us. As we grope to come to terms with our lives, we generally find ourselves in one of two situations. The question "What about me?" is usually seen in terms of whether we feel we have succeeded or failed. If the reply is a happy one, it is crucial to have the opportunity to savor the triumph. If it is a disturbing one, middle age becomes our last, often desperate, chance to make up for lost time.

Let's consider first those who feel that they have made it. They may realize they have lost the vigor and physical beauty of their youth. But they are able to look instead at the wisdom they have garnered over the years. Thus they may feel that the tradeoff has hardly been a lamentable one. As one corporate executive put it, "Sure, I'd like to look as trim as I did in my twenties. But I sure as hell wouldn't want to be that age again. You just can't put a price on the autonomy or the authority I've acquired or the self-confidence and the ease I feel in my relationships. That only comes from experience."

Along with this feeling comes the belief that we know how to handle ourselves well in almost every situation. Instead of feeling driven by our obligations, we are now in charge. The world has become a familiar place in which we can play a competent role. As a cosmetics saleswoman said, "I understand why they characterize middle age as the command generation. We don't operate in a trial-and-error fashion the way kids do. We're generally self-reliant and independent. And it's rewarding and exciting to find that we see things in people and books that no one younger can really perceive or appreciate."

The job is another area of satisfaction. As a banker explained, "I'm not as young as I used to be, but I still get much more done than the young hotshots around here. I know how to insulate myself from the people who annoy and furstrate me. I know how to cut through the red tape and make the best use of my time. I know what decisions I had better make myself and when I ought to delegate my authority. I have the edge over these young guys because I know how to make my institution work for me. All of that, naturally, can only come through time and experience."

We may also find that we have begun to receive the deference and respect that goes along with our position. We are consulted when important decisions are made. Our advice, support, and approval are sought by our younger colleagues.

And so a man's personal time and energies take on a new meaning. They become more precious to him and more his own. He no longer has to push himself as hard because he is financially secure enough to purchase most of the material comforts he desires. And he knows how to manage his time in the most fruitful way. Often he faces a turning point—he can either expand his interests and activities, or he can stagnate. To grow, he has to redirect his energies. This may mean spending more time at home with his wife or turning to his community—to politics, art, sports, literature, or other hobbies.

Many of us have been forced to give up what we wanted to do because the things we *had* to do demanded the best part of our time and energy. Over the course of the long struggle, we may have forgotten that life can be structured in any other way. But we must recognize middle age as a fresh stage of life. The scope of our responsibilities narrows and changes, with the resultant need to cultivate and rediscover interests that are more personal and self-centered. New outlets must be found to provide as much gratification as did those that are no longer available. The wear and tear our body has endured must be respected. The practice at readjustment is indispensable, since it is a skill that we will use again to confront the next stage of our life—old age. The new hobbies and activities we acquire now will help make our sixties and seventies richer and more purposeful.

Perhaps the need to be flexible appears more clearly to middle-aged women than to men. After the children leave home, their life's work has begun to draw to a close. Their husbands will not have to face this problem squarely until retirement. A middle-aged woman may take great pride and satisfaction in a job well done. It may be a relief to have most of her past responsibilities off her hands. But she also has feelings of emptiness and a loss of identity and usually must begin to look around for other activities. If she is fortunate, she may be able to bring her feelings of competence and accomplishment to a new career. Unfortunately, some of the most successful women arouse their husbands' jealousy. As one architect put it, "My wife went back to school, got a doctorate in English, and now is teaching at a large community college. It has opened up a whole new world for her. The only thing I have to look forward to is putting up a new building, then another, and then another."

Often people discover that middle age is like a second honeymoon. Their marriage has become something sturdy and long-lasting. The private, shared history of burdens and successes may stimulate a renewed intimacy and sexual ardor between spouses. One woman described her situation in these words: "We're together constantly now, and I honestly believe we've never been happier. I don't worry about what the job is doing to him any more."

Another set of middle-aged adults, however, does not feel that they have accomplished all they were aiming for. This realization makes them painfully aware that life is slipping away. As desperation mounts, they may see embarking upon an entirely new direction as the only possible way out of their difficulties. Unlike the other group we discussed, the prospect of death for them makes the loss of their youthful looks and vigor terrifying. If they lived most of their lives with a low self-esteem, their looks perhaps were the only thing in which they took pride.

For such people the need to recapture their youth can be anguishing. Self-esteem cannot be restored if it depends upon our ability to reverse the passage of time. As often happens, their marriage may have turned out to be a disappointment. Animosity and indifference that may have been suppressed for the sake of the children emerge. Past rationales for compromise disappear, especially since the couple is now alone together. The bad feelings one partner may have had about his or her lifetime occupation may contribute to the sense of discomfort. During middle age a man may conclude that his choice of work was wrong, that his talents have been wasted or misapplied, that his ambitions have been stifled, and that he has amounted to little in life. If he believes that he has been bored by his job, overlooked, or underpaid, the feeling of self-disgust may become overwhelming. The only conceivable way of coping with this problem would be to search desperately for another job. In general, people like this man do not have the self-assurance and confidence that they have mastered the course of their lives. They may feel, instead, that in every major respect life is beyond their control.

Not all women think of their years of motherhood as rewarding. One woman described her feelings this way: "I just don't care much any more. I feel more disgusted than old. All my children are married, and I don't know what to do. I don't play tennis, I don't have any marketable skills, and I'll be damned if I will accept some menial job. If I weren't such a coward, I think I'd probably do myself in. Since my children got married, I feel so alone. I wish they'd waited."

All that we have just said about middle age brings out clearly why a declining parent can pose serious problems for an adult son or daughter. All of us need the opportunity to resolve the issues of our new stage of life patiently and gracefully. Our self-examination and emotional turmoil are really a form of work, however privately undertaken or discreetly handled, and each of us must do it on our own. *Working through our feelings*, in fact, is the phrase psychoanalysts use to describe the experience. To "get the job done," we must have control of our time and energies. We must be unencumbered by other pressures and responsibilities. These are the years when we judge whether we have had a reasonable opportunity to lead a fulfilling life. It is a time to emphasize self-gratification instead of self-denial, a time for rewards instead of more struggle. Some people discover that this means savoring happily their social and financial prosperity. Others, who do not have the material resources they need, may have to switch jobs, cultivate a new set of friends, or move to another town.

No one would deny that some middle-aged adults have always had a loving, intimate, and problem-free relationship with their parents. The attachment they have for their parents has always been undisturbed by ambivalence, resentment, or conflict. As their parents grew old, these children sympathized with them over each new impediment. If their mother could no longer cook her own meals, they felt with her and took action out of a sense of mutual loss. If their father had his driver's license revoked, they themselves felt deprived of an ability and a source of freedom.

Perhaps these sons and daughters took it upon themselves to prepare their parents' meals or perform the errands the parents once ran themselves. The parents' dependence, however, amounted to new demands upon the offspring's daily lives and routines. But this new situation did not leave such children with private reservations, nor did it strain their relationship with their parents. They never felt even a passing wish that the new demands of their parents should come to a halt. In approaching a book like this one, the interest of such a son or daughter would probably extend no further than curiosity about a particular medical complication of old age.

The truth, however, is that this happy picture is not typical. It embodies an ideal or a standard against which some of us believe we should measure ourselves. Perhaps a part of us wishes we had, in fact, a relationship with our parents that fits this description. But as a fantasy it more closely resembles the situation of a hero in some pulp novel who effortlessly attracts every woman he meets. Such a situation can hardly be looked upon as a description of reality.

In fact, it is correct to state that usually the problems of aging parents fall at the doorsteps of middle-aged sons and daughters at the worst possible time. In most cases the two generations have been living totally separate, independent lives for the past twenty or thirty years. Their relationship may have been cordial and pleasant, but the personal involvement stopped short after the birthday or holiday celebrations. It does not really occur to most people that their parents are steadily declining and that they may one day need outside assistance.

This "lapse" is not really our fault. Our culture and values must be held largely responsible. The old European standards are all but extinct in the United States. We do not live within families that are large, closely knit networks of fathers and sons, mothers and daughters, uncles and aunts, grandparents and cousins. Many people today have relatives spread randomly across the country—relatives with whom they may have no contact whatsoever. It would be wholly inaccurate to assume that elderly parents are the shared responsibility of the modern American family.

Nor does the American culture consider aging parents to be titular heads of family or household, entitled to direct and run the lives of the younger generations and due all deference and respect. Quite the contrary, most of us are expected to leave home, and we look forward to living a self-sufficient life as soon as we can. Attempts of an aged person to intrude into our daily affairs are seen as unreasonable. Our culture also views the elderly as embodying the personal characteristics we value least. We worship youth, beauty, strength, wealth, novelty, and self-reliance. The old, by and large, do not possess any of those qualities. We view their appearance and limitations as little more than liability.

This does not mean, of course, that a part of us all does not feel we ought to assume major responsibilities for our declining parents. It is probably a universal impulse to feel that we owe them the sort of support they provided for us in our childhood. We may pay a steep tribute to that sentiment, however. It comes in the form of a tremendous guilt over our wish to place limits on our involvement. Worse, it can impel us to undertake new obligations that never seem to acquit us, in our own minds, of our overall debt. Never being able to do enough for our parents accounts today for no small portion of the world's supply of resentment and frustration.

We may have these feelings regardless of the treatment we received as we grew up. Parents may have been utterly uninvolved in their daughters' youthful problems. Fathers may have been overbearing enough to attempt to break up their sons' marriages. The generations may have been out of touch over the years because they genuinely disliked each other. Even so, if a parent becomes frail and sick, friends and neighbors and ministers, priests, and rabbis may make us feel inadequate and insensitive in various ways if they believe that we are not as involved or concerned as they think we should be. They do not see the old quarrels and old fights when a daughter who wanted to be a professional woman was told that she should never pursue a career but should get married and raise kids, just like everyone else.

Nor do such well-meaning outsiders appreciate the potential negative consequences there may be from a greater involvement on our part. Most parents, surely, do not intentionally set out to be a burden, but their new demands really *do* deprive some sons and daughters of the opportunity to lead fulfilling and well-adjusted lives. Their demands really *are* an interruption of the private emotional work that we need to do. The time and energy it takes to care for our parents may be equivalent to the investment we have made in our own children.

We as offspring may not be aware that our parents do not benefit from help that is given solely out of feelings of guilt. If our new responsibilities drag on for years, most of us will inevitably feel that life has cheated us. Responding out of guilt then simply trades one set of emotional problems for another, which may become far more serious and destructive.

In an area as emotionally complex as the parent-child relationship, a realistic and practical stance may seem heartless or impossible. It is neither, however. You may have your husband come home from an evening with his mother and tell you how much he loves her and how he hopes to take care of her forever.

But next week he may return home and bitterly complain that he cannot stand the sight of her and that she ought to be placed in a nursing home the very next day. People have contradictory feelings about their parents, and these feelings exist side by side. It is wise not to interpret a single feeling alone as our main one.

This problem cannot be solved in traditional moral terms. Instead it must be approached by weighing and evaluating alternatives that afford assistance to parents with the least amount of anguish and conflict for yourself and your family. The personal difficulties you may have in relating to your parent, whether you realize it or not, are serious, legitimate limitations on your ability to provide effective care.

An elderly parent thrives best if he or she is able to live independently. It is the best of all *possible* worlds for him or her. No one would dispute this. Being a thoughtful, sensitive son or daughter should never be incompatible with the right to pursue your own happiness without the burden of excessive responsibilities. This last concept, needless to say, is not easily accepted. Much important help for you and your parents exists in the variety of social programs and services that are finally beginning to develop all across the country. Until our society catches up fully with the need for social programs and a public attitude more accepting of and responsive to the elderly, the initiative lies largely in your own hands.

In the next part of the book, we shall take a look at the changes your parents undergo as they age. These changes are the very reasons that they will one day need your help.

II

A Litany of Loss

3

What Is Behind the Aging Process?

The human body embarks upon a process of slow, continuous change from the moment of conception. What the mainspring of this process is and why it inevitably brings the body to the physical state we call old age are still a mystery. Some scientists speculate that each of us carries a personal program or set of internal messages that directs the process of change. This, they presume, is passed on to us at conception through the genes and chromosomes of our parents. Thus it is conceivable, though unlikely, that if we ever discover the dynamics of this set of internal messages, we might be able to program ourselves in such a way as to retain eternal youth.

Another school of thought believes that the body wears out as naturally and inevitably as any machine. The human body does not age in a uniform way, nor do all its parts deteriorate at the same rate. An aged person's kidneys may function poorly, but his or her heart may be as healthy as that of a younger person. So if a system of artificial devices could be perfected to replace parts of the body that have worn out, life might perhaps be indefinitely prolonged. The second possibility, however, is just as remote as the first one. In fact more people live into their seventies and eighties today because many contagious and infectious diseases that once decimated human populations have almost been eliminated. The speed and severity of our aging tend now to be more influenced by such self-imposed cultural and social sources of stress as an unhappy home life, a high-pressure career, poor eating habits, lack of exercise, and the abuse of alcohol and tobacco.

Even if *these* problems did not exist, the truth is that the human body has just not been designed to live more than about 125 years. The body begins to wind down physically in a variety of ways. An important first concept with which to view old age is to see it as a stage of life that has been approaching inevitably and that cannot be denied or forestalled.

The difference between our own aging and that of our parents is that for them the changes are greater in number and more advanced in character. At the ages of sixty, seventy, or eighty, our parents enter a period of life generally marked by a dwindling ability to defend themselves against illnesses and a greater vulnerability to serious injuries. The overall speed at which our parents' bodies physically deteriorate is much greater than that at which our own bodies do.

We do not doubt for a moment that many elderly people enjoy excellent health. On the whole, though, a multitude of physiological changes have occurred that result in an overall physical decline. It began long ago. It may level off at times. But its course is irreversible, and in the long run the elderly become worse physically, not better.

No matter how robust and independent your parents are today, their physical deterioration and death are inescapable. Many middle-aged sons and daughters consider these truths unacceptable and refuse to permit them fully into their consciousness. There are several reasons for this development, all of them quite basic and normal. Let's go over a few of them together.

First, our society dreads old age, which represents somehow a sudden and total physical disintegration. To the degree that each of us imagines our own old age as a time of dependence and catastrophe, we find it hard to face squarely the image of such a condition in someone close to us. Many of us react in this way even though, statistically speaking, physical disasters strike only a relatively small percentage of the elderly. Alzheimer's Disease, for example, may affect only about 8 percent of the over-65 population. At any one time, no more than 5 percent of older persons will be living in long-term care institutions. The reality is that the vast majority of older people do quite well, but the negative image continues to influence the public view of old age.

A second reason has to do with the nature of the relationship between parents and children. In early childhood we all formed ideas concerning our parents that we have carried with us throughout our lives. During infancy most of us, for example, wished in rare moments of rage and frustration for our parents' death. We found this impulse so monstrous and unacceptable, however, that it had to be disavowed almost as soon as it was felt. We largely resolved these feelings as we gained our independence in life. But they may still linger sufficiently to make us uneasy or guilty when even a passing or legitimate thought about a parent's death runs through our minds. Though such feelings are quite common, no one wants them. An adult who openly expresses an eagerness for a parent's death—unless the wish comes out of compassion for the suffering the parent is enduring during a terminal illness—would seem to most of us cruel or peculiar.

Then too, middle-aged persons who are constantly bothered by the demands of their own adolescent children, or who have had to postpone some of their own pleasures, may just not want to face the prospect of new responsibilities toward their parents. On some level they secretly believe that their parents' physical problems, for example, may automatically become a new set of problems for them. Instead of openly declaring that they do not want this new burden, they seek to dismiss the entire situation from their minds.

There is also another "built-in" reason why sons and daughters often remain in the dark over their parents' physical losses. It is due to the nature of their relationship with the parents. By this we mean that we approach our parents and our own children in very different ways. Our culture neither asks nor expects us to be deeply involved with our parents after we reach adulthood. The roles you and your father developed toward each other are something fundamental and deeply ingrained inside both of you. During the most impressionable years of your life, he was the independent, powerful figure on whom you depended. As you grew up, your major concerns were centered around your own needs. You had no reason and little motivation to evaluate your parents in terms of the overall adjustments they, too, were making to life.

Just as you expect the Mississippi River to continue to flow day after day into the Gulf of Mexico, you also believe that your relationship with your father will continue to conform to your understanding of the natural order of the world. It does not matter how little or how much you are involved with him; you expect him to be what he always was to you. On an emotional level an elderly father's dependence upon you may seem like an unnatural and unwanted reversal of your proper roles. After all, the Mississippi is not supposed to reverse its current and head for Canada!

The dependence of your children on you, on the other hand, does not require you to make any far-reaching emotional reversal of your attitude. Beyond that, the experience of watching a direct product of your love and labor grow up to be strong, happy, and self-sufficient is very different from watching a parent become progressively vulnerable, discontented, or dependent. An elderly parent does not come to you like a newborn child, naked before the world. Your father or mother brings, instead, a complex relationship with you that stretches back for decades. While you naturally associate a young child with a bright future, it would be unusual to feel that way about a parent in his or her early eighties.

A commonly felt wish is that our parents would live forever. Affection and respect may play a part in this desire, which probably reflects what Mom or Dad represented to us as we grew up. They were the sources of stability, security, and order. We depended upon them for love as well as for meeting our physical needs. They were the first human beings, and perhaps the only ones, whom we comfortably perceived as put on earth exclusively for our benefit. They protected us when we were sick or frightened. The permanence of their existence has served as a fixed point of reference in our lives. No matter how self-sufficient we may now be, the prospect that they may leave us alone in the world, that they may abandon us, is unthinkable. Then too, we all long in our hearts for someone to be around to fulfill our needs—as our parents once did, and in some cases still may. So while we have no trouble admitting the reality of death when it comes to strangers, we usually do not bring the same casual acceptance to the prospect of our parents' death.

At bottom no one believes in his own death. This might also apply to the death of one's mother and father. The defense mechanism many of us use to live with what is emotionally unacceptable for us is *denial*. For all practical purposes we block from our minds the recognition of an unwanted fact. In some instances this tendency serves us well. Our children, for instance, will also die one day, but there is little reason to let such a thought dwell in the center of our consciousness. But in dealing with an elderly parent, denial serves us poorly. The denial of the possibility of a parent's death may easily lead to our denial or inability to see the lesser changes and losses our parents are encountering. This impulse can blind us to our parents' real physical problems and the emotional stresses that go along with them.

It is in this way that the physical losses of our parents tend to become progressively more serious until a dramatic accident or problem occurs. The truth may only emerge then like a sudden shock when your dinner is interrupted by a phone call from your father's next-door neighbor. You may be told that Dad has just fractured a rib in a fall down a flight of stairs. Only then do you discover that Dad has been having dizzy spells for quite some time. His fall may not have been in any way connected to your conscious negligence, but you may now begin to torment yourself with this thought.

A parent's physical difficulties, in fact, are what most often brings you back into regular contact—something you may not have had for decades. The sort of experience we have just described can be avoided, however, if you become more sensitive to the kinds of risks, behaviors, and special needs your parent is likely to exhibit as his or her physical deterioration accelerates. Your willingness to overcome the natural temptation to deny the fact of your parent's decline is an important step. It may pay off for both of you in several ways.

Old age is characterized by losses. But the severity of them may vary a great deal. Each parent's body is affected by some changes, while relatively unaffected by others. Your father, for example, may suffer some loss of hearing and yet have hardly any problem with his eyesight. To admit that isolated, specific problems exist is also to recognize the overall strength a parent has. This may provide you both with some emotional relief as well as the perspective necessary to build upon these strengths.

The elderly are prone to serious accidents and are more often the victims of fatal mishaps than any other age group. This does not mean that a catastrophe lurks behind your parents' every movement. But again, facing up to an inevitable series of declines is the best way to start providing your parents' home with essential safety devices, some of which will be discussed in a later chapter.

The medical profession has long maintained that preventive medicine can enhance good health and independent functioning in a way that crisis medicine simply cannot. Instead of coping with physical catastrophes after the fact, you can assure the quality of a parent's present life and even prolong it altogether by recognizing and responding to changes and problems. The important point is this: *Take action against these problems when they are small ones*!

Working to achieve a perspective that acknowledges a parent's strengths and weaknesses as well requires some knowledge of the physical processes at work during old age. One of the purposes of the medical discussion to follow is to both fortify and reassure you. The unknown can be frightening at first. As you cultivate your own independent point of view, our discussion may enhance your ability to become a more effective counselor—one less bothered by frustration or vulnerable to complaints of neglect.

In reading about the most common laments and hazards of aging, many of us are prone to feel a series of false shocks of recognition. At first glance every symptom described seems to exist, in one form or another, in both your parents and yourself. It is practically impossible for all of these potential problems to disrupt the lives of your parents. As long as possible changes are kept in mind, monitored, and guarded against, your parents should remain at their ordinary level of daily functioning. It should also be stressed that the expectations we have for our own health or for the health of our children are not those that we should have for our elderly parents. We expect our own health to improve or remain steady. We expect the health of our small children to become increasingly sound. The most reasonable and appropriate approach to the health of our elderly parents lies in trying to identify and *minimize* the speed of their *decline*.

The overemphasis commonly placed on disease and dysfunction in old age is reflected in newspaper and television accounts. We refer to stories about a kindly old man in his nineties who still works part-time. He is usually asked for his secret for vitality and, shortly thereafter, how much longer he expects to be among the living. These stories imply that alertness, physical fitness, or usefulness among the aged is an exception bordering on the miraculous.

But it isn't so. A survey published by the National Center for Health Statistics concerning elderly people with chronic physical problems found that practically all of them described their limitations as just an inconvenience or a discomfort. So while people sixty-five years of age and beyond confront a greater assortment of serious health ailments than any other age group, these conditions hardly spell total incapacity.

The outlook aged parents cultivate toward their physical status may also make a great deal of difference in the quality of life they enjoy. For example, many sons and daughters listen uneasily as Mother describes her health as good, even though it includes arthritis, poor hearing, and lower-back pain. Such a parent is not kidding herself. She has learned that these conditions are all common in old age. Although there may be no cure for them, she has gone beyond the initial anxieties that these losses may leave her helpless and isolated. She has found that, as she adapts, life can still hold gratifications. And she is right.

People adapt to physical losses as well as to other changes in their lives. Sometimes the adaptations are minor and can be accomplished almost automatically, as when we learn to readjust to where the local grocery store has located the breakfast cereals in a periodic reorganization of its shelves. When an elderly person adapts, however, it may appear to be something dramatic, as when a parent first makes use of a cane.

Such adjustments are also made by people in your own generation. Let's consider one such situation.

> George Norris, a middle-aged lawyer, recently under went a change that illustrates the process elderly people experience on a grand scale. George had always been an avid tennis player. Not long ago he found that he just wasn't covering the court and returning those once easy shots. He was becoming winded sooner and feeling just a little more muscle ache after even the first set. He suspected he was getting "over the hill."
>
> This thought made him particularly angry and depressed because tennis had always provided him with more than important physical exercise. He took pride in his game and considered his skill a real personal accomplishment. He rejected fairly soon the notion of giving up the game. Instead he accepted the change as permanent and began to adapt to it. He modified his style of play and decided to engage in more doubles matches. He could now share the running with a partner and enjoy a longer period of play. It was not a perfect substitute, but it insured him of an ongoing source of pleasure.

Surely not all parents can, or know how to, assume an attitude of acceptance and an overall strategy of adaptation to physical changes as George did. Perhaps no one can sustain such feelings at all times. But when a parent fails to do this altogether, he or she can bring a great deal of needless discouragement and frustration into his or her life and yours.

Most elderly people, of course, do not readily accept the changes taking place inside them. A common response is to refuse to face up to the need for adjustment. The denial that serves your needs serves a parent's, too, though for somewhat different reasons. It springs in part from the universal wish to remain alive and well and from the fear of discovering a disabling or terminal condition.

An elderly parent's denial, then, is a natural and understandable effort to cope with what he or she cannot face. Successful aging requires some acceptance of one's condition. And you do not help your parent by reinforcing his or her tendency to denial. Beyond that, by creating such an unrealistic pattern during middle age, you run the very real risk of falling into the same dangerous situation when you yourself begin to wind down physically. Ultimately you may subject your own children to a nonacceptance of the aging process.

Perhaps it should not be surprising that many aged parents so fear the reality of physical change that acceptance becomes difficult or impossible for them. It is, in fact, one of the most difficult psychological adjustments human beings must make, for so many changes seem to be occurring at the same time. It can create the feeling that our life is about to crumble away.

There are other changes, however, that take place so slowly and over such a long period of time that a dramatic event that would normally bring the change to your parent's attention never occurs. How, for example, can your mother be absolutely certain that the extra puffing and pain she feels after climbing a flight of stairs is anything more ominous than a temporary discomfort she has felt every day for years?

Perhaps the parents who trouble middle-aged sons and daughters the most are those who magnify every bodily change. Perpetual complaints may be all you hear, and it may seem that every day brings a new pain or itch. After a while you may quite naturally begin to resent bitterly having to listen to such gloomy accounts. In these circumstances a parent's behavior may be due to the complicated psychological changes that accompany aging. There are many pains and ailments of old age that are real indeed. A wealth of medical data backs up many parents' claims. If your father, for instance, has always been cautious and reliable about his health problems in the past, an increase in complaints on his part surely warrants medical attention. Both of you will be far better off finding out if his pain in the chest is just gas or a symptom of heart disease. It is often hard for the elderly themselves, when suddenly confronted with a whole combination of physical changes, to be sure in their own minds about what is serious and what is not. The experience of our deteriorating physical capacity is frightening, for in some ways it amounts to unexpected reminders of death.

But it cannot be denied that for some parents there is a heavy emotional component to their complaining. Part of this comes from the natural, human wish to gain sympathy and consolation for our hurts. It becomes aggravating to children, unfortunately, when physical problems are used to receive from a son or daughter reassurance and warmth that the parents do not believe they can get in any other way. Your mother, for example, may wake up in the middle of the night, frightened and lonely. She knows that she could never reasonably call you up at two in the morning over such a "silly" reason. So, instead, she imagines that she has a heart murmur. It is important for you to understand that she has awakened you out of a genuine concern. She is really not trying to burden you with her problems or ruin your sleep in the process. Unfortunately, the heart murmur of loneliness she feels might be dismissed by many children with a hasty reassurance such as, "Cheer up. It'll be all right in the morning!"

This kind of parent usually provokes precisely the response that is the direct opposite of the one she truly wants and needs. The more she pesters her children with calls and complaints, the more her children come to resent her and seek to withdraw from the situation.

Often sons and daughters who become embittered and fed up with this problem are those who do not enjoy a good relationship with their parents and probably never have been truly close to them. This does not mean that such children are cruel or insensitive. Many have a long history of wounds and resentments associated with their parents. Perhaps it would be unreasonable to ask them to respond to their mother or father in any other fashion.

We shall discuss in Part Four the services existing in many communities that can allay a parent's physical anxieties more adequately than you can, and, in the appendix, you'll find a listing of some specific resources to contact. Here, though, we should emphasize how important it is for children to be able to decode the message their parent is sending to them. Your response to an ache in the leg should really be different from your response to an ache for human contact. If your relationship is unusually strained or burdensome, a solution might be to set formal limits on how often the two of you are in touch. Perhaps, for example, you and your parent will agree to check up on each other Tuesdays and Saturdays.

But the most effective approach to this dilemma is usually one that may sound painful to many sons and daughters. That is, try calling your mother first, even when she has no reason to expect to hear from you and when there is no emergency or specific business to conduct. Calling simply to check up and see how she is doing often lets her know someone is there for her—someone concerned about her and ready to help out if need be. This usually gives her the emotional reassurance and confidence she has been asking for in the first place. The more secure she feels, the less she shall need to search around—on an unconscious level—for a painful excuse to make sure she has not been abandoned.

Let's assume your father is complaining about his health problems in such a way that his children are left with the feeling that he expects them to do something about the situation, such as curing the health problems once and for all. If you try to get some perspective on this situation, you may be able to discover just what Dad is seeking. Set aside for the moment whatever guilt or anger his complaint may provoke in you. Your parent is undoubtedly demanding something be done about his health. The implicit burden of responsibility you are left with is simply an aspect of his *misplaced* demand.

People who have been swindled can go to court and sue to receive compensation for the damages they have suffered. But when the human body deteriorates, as Dad's body is doing, the losses are usually permanent. Cells tend not to be replaced as they were in childhood. If the deterioration involves your parent's hearing, for instance, he may never again hear as well as in the past. Often a hearing aid is an unsuitable replacement. Deep down, your parent may feel this is unjust. What has he done to deserve this punishment? It is an outrage, he feels. His anger has nowhere to go. Satisfaction for the insult cannot be demanded from fate, God, or the central nervous system. So he turns to you, and you must give him some sort of response. The wish you have for full restitution of Dad's hearing also carries threatening and discouraging feelings for him. Your disappointment if his hearing cannot be restored can prove to be an extra burden for your father. And what if his hearing is lost altogether? You should handle the medical problem by consulting qualified medical authorities. But the personal and emotional problem is basically one that you as your father's son or daughter cannot sidestep.

Generally the effects of sickness and physical deterioration will be quite evident to your aged parents. A loss of self-sufficiency may show up, for instance, in some of the simple things they have been doing all their lives. Dad may begin to find he cuts himself more often while shaving, or Mother may find that she can no longer open the vacuum-sealed jars she put away on the kitchen shelves. Or both of them may now find buttoning up a coat a major effort.

Facing the thought of not being able to perform functions like these effectively implies accepting the fact that something is wrong with oneself. The cuts on the face and the unbuttoned coat are signs of a declining self-sufficiency. They are also messages to the rest of the world and to oneself that things have changed. Covering up and pretending that these problems do not exist are natural human devices used, and needed, to preserve your parents' self-esteem. Mom and Dad may not be able to bear having their protective security removed from them.

Sons and daughters often only see the tip of the iceberg of their parents' physical problems. But these problems are serious events. As a result some elderly parents may become so depressed that they lose interest in their physical status or in "keeping up appearances." Most are embarrassed, afraid, and ashamed of the changes taking place in their daily lives as a result of their physical decline.

Every loss becomes further evidence that they are not what they once were. Referring to themselves as "decrepit old men" or "bags of bones with one foot in the grave" are common expressions of this sense of despair. Such emotion, by the way, often annoys or embarrasses their children, who respond with a denial of their own by either changing the subject or telling their parents it simply isn't so bad. But ignoring a subject so important as your parents' physical deterioration is no real reply. In the next chapter we'll go into more detail on this topic.

4

How Do Common Physical Changes Affect Your Parents?

We now want to take up some of the specific ways in which the physical changes of the aging process show up. Most of the changes are quite obvious and come as no surprise. But by taking a fresh look at them, we may be able to understand a little better how your parents experience old age. In addition, the discussion may help you learn more about your parents' difficulties and enable you to alleviate the changes somewhat or at least compensate for them in some way.

PHYSICAL APPEARANCE

As the years pass, all of us look older, and usually we can accurately surmise someone's chronological age at a glance. With each age period of life, we associate a certain set of expectations and value judgments. If we were asked for a list of the signs that distinguish old age, we would probably include wrinkled skin, baggy eyelids, white hair, and baldness. Pressed further, we might add that the once shapely curves or firm angles of the body would have sagged. We might add teeth that have now worn down, a chin that seems closer to the nose than in the past, and a nose that has become longer and thicker. Particularly if we are thinking about our parents or people we have known over the years, we soon realize that the whole profile and bodily appearance have altered.

Notice, too, our judgment is not based on any one characteristic but rather on an *accumulation* of details. Our expectations are, for example, that a man's face should be more wrinkled at age seventy than at sixty and that a woman's hair should become first gray and then white as she ages. We take it for granted that such changes are gradual, ongoing, and inevitable. We also know that in extreme old age the changes in appearance may come fairly quickly.

Our society uses a revealing expression to sum up this process. We say, "She has lost her good looks." Thus we see the change in appearance as a *loss*. This concept is crucial to an understanding of how your parents themselves perceive their old age. It is perhaps their overall experience.

The expression we used stressed *good* looks. Since one's appearance is not a moral issue, by "good" we really mean "youthful." In other words, youth is the equivalent of beauty in the United States. In some cultures, however, the physical signs of old age are regarded as precious and enviable. They imply stature, maturity, and a special and valuable wisdom that comes exclusively from long experience. Parents in the United States who draw upon an ethnic background of esteem for age have to do so in spite of our culture, for in this country we stress the rapid obsolescence of experience and knowledge. Old age is more likely to be associated in most minds with uselessness. A change in your appearance means you have *lost* your beauty.

Fashion models to the contrary, this particular change need not interfere with successful living. It has no bearing on whether your mother can hold down a job, handle her mail, or pay her bills. Nevertheless, the "loss" of looks may be a major—though often undiscussed—part of her anguish and concern.

There are several reasons that sons and daughters overlook or dismiss lightly their parents' possible depression over lost beauty. In old age, after all, there are plenty of potential or real medical problems of an acute nature to worry about. The loss of looks is a very subtle form of disability in comparison. In addition, most children are neither eager to view nor accustomed to seeing their parents as sexually attractive. Many children are simply unaware of this aspect of their parents' lives.

As a group, the elderly are not expected to be attractive. An aging Cary Grant or Ingrid Bergman still drew the admiring gaze of the general public, but they were exceptions. We can safely assume that many of our elderly parents are sensitive to the changes in their appearance. One does not simply lose beauty; one also receives in its place the feeling that one has become ugly. Indeed, *ugliness* is one of the terms our culture uses to define old age.

Many parents, of course, succeed in retaining a good measure of their attractiveness. The assumption that all elderly people are sexless is simply one more way in which the aged are lumped by our culture into a gray, undifferentiated mass.

To understand the values we place on old age, we need only examine the basis of the advertising industry's successful appeal to our secret wishes, anxieties, and fears. Crudely put, the equation is: physical attractiveness equals sexual desirability. An elderly woman has only to look in the mirror to see that her days of youthful beauty are over. A good part of everyone's self-confidence and worth is anchored to their good looks. Can we not, then, understand the proverbial aging woman who has put on so much lipstick, jewelry, and perfume in an attempt to appear youthful that she has heightened her losses and appears all the more desperately unattractive?

To realize in part how such a parent experiences her loss of good looks and why she tries to cover it up and deny it, simply remember your own jolly discovery of your first patch of gray hair a few months or years ago. Maybe you yourself made the discovery one morning as you groomed yourself before a mirror. This is what happened to Paul Hollander, a successful, middle-aged businessman, whose story may prove illustrative.

It was an unpleasant shock for Paul to note the gray patch of hair above his right ear that morning. He bent over to take a closer look and focused the light carefully in the hope he had imagined the gray strands. He double-checked, swallowed his hopes, and finally had to accept the reality—for the time being.

Paul walked into the breakfast room looking morose and irritable. His wife dutifully asked what was wrong. For a moment Paul was tempted to ask if she had noticed anything. But he just said, "Nothing's wrong." It would have been depressing to hear her reply, "It's been there for quite a while." But since she had never mentioned the gray patch, he felt that perhaps he might be able to conceal it, like a secret.

Here we see how the change was brought to Paul's attention. Although the graying process had been taking place slowly and unobtrusively, its discovery came as a shock—a dramatic event.

Some weeks later Paul noticed a second gray patch. Although he had never wholly forgotten his sense of loss over the first patch, his second experience of loss was less intense. It was easier to shrug it off, accept it, and go on. Subsequently, of course, the gray hair was no secret at all, and Paul Hollander became less interested in the graying process.

There was a curious side effect to Paul's experience, though. He had become a bit touchier on the subject of aging. One evening his daughter called home, collect, from college. She made a passing reference to a stodgy professor as "that old man of fifty." He quickly corrected her, as he put it, for her loose and erroneous use of an adjective. His wife just as quickly pointed out to him how overly insistent he had been with his daughter.

Yet it was beyond Paul, as it is beyond most of us, to appreciate the same emotion or approve of the same need in his elderly parent.

Every year Paul's church held a benefit dinner. This year his mother, who was a widow in her late seventies, began her preparations for the event a month early. Paul's wife received almost daily phone calls about which dress, shoes, jewelry, and hairstyle should be worn. Paul, too, was drawn into a series of questions like "What do you think?" and "You don't think I'm being silly, do you?" He reassured his mother, though he privately felt that her behavior was somewhat pointless, pathetic, and embarrassing. But he hadn't the nerve to tell her that she ought to accept her age and act it. What difference did it make how she looked? She was not an ingenue. She was an elderly woman. She was his mother!

The big night arrived, and when Paul came to pick his mother up, he had to wait in her living room while she called his wife on the phone for last-minute advice. After a great deal of grooming and primping before the mirror, his mother finally made her entrance. Although the bracelets, hairdo, and dress all struck him as somewhat loud, he greeted her with a perfunctory "You look fine."

Then they set out together. As they checked their coats, they bumped into a middle-aged business acquaintance of Paul's. When the other man immediately complimented Paul's mother on her dress, she smiled and blushed. During and after dinner she whispered first to her son and then to her daughter-in-law that she thought Paul's friend a very sweet man. Later, when Paul was alone with his wife, he could not get out of his head how "shameless" his mother had been, courting the attention of men far younger than herself. What was wrong with her?

Paul Hollander could hardly be faulted for reacting as a son. Nevertheless, he should have realized that women—far more than men—have been taught to value themselves for their physical beauty. His mother was reacting to a very real threat that as she became less attractive, people would no longer esteem her as a woman. Her elaborate preparations were just another way of asking for the special sort of consideration she had enjoyed for decades.

As a rule, the elderly do not cut a dazzling image, and they know it. This message is delivered to them in many subtle ways. They can scarcely be faulted for feeling the same twist in the stomach any of us would feel if a spouse informed us that he or she has not found us physically attractive for the past dozen years. In our society males have a relatively easier time with the changes in their appearance. When a man ages, he may even be considered distinguished. Cary Grant still appealed to members of the opposite sex in a way that Gloria Swanson did not. The "dignified look" of old age is more apt to be a polite phrase than a term for describing most of the elderly people we know. And it seldom is applied to elderly women. Since there is no advantage, real or imagined, in looking old in the United States, it should not surprise us that many old people strive mightily to look as young as they can. Elderly men are not immune to this impulse, as the following example illustrates.

> Every two weeks a former furniture salesman now in his eighties used to take his twenty-three-year-old granddaughter out for dinner. During one of the meals, she asked him what sort of hair oil he was using.
>
> "It's nothing," he said, somewhat startled. "Just something I picked up last week."
>
> "That's too bad," she said. "I used to like your hair much better when you just used water and a comb to groom it."
>
> The grandfather quickly decided to give up his new hair oil, and he hasn't used anything since.

Of course here was a man who had long been coping with and resigning himself to the same sorts of problems Paul Hollander had been experiencing. While he may have come to accept his losses over the years, his pleasure in being considered handsome and dashing was just as much a part of his emotional needs and makeup as it was for persons many years his junior. Of course his granddaughter was not an object of his romantic interest, but this elderly gentleman, like each of us, remains terribly sensitive to the physical impression he makes. And, given the conditions under which he lives, whatever attention and respect he receives in that regard is meaningful.

The need to be noticed and considered desirable is something many people never lose. In attempting to overcome the stigma of age, elderly parents may choose among several possibilities. They may wear youthfully stylish clothes; they may become more fastidious in their grooming or more artful in the use of cosmetics; and they may also "act younger" by emulating the slang, opinions, and activities of the younger generation. Our elderly parents may even try to recapture a youthful figure by means of exercise, diet, or plastic surgery. Unfortunately, our culture tends to frown on many of these choices. Physically beneficial as yoga may be for a parent or exciting as the results of a face-lift may be, in most people's eyes such improvements can never "make up" for the real defects of age. Yet slimming down does make people look and feel younger, and as a result they may well feel better about themselves. On this score there are small things a son or daughter can do to help. Children should make a point of taking their parents' looks seriously. You should compliment them in some way whenever possible. You should, if possible, be instrumental in encouraging them to dress tastefully. Daughters or sons, on their own initiative, might suggest that a trip to the hairdresser or clothing store be taken in tandem.

If your relationship with your parent is marked by unusual tensions or discomfort, however, you should feel free to disregard the suggestion of a joint shopping expedition. But there are advantages to these kinds of activities, if you can handle them smoothly. They are structured; they have a clearly defined time limit and purpose; and they accomplish something tangible, useful, and positive.

SEXUALITY

Loss of beauty is only one of the meanings associated with your parents' change in appearance. It also implies to your parents and those around them a loss of sexual vigor.

There are a host of myths and misconceptions about sex in old age that abound in our culture. They generally run as follows:

—Beyond a certain age—no one knows precisely when—people are physically incapable of engaging in sexual intercourse.

—Even if they could do so, they really shouldn't. The whole idea makes *us* somehow feel squeamish.

—No children can be produced at this stage, so sexual activity must be unnecessary.

—Not only does sex in old age seem unnatural, but it might put too great a strain on the heart.

—We may think that sex is a health hazard, since we know that the elderly should avoid all forms of stress and excitement.

—Anyway, we have heard that normal old people no longer care for sex. They are probably as indifferent to the subject as they might be to a favorite toy or doll they enjoyed in childhood. Despite the jokes about dirty old men, most of the elderly people that we ourselves know have a vacuum where their sexual appetites, interests, dreams, fantasies, conflicts, and outlets used to be.

Most of us have always had difficulty picturing our own parents engaging in sex, despite the indisputable evidence of our own presence as proof that they must have! The logic of our reticence commonly leads us to infer that now that our parents are old, they *surely* abstain altogether. And by extension we feel that all other aged parents are just as inactive.

The plain truth is that all these speculations just mentioned are nonsense! There is no biological time clock in the human body that erases sexual feelings or longings. Researchers like Alfred Kinsey and Masters and Johnson have found that sexuality can and does play an integral part in the lives of aged persons. Recent research has disproved many of the old myths and found instead that sexual activity enriches the lives of the aged. It may often be quite therapeutic, especially for the heart. The traditional argument that sex is only justified as a means of procreation may still be preached in some quarters, but new knowledge and changing social norms have led to a greater understanding and acceptance of sexual activity as an important contributor to our personal mental health.

Our parents as a rule continue the same patterns of sexual habits and interests they developed in their younger years. Those who found sex a gratifying, indispensable activity usually continue to do so. They may be more likely to seek a new partner if their spouses have died. Those who felt sex was a duty or a chore in their middle years will probably not miss it in their seventies and eighties.

It is true that a decline in sexual activity occurs. Although women generally reach a plateau of sexual drive in their thirties and maintain it most of their lives, men gradually decline from the peak they attained in their early twenties. Elderly men are less capable of rapid and prolonged arousal and have lost the ability they once possessed for frequent ejaculation. Few people, though, think of anything so personal and complex as their sexuality just in terms of biological facts.

Research on human sexual behavior has served a useful purpose. It has contributed to a greater public understanding of the topic and has helped change many misleading and often inhibiting social attitudes. There is still a long way to go, however, before our culture achieves an entirely correct perspective. As it is, elderly parents are not recognized as the sexual beings most of them are. On this basis they have often been deprived of the degree of respect, recognition, and individuality that the rest of us take for granted.

Then, too, we should recall that human sexuality takes on many forms and outlets, including some that may escape our attention. Making love may enhance the self-esteem of elderly people and allow both partners to express and receive tenderness. When a parent lives alone, masturbation may help temporarily to relieve his or her loneliness, boredom, and frustration. Beyond that, though, everyone needs to be touched, hugged, and held. Often an aged parent has no one—neither close friends nor family members— with whom to find spontaneous and warm human contact.

A recent news story that received national coverage illustrates just how starved the elderly can be for affection. Social workers for a Florida nursing home were seeking a fresh solution to the problem of the low morale that afflicts many residents of such institutions. Like every nursing home, this one had its share of clients who had been deaf, mute, or catatonic when they entered. The daily activities of such clients were obviously minimal and consisted largely of sitting and staring into space. Other residents were not much more animated. They were depressed, irritable, and prone to spells of weeping and bitter complaining. As an experiment, the social workers collected some dogs and cats and presented them to various residents as pets. The results were astonishing. As the animals developed an attachment to their owners, the elderly took a new interest in their own lives and surroundings. The physical demonstrations of affection that the pets conveyed stimulated some patients, who had neither spoken nor responded to a word since their admission, to laugh and cry and speak.

We needn't look only at such extreme examples to see the unfortunate consequences of our traditional sexual stereotypes. Many aged parents feel they must conform to one or more of the generally held beliefs about old people. As a result they may feel too embarrassed to admit—let alone openly discuss—the sexual relationships they may have found and may want to pursue further. They may be hesitant to begin dating for fear that relatives will disapprove of their actions and that friends may tell them not to make fools of themselves. A passing sexual thought—even the need to be hugged once in a while—may be repressed because for a person of their age it may seem something shameful or unnatural.

The scope of our aged parents' sexual fantasies, conflicts, and needs is still an unexplored area. It is such a wilderness, in fact, that a Duke University researcher has labeled the elderly "a sexually oppressed group." Our culture's so-called sexual revolution has resulted in much openness, attention, and freedom of expression for younger people. But it has left the sexual problems of the elderly virtually untouched. Neither Kinsey nor Masters and Johnson dealt to any great extent with this topic.

Sons and daughters should certainly be aware of these needs of their parents and might even obliquely raise the subject and explore it if Mom or Dad is keeping troubled feelings locked up inside. There is no hard and fast rule on this point, however. It would clearly be inappropriate to urge an elderly widow who has no emotional outlets to become promiscuous. In general, your parents should be encouraged to fulfill their strivings and express their concerns to the limit of their capabilities and the prompting of their hearts. Continuing normal social contacts with friends and neighbors is an important substitute for the basic sexual needs that are no longer easily met during old age.

SLEEPING PATTERNS

Another general misconception can cause undue concern to elderly
parents and those around them—one concerning sleeping patterns.
Most people assume that the older we get, the more sleep we need
to stay healthy. It is true that, as a result of general activity, the
elderly tend to tire faster than younger people, but that has nothing
to do with how many hours of sleep they need at night.

Many aging parents become fearful when they find that they
need less sleep than in the past. People who always needed eight
hours a night may now find that they are suddenly getting along
quite well on only six hours. While they once slept so soundly that
they would remain undisturbed if a train rushed through the bedroom, they now are waking up several times a night. Some parents
may fear that they are now insomniacs or are turning into emotionally troubled people.

This type of concern may be another instance of how frightening an unexpected, though perfectly normal, physical change can
be. The amount of sleep we need changes throughout life. In infancy we usually require a great deal. The need gradually tapers off
through adolescence and then may increase or decrease somewhat
during our middle years. Scientists have discovered four stages of
sleep, of which the last is the deepest. In old age that last stage
commonly disappears. Often an aged parent must lie awake for a
longer time before sleep comes. The sleep of the aged is often
lighter and more prone to frequent awakenings.

Sons or daughters who listen to complaints and fears over this
problem should keep a few concepts in mind. If a mother or father
has always been an emotionally troubled soul, the present worrying
may just be an old habit that is becoming more pronounced. If the
fears are based on this change alone, you can most likely reassure
your parent that everything is fine—just a bit different. On the
other hand, if a parent is experiencing a mounting set of physical
problems or is becoming emotionally overwhelmed by old age, the
change in sleeping pattern may be a result of his or her pressing
conflicts. If this is so, the best solution would be to consult a
physician.

As a general rule, though, you may be able to help your
parents accept the change in their sleeping patterns. They should
not force themselves to take too much sleep. Studies have found
that the elderly who regularly get ten hours or more of sleep each

night are more likely to suffer a stroke. So moderation in sleep, as in everything, seems desirable.

EYESIGHT

Most elderly people have met with a decline in one or more of the five senses: eyesight, hearing, taste, touch, and smell. But the most serious problems usually come about as a result of impaired vision and hearing. People who are losing the ability to watch and listen to the world that surrounds them are not only being forced into isolation and dependence but are also vulnerable to serious accidents.

Our eyes may deteriorate in several ways. Light passes through the pupil of the eye, and an image is brought into focus by the lens. The retina receives the picture, and the optic nerve conducts it to the brain. Commonly in old age the pupil becomes smaller. It does not adjust as efficiently or automatically to the amount of illumination around it. Gradually it may become fixed and not react at all to changes in light or darkness.

This means that the pupil cannot expand enough to afford proper vision in a darkened place. It becomes difficult to distinguish objects in the dark. Elderly persons who are unaware of or refuse to acknowledge the onset of this loss are liable to meet with a number of nighttime accidents. In the house, for example, your mother may not be able to travel safely from the bedroom to the refrigerator or bathroom without switching on the lights. Not to do so could be akin to walking through the house with her eyes half closed.

Turning on the lights is a simple instance of successfully adapting to a loss. Such an adjustment sounds like a relatively smooth one to make, but it presupposes that Mom recognizes and respects the new limitation. After all, your mother has made such small trips all her life. Isn't she intimately familiar with the layout of her house and the arrangement of the furniture? Almost everyone has at one time or another been rewarded for such overconfidence with a set of toes stubbed against a half-opened closet door or a knee banged hard against a chair left in the middle of the kitchen. Unlike the rest of us, who merely grunt or swear for the few minutes that the pain lasts, Mom may receive a bruise that makes her miserable for days. Worse, she may lose her balance and have a nasty fall.

Without routine medical examination it is difficult for elderly persons to perceive a subtle decline in their vision. When young people or middle-aged people stumble in the dark, they do not conclude that their vision is failing. Instead they assume that they have been careless or the victims of malevolent, inanimate objects and promptly forget the incident. It shouldn't be surprising, then, if your parents' thoughts run along similar lines.

Elderly persons often need more light than younger people to carry on with assurance the mundane routines of daily life. When such light is unavailable, they may face anything from annoyance to severe harm. If all that is needed is greater wattage to read or prepare dinner, it may just be a matter of your switching light bulbs around the house.

There are other situations, however, where a simple remedy is impractical. Such situations may lead to behavior that either mystifies or confuses you, as the following case shows.

Eleanor Hertz had never been very close to her father, a man in his middle seventies who was now living alone. She managed to overcome her reluctance, if not all of her guilt, and one night phoned to invite him out to dinner at a swank French restaurant. He accepted, but the moment he entered the dimly lit place, his mood seemed to darken, too. When Eleanor asked how he liked the restaurant, he grumbled, "No one but bats could enjoy themselves in this cave." Before the expensive evening was even under way, Eleanor was already paying a high emotional price in censure and abuse.

After they sat down and were handed menus, she could quickly sense her father's impatience. He barely glanced at the list and ordered steak and mashed potatoes—ordinary American fare. As the waitress left, Eleanor chided him in a not altogether jocular tone, although she felt guilty the moment the words leapt out of her mouth. "Here I take you to the best French restaurant in town, and all you want is steak!"

Dad merely shrugged, and as the evening dribbled downhill, Eleanor prayed she would keep a memory of this encounter vivid enough to cure her of any similar well-intentioned gestures in the future.

The pity was that her father was unable to admit that his eyesight had failed to the point that reading a menu was almost impossible. It was just easier for him to pretend that he had not lost anything—the setup of the restaurant was at fault. He might have liked to ask for a flashlight or even request his daughter to read the entrees to him. But the fear of looking foolish as well as the anger he felt over the situation kept him from doing any such thing. The last thing he wanted to eat was steak and potatoes, but at the moment he felt he had no other choice. Dad was covering up for his deficiency—and unfortunately he was convincing.

Eleanor was not clairvoyant enough to grasp the reason for his short temper. She did not know how successfully he had convinced her that she could not reasonably expect anything but a repeat of his hostile performance the next time they might meet.

Another aspect of visual decline occurs when the pupil of the eye can no longer respond adequately to glare. From age sixteen on, the span of time a person needs to recover from glare doubles every thirteen years. An elderly person, then, may need five times as long to adjust to glare as a teenager. It also means that the period of temporary blindness has vastly increased. We all know how painfully blinding it is to step into the bathroom on a sleepless night and turn the fixture on to locate something. The experience is so miserable that most of us flick the switch only as a last resort. While young children may need only several seconds to attain normal vision, our parents may need several minutes.

Even if the changes in the pupil of the eye easily escape our notice, problems with the lens are another story. Signs of wear in the lens are among the earliest unwelcome hints of aging most of us receive. Usually the wear makes itself known by increasing difficulties in reading fine print. At the other extreme, we may have trouble making out what a highway sign far down the road has to say.

The lens expands and contracts to bring objects of every size and at most distances into focus. As some of this elasticity is lost, bifocal glasses may become necessary. Any middle-aged son or daughter who has put on bifocals realizes how much of a nuisance it may be to coordinate vision between the two areas of the lenses. Since your parent may have lost some physical agility, poorly illuminated halls and stairways can turn into major hazards. Stepping off a curb or down to the first stair of a stairway and locating the first step up a stairway are actions we all do without much thought every day of our lives. But if our parents cannot make out a stair in the dark or coordinate the proper section of the bifocal with the action of their feet, they may be in for difficulties. At the very least they may get to the point where such simple acts demand caution and full concentration.

Concentration is one of the ways the elderly adapt. As their eyesight becomes less reliable, a greater deliberation has to make up for the difference. This is a healthy, natural response. Too often, unfortunately, sons and daughters watch the extra effort with dismay. It makes them uncomfortable and perhaps sad to see such a clear-cut loss. But it would be far better as well as more accurate to admire the strength that successful adjustment also represents.

Both you and your parents would be fooling yourselves, however, if you consider these extra efforts to be perfect substitutes. A net loss has taken place. The difference between what was and what is, is irreplaceable to a degree. Elderly parents whose eyesight has deteriorated may climb and descend a familiar, dimly lit stairway by counting off the steps. If they miscalculate, as happens at times, they may take that first stride when they still have a step or two to go. A painful fall or accident may be the result.

Other changes may make the streets dangerous at night. As it becomes more difficult to distinguish objects in the dark, everything appears to have blended into a uniform color. While driving, your parents may not make out a line of cars parked on a narrow residential street or a pedestrian stepping out between two parked automobiles. Often the visual field narrows, which means that your parents may no longer perceive cars or people on the periphery of their field of vision. Often an elderly man or woman may step into the street without noticing a car that has just turned the corner.

Aside from added caution on the streets at all times, our parents are dependent on the municipal government to reduce the possibility of such problems. Incandescent street lamps, which are in almost universal use, produce a painful white glare. Replacing such bulbs with sodium light-yellow illumination would be a big improvement. This kind of light reduces glare and makes for more rapid adjustments. Brightly painted curbs, stairs, and street signs are easier for the elderly to spot, even in the dark.

Improvements of this nature do not make for burning public issues. Politicians are unlikely to base their campaigns on such a platform. But the pressure of community groups can make a difference, especially in neighborhoods with a sizable elderly population. As soon as people like yourselves become sensitive to the specific kinds of "small" changes in vision that can make a great deal of difference, much of the battle will have already been won.

Another physical change that may *seem* small but is significant occurs around age sixty, when the lens loses some of its transparency. It starts to yellow, which affects the eye much as a color filter affects a camera. When this happens, your parents may confuse colors. The eye may be unable to pick up and send the color of red and green objects to the brain. Since those two colors are used in traffic signals, this situation might lead to trouble. In addition, cataracts, which become more frequent in old age, cloud the lens of the eye, impairing vision further.

Clinical descriptions alone fail to convey the physical and emotional obstacles that confront the elderly with these visual problems. To get a better idea of these problems, remove the cellophane from a package of cigarettes and place it across your eyes. Before long the total blurring of your vision will make you impatient and angry. You will probably feel foolish and embarrassed over your appearance and more than a trifle helpless. It can finally make you so self-conscious and infuriated that all your willpower may not be enough to keep you from tearing the material from your eyes. Your elderly parents may feel all those things. But they may never come nearer than wishful thinking to the relief you experience by removing the impediment.

In real life, of course, elderly parents do not lend themselves easily to these sorts of educational lectures. Whenever the human element is involved, especially in a parent-child relationship, some degree of strain and misunderstanding may be almost unavoidable.

Every two years John Marsh used to fly down to visit his parents in Fort Lauderdale. But his most recent visit started off with a shock. After unpacking his luggage, he walked into the den and saw the color television set tuned to a sporting event. His father entered and asked him to sit down. Then they both began to watch a screen that seemed to John to be nearly psychedelic. Everything—the fans, the players' uniforms, the field itself—appeared in an exaggerated, almost grotesque color. John sat and waited for his father to take notice and make the obvious readjustments on the TV set. When this did not happen, John tried to sit there calmly for a while. But the picture was so radically strange that it was soon impossible for him to concentrate. Finally he got up and returned the picture to normal. His father grew silently uncomfortable, looked uneasily at the game, and then became quite fidgety. At last, without saying a word, he left the room.

John was stunned, for he could not fathom what terrible thing he had done. How had he so quickly and thoroughly insulted his father? "Maybe," he thought, "this is the old man's way of saying he doesn't want to see me. Or maybe he's angry I don't visit more often." For a few moments this made John feel terribly guilty and then terribly mad. What an irrational, punitive way to treat a son! The old man should only realize how difficult it had been for him to arrange this excursion.

Ultimately John began to wonder if his father had been struggling to reveal some awful secret. Of course! What an insensitive son he was! Here he had started watching television practically the moment he walked in the door. He had even gotten all worked up because the dumb picture was out of focus. Meanwhile, his father had been trying desperately to tell him about a fatal illness or some emotional trouble—or even perhaps that he's broke! Or, God forbid, perhaps his father was slipping into senility and had actually forgotten that his son was in the room.

Fortunately, the problem was far less monumental. John's father had been abruptly reminded of a loss. His vision had changed in such a way that it distorted his perception of color. He had been compensating for this when watching television by exaggerating the screen's colors. By making that adjustment, the picture would become what he perceived as normal for him. Naturally he did most of his viewing at home, where he could be comfortable enough with his loss to forget that an "outsider" such as his son might be terribly puzzled.

And so the elder Mr. Marsh found himself in a bind. He could confess his loss or cover up and say nothing. Both options seemed unpleasant. It would be depressing to bring up the problem, since it would leave a general feeling with John that he was changing for the worse. He was quite familiar with that emotion. Since it only made him feel bad and improved nothing, he would just as soon skip it. Besides, it would draw unnecessary and embarrassing attention to himself. He did not see himself as a complainer and didn't want anyone else to think he was one either. His son would probably ask him questions, express solicitude and concern, and insist that every effort be made to find a doctor to help. But all this to-do would make him feel even more uncomfortable.

Mr. Marsh asked himself what would be gained from such a discussion. His son would probably insist that the television be adjusted to compensate for his loss. Much as he had been looking forward to watching the upcoming bowl game with John, he just wouldn't be able to relax knowing someone else was quietly jumping out of his skin for his benefit.

It was far better to say nothing. Part of him, though, was quite irritated. An old man just can't say, "Look, this is my house, and when you fiddle with the buttons, you're ruining one of the few things I really enjoy. So if you don't mind. . . ." A pleasant routine had been taken away for the duration of his son's stay simply because, when it comes down to making "legitimate" demands, a loss always seems to take a back seat to a normal condition.

Of course, not all parents are as uncomplaining as Mr. Marsh. We can see, though, how perpetual an interference some of these changes can be. Depressing or exasperating as it is to listen to complaints from our parents, the case of John Marsh and his father illustrates an important point—how much annoyance physical problems can cause for the elderly, and what a large role they occupy in their thoughts. In some ways they can be compared to steep debts. You can't make the problem go away just by taking a nap or going to a movie.

Even so, we must always keep in mind the fact that the rate of change and the degree of loss will vary widely from person to person. Although the percentage of elderly people who become nearly blind or deaf is larger than that of any other age group, the vast majority of them are not in bad shape. A study conducted in St. Petersburg found that over 80 percent of the elderly in a local institution had sufficient vision to function properly. Among the aged population of St. Petersburg as a whole, the figure was 90 percent.

HEARING

We don't know how many of the people in St. Petersburg were hard of hearing, but it would not be surprising to learn that almost all of them had hearing problems. In fact the decline of this particular sense is just about universal, since it begins for most people as early as age twenty-five. The process, however, is so gradual and continuous that it usually cannot be noticed. It starts with a reduction in the ability to hear the high-pitched sound waves. Since these are far beyond the range of normal hearing, their slow loss probably doesn't make much difference in our lives.

You may be disturbed, however, if you discover one day as you are attending an opera that you cannot hear the soprano's aria—she seems to you to be only going through the motions of singing. If hearing loss progresses, of course, more practical problems will arise. The range of difficulty may vary from failure to hear the door bell when in a distant room to inability to make out the whistle of a train or the honking of an approaching car.

In some cases a hearing loss may be reversible. For example, wax may build to the point of blocking off the middle ear. Once the ear has been cleared out, however, the problem is gone. More often, though, changes in hearing are permanent. If a nerve in the ear or central nervous system deteriorates, it cannot be restored.

It is not difficult to recreate—let alone imagine—the impact a hearing loss may have on a person. By simply plugging up your ears for a few minutes, you can feel the sense of utter isolation, self-consciousness, and embarrassment at being unable to know and respond to what is going on around you.

In dealing with mechanical things, our aging parents can adapt with fair ease, at least within their own homes. They can turn up the volume of the telephone bell, television set, radio, or record player. If sons or daughters are jarred by the level of noise in their parents' house, they should remember that a compensation for the hearing loss has probably taken place.

When your parents go out into the world beyond their home, however, the problem gets a little stickier. All of us have been to a movie theater where we were unable to hear the sound track properly. Although we may not always have complained to the usher about this situation, our hesitancy probably was due to a reluctance to make an issue of it. But we were not surprised if a group of adolescents in the movie house began to shout, "Sound! Fix the sound!" We always assumed the fault was with the theater, not with our ears. By contrast, elderly people at the same movie performance might believe that the fault was with their hearing and feel that they had no reasonable grounds for complaining to the theater management.

Regardless of whether our parents are inside or outside the home, the loss or decline of their hearing can be tough on them, especially if it interferes with their ability to hold conversations. Turning up a radio is one thing, but asking a friend to repeat every sentence at a near shout is another. Hardly any of us can keep an even temper while talking at the top of our lungs, and our aged parents are well aware of this. Rather than watch our exasperation or "cause trouble," they may often just nod and smile and then let the conversation drop. You may discover that some agreement you thought had been made and understood turns out to be no agreement at all. This situation may simply be the result of your parents' efforts to cover up the fact that they could not make out clearly what you said in the first place.

Feeling left out of things is no pleasure at any age, as the following case brings out.

Mrs. Dougal, a grandmother in her early eighties, always looked forward to the gathering of the clan for the holidays. She no longer saw her family regularly and very much wanted to catch up on what each of them had been doing. Her son Marty, on the other hand, was always uncomfortable and bored at family get-togethers. He had very little in common with his relatives and came only out of a sense of duty.

After dinner his wife and sister-in-law cleared the table and then adjourned to the kitchen to wash the dishes and put away the leftovers. All the other relatives leaned back in their seats as the gossip, small talk, quips, and political backbiting began in earnest.

Before long Marty contracted a case of what we may call social deafness. The conversation turned gradually into an incoherent din and, as his private thoughts and worries took over, soon became practically inaudible for him. Every once in a while, if his preoccupations got too upsetting, he immediately zoomed back to listen to the talk around him. Within moments he had an exact bead on what old joke or silly political prejudice was being retold. Each time he tuned his mind in again, he felt sharply bored, isolated, out of place, and itching to go home.

During Marty's fourth reverie of this kind, his ears caught a burst of sharp laughter in the kitchen. He heard his wife mention his name and, for the next few moments, strained to piece together what was being said. The subject was finicky eaters, and he had evidently taken first prize. Well, he had lived with that label for years, and so he slipped back into another reverie until his brother jolted him out of it by asking him a direct question. For a moment Marty was flustered. He looked around and then had to admit he hadn't been listening. His embarrassment, though, was milder than his brother's ironic wonderment that Marty had found their conversation less than fascinating. Marty insisted that, on the contrary, the talk was totally absorbing. The company laughed, and the talk moved on.

Unlike her son, Mrs. Dougal had all along been making a real attempt to take in every scrap of conversation and, on occasion, contribute to it. It had been a wearing, frustrating experience. Her hearing was poor, so she had to make a concentrated effort to listen. She had to summon all her attention for each speaker. If she did not, she was simply left alone with her own thoughts. Again unlike her son, Mrs. Dougal knew that this state of isolation was a monotonous, confining aspect of her daily life. As the talk grew more rapid, it was harder for her to keep up. The laughter from the kitchen and the gossip associated with it were no distractions for her—they might as well have been taking place in the house next door. Despite all her alertness and attention she was still missing out.

Just then Marty's wife entered the room with the after-dinner coffee. For no apparent reason she asked if anyone had heard from Cousin Laura, a woman in her late fifties who lived in Cleveland. Someone responded that Laura's eighteen-year-old daughter was said to be pregnant. Eyebrows were raised, and Mrs. Dougal, noting this, ventured to say how amazed she was that a woman that old could still conceive.

Eyebrows rose still higher. The surprise was directed at Mrs. Dougal, who had not caught the daughter's name when it was mentioned. Unlike Marty's lapse, Mrs. Dougal's lack of comprehension made her seem foolish in the clan's eyes. Some wondered if she was apt to become confused, if her attention span was decreasing in her old age. When her daughter corrected her, Mrs. Dougal smiled a little sheepishly and lapsed into the same sort of reverie into which Marty had retreated. But this was exactly the kind of isolation she had hoped to avoid on that particular evening.

If we reflect on this incident a bit, we shall realize that there was nothing malicious in the mistake the family made about Mrs. Dougal. After all, some elderly persons do become disoriented and inattentive. Although such changes are disturbing, they are not nearly as prevalent—let alone as inevitable—as some of us may believe. Far more confused and quizzical responses among the aged are results of simply not having heard all that was said rather than some sort of brain or memory dysfunction. So part of the difficulty sons and daughters may have in dealing with elderly parents is learning to guard against jumping to conclusions of this nature.

There are two practical ways in which aging persons can compensate to some degree for a loss of hearing.

Lipreading classes have only recently begun to find acceptance and usage among the aged. Still they are not the first remedy that comes to either your mind or that of your parents. Obviously lipreading cannot restore lost hearing, but it does improve the ability to understand what is said. Although that in itself is no small benefit, your elderly parents would have to be highly motivated to take this step. Not only does it take a lot of work on the part of your parents, but it also requires them to admit that they have a hearing problem for which they need help. Then it requires them to register for lipreading classes and attend them regularly.

Another, more common, remedy is to consider use of a hearing aid. Unfortunately, most people expect the hearing aid to correct the problem as neatly as glasses do poor vision. Usually, however, this is not the case. As a result many misinformed elderly may experience an initial feeling of disappointment and decide to put the listening device away unused in some dresser drawer. This reaction may be due to some unexpected physical discomfort involved in getting used to the hearing aid, or some elderly may perceive the hearing aid as a symbolic proclamation to the world that their nervously concealed "weakness" exists in fact. As a result they will probably feel a great deal of psychological uneasiness when they start to use the hearing device.

Once the use and the limitations of the hearing aid are understood, however, you should be able to anticipate and handle the most common complaints of your parents. Such understanding may alert you when it may be better to spare yourself the aggravation of fruitlessly extolling the virtues of an aid that Mother or Dad simply will not use.

Perhaps the best way to understand the difficulties of using a hearing aid would be to compare and contrast the principles on which eyeglasses and hearing aids are constructed. There are, for example, two primary ways in which people's eyesight usually deteriorates. In the majority of cases, people with a vision problem can still see the world. They can take it in and adjust to as much light or darkness as everyone else. But they simply cannot bring objects into focus beyond a certain distance. The problem can be solved, however, on the basis of mathematical principles that have been thoroughly understood for many years. As a result people can put on a pair of glasses especially prescribed for their eyes and enjoy normal vision from that moment onward. This remedy is as uncomplicated as slipping into a pair of slacks. Usually the only instruction anyone needs is to be sure to take the glasses off before going to bed or if a headache develops. We have to learn to wash them if they get dirty, to avoid stepping on them, and to keep them away from the dog.

At one time glasses carried something of a stigma. They were supposed to be reserved for old fogies, studious boys inclined to be effeminate, and girls at whom men seldom made passes. But this has all changed! During the late sixties, for example, the wire-rimmed version, or granny glasses, was considered highly fashionable by college students.

Unfortunately, deteriorating eyesight may also confront people with a second kind of eye trouble—a gradual, destructive process that leads eventually to blindness. A nerve or some other irreplaceable part of the eye mechanism may degenerate or be destroyed. The world then dims and gradually becomes as imperceptible as a stage behind a purple velvet curtain. High intensity light cannot pierce it. Glasses cannot help one see through it. Nor would we expect eyeglasses to help against this form of defective vision.

When someone becomes hard of hearing, the result is often similar in a way to the second kind of defective vision. A nerve or some other irreplaceable part of the ear mechanism may have permanently worn out. This may not lead to absolute deafness; in fact it usually does not. But sounds now become muffled or cannot be heard at all. The principles behind most cases of hearing loss are not wholly known. Here it is not a matter of straightforward mathematical ratios. The ear does not have the tremendous ability to focus and adjust to levels of sound as the eye does to objects and light. A young mother who can hear her baby crying upstairs while she is in the kitchen in the midst of a raucous party impresses us, for example, even though our own eyes perform analogous feats of vision every day and as a matter of course.

A hearing aid is ruthlessly indiscriminating. It amplifies all sounds equally, from the neighbor chatting over a cup of coffee to the garbage truck moving in the alley. It does not select out and focus in on precise sounds at precise distances, as a user may desire.

Often hearing aids provide adequate assistance, and sometimes they do far more than that. All the same, a hearing device is far from an ideal substitute for the real thing. The hard truth is that no perfect solution for serious hearing losses has yet been discovered.

Glasses provide a fairly unobtrusive and distortion-free correction. Hearing aids, however, often make a humming sound, which in itself can be an annoyance to the user. This problem may be alleviated as the devices are refined. In the last thirty years the devices have improved as our technology has become more sophisticated. They have become smaller and now run on transistors. This makes them more dependable than the old battery-run sets, whose batteries quickly ran down and needed regular replacement. Although hearing aids are much more reliable today than in the past, you still have to follow detailed instructions for their use and upkeep.

To these generally unanticipated "technical" problems of hearing aids, our society has also added the unfortunate prejudice of fashion. Hearing aids on the whole carry a stigma that most middle-aged sons and daughters may not fully appreciate. An attractive woman in her sixties, for example, can wear a pair of glasses at all times without calling any particular attention to a physical problem. Hardly a soul will find that her appearance has seriously deteriorated because she has begun to wear glasses. Were she to start wearing a hearing aid, however, many people might take notice. It would often be perceived as a sign that she has become old, and it would unquestionably affect her cosmetic appearance in an unfavorable way. If you pause for a moment to imagine how self-conscious you yourself would feel if you had to start wearing a hearing aid tomorrow, perhaps the reluctance of a parent to do so will become more understandable.

Many elderly people have also been disappointed—to say nothing of being misled and swindled—because they purchased an aid under the mistaken impression that their hearing problem was a "standard" one for which any "standard" device would do.

That simply is not so. A wide range of hearing aids is available for a wide spectrum of individual problems. For years, however, unscrupulous firms have ignored this fact in order to sell devices through the mail on the basis of appealing magazine and newspaper advertisements. No one would think of ordering prescription glasses this way. But unfortunately the elderly are sometimes an easy mark.

If your mother feels that she could benefit from a hearing aid, you would do well to see that she is examined and fitted at a licensed hearing aid center. They may mean some extra effort on your part, for these outlets are not as common or well known as optometrists' offices, but they are just as reliable and professional. The people in licensed centers will not sell a device if it is unnecessary or superfluous, and they are quite conscientious about follow-up care.

Ideally, if a parent complains of a hearing loss, the first step is an examination by a physician. If he or she indicates that a hearing aid may be helpful, you should help your parent find the nearest center and—to the extent you are able—learn for yourself what limitations the new device brings with it. Your parent can best adjust to the aid if he or she accepts the new situation and decides to improve it in whatever ways are possible.

Often, however, a parent may not complain at all about this particular loss. In such instances it is not unusual for sons and daughters to take the initiative and express the necessity of having their father or mother checked out and outfitted. Unfortunately, this propensity, which is done out of concern and a desire to be helpful, may push your parent too quickly into facing a painful truth. Trying to get Mama, for instance, to use a hearing aid before she is ready to admit she needs one can easily result in conflicts and arguments. Even if you "win" such a battle, everyone usually loses in the long run, as the hearing aid may somehow get broken, misplaced, or buried in a closet.

It is especially important for sons and daughters to keep this last piece of advice firmly in mind. The most lasting, positive adjustments to physical losses come when our elderly parents are ready to face and accept the loss on their own terms, in their own way. As a rule, unless there is an imminent threat to life, limb, or personal safety, parents should not be *pushed* into admitting the severity of their losses. The well-intentioned pressure will probably be resisted and resented. This is in part because your parents need to feel—perhaps more than ever now—that they are still autonomous, self-reliant adults capable of making their own decisions and taking responsibility for their own welfare. For many parents the passive, dependent role is a very painful one to play. And so while you may hear yourself making suggestions that are clearly in your father's own best interest, he may simply suspect that you feel he is incompetent, deteriorating, and clearly in need of heavy-handed supervision. He may need to openly reject your good advice, think about it privately, and come up with a decision that is now his own. Don't be too upset with this initial need to reject your good ideas. It's part of the necessary work involved in maintaining one's dignity and self-direction, which are no less important than improved hearing.

In handling a parent's complaints about a hearing loss as well as any uneasiness you yourself might feel over this symbol of your parent's decline, perhaps the most appropriate and effective tack is to assume that this device will provide Dad with a choice. Without it, he might well be involuntarily prohibited from casual contacts and involvements with others. You might remind him—and yourself—that a hearing aid may be a pain in the neck at times. It certainly isn't perfect, and no one would pretend otherwise. But if it allows him to listen to what may even be a distorted version of a holiday's festivities, he is far better off than were he confined to seeing the animation without being able to comprehend or participate in it. If a hearing aid allows him to be more involved and—just as important—if it enables people to be more in touch with him, its benefits are sizable.

The overriding principle, after all, is having your parents remain self-reliant participants in the world around them. And sometimes this means that they, like all the rest of us, would prefer to shut the world out temporarily. There is nothing unnatural about this. Sometimes it is psychologically essential to do so. And so it sometimes happens that aged people who are sitting with members of their family may suddenly confuse or offend them by shutting off the aid. It may be, as their children tend to assume, that this is their parents' way of saying they are angry or bored. If so, there is no need to be afraid of those emotions. We all have them and are all entitled to them, but we usually snap out of them eventually unless we have made it a practice to shut ourselves off from the outside world. Just keep in mind, as we saw from the case of Mrs. Dougal, that participating in a conversation when you are hard of hearing can be a demanding, draining experience. People become tired. Snapping off the hearing aid may just mean that the strain of listening and the electronic hum has finally gotten to Dad or Mother. It may also mean that your parent is trying to be economical by conserving the set.

TOUCH

If your elderly parent is blessed with good fortune, perhaps he or she may even be able to say that the only sense considerably diminished is the physical sense of touch. The ability to distinguish between burlap and velvet while blindfolded is not what is meant by touch here but rather a growing numbness to pain and other stimuli under certain conditions. In old age this sense often deteriorates.

At first glance some middle-aged sons and daughters might feel that such a loss would be welcome. "You ought to meet my mother, who's the living contradiction to this problem," such an offspring might think. "Not a week goes by when I don't hear in exquisite detail about the stabbing, shooting pains along her arms and legs. In fact I hear about every twinge there is."

The deterioration of the sense of touch might sound like a godsend because, after all, what could be more desirable than an invulnerability to suffering? And it is true, as studies have found, that in some cases certain minor surgery can be performed with little discomfort.

But pain, we must remember, is a warning device. It tells us that our body is in danger and urges us to do something about it. If our body does not receive this message, it becomes vulnerable, if not downright defenseless. An elderly parent's insensitivity to pain is usually not absolute, and, for the most part, we should be thankful that it is not.

Being unable to receive signals that something has gone wrong within the body can be disastrous. It can mean, for example, that an elderly parent may be unable to detect a mild heart attack. If such an event occurs while your mother is out walking, even more serious damage may be inflicted as a result of a fainting spell and subsequent fall. There are, of course, a number of lesser, more everyday hazards, which have to do with such things as hot baths, heating pads, and kitchen burners. Insensitivity to pain may in good part account for the fact that elderly parents suffer three times the number of scalds and burns as their middle-aged sons and daughters. It may take Mama far longer to feel just how hot that bathwater she has stepped into really is. If the circulation in her legs is poor, she may never feel the damage a heating pad causes during the night. In the kitchen she may touch a live burner and pull away only after she has received a severe burn.

TASTE AND SMELL

The losses that may have the least significance in a parent's every-day life may be those of taste and smell. In old age the taste buds around the tip of the tongue, the ones most sensitive to sweetness, may atrophy. If this happens, sweet dishes and drinks may seem bland or bitter. On the other hand, a parent's sensitivity to the taste of salt may increase. And so a mother-in-law who has begun to find the meals her daughter-in-law prepares unbearably salty should probably be served food she can season herself at the table.

Since most of the elderly, like the United States population as a whole, live in urban areas, the decline in our sense of smell may sometimes be construed as a blessing in disguise. But gerontologists point out that this can make the elderly oblivious to such things as an open gas jet or burning material. The gas companies in many states, however, have begun to lace their natural gas with an aroma that resembles rotten eggs. As this program gains momentum, your parents, to be sure, will all breathe a little easier.

OVERALL STAMINA

Perhaps there is no better-known, if somewhat exaggerated, example of how the body wears down and how people can cope with this phenomenon than the aging professional athlete. As a line-backer nears forty, he usually stops trying to knock aside every opponent and chase all over the field at every play. He knows that he becomes exhausted more quickly and that he can no longer depend upon sheer brawn and stamina as he once did. If he has a history of injuries, as most athletes engaged in professional sports do, he knows that indiscriminate contact and stress can now put him out for the season or for good.

A good athlete has continued to survive all those years in the league because he uses his head as well as his chest and legs. He has gained in experience as his physical prowess has diminished. Perhaps it hasn't been a perfect trade-off. But it has been valuable enough to extend his career a few extra years. And so he now figures out beforehand where the play is likely to go and just how he can use his full energies to make them count the most.

Our elderly parents, of course, have slowed down even more than the linebacker, and the ways in which they have done so are often vivid and painful to witness. They may not only be unable to run errands all day as they once did, but they cannot even walk as far at a stretch. Their physical decline may give them an entirely different perspective on how to structure their time and activities. When most of us set out for an afternoon of errands, for instance, we usually plot out beforehand how we can most speedily and efficiently get to the most stops in the hours we have set aside. An elderly mother, on the other hand, may have to figure her schedule on the basis of how far she can go before she becomes too exhausted to continue.

In other words, biological changes have now advanced to the point where your mother's stamina and reserve, among other things, have been drastically reduced. Along the way her step may have lost its briskness, and her gait may have changed into a kind of shuffle. She may now bring her feet directly up and down or walk with a waddle.

Elderly persons do slow down, and they need more time to walk across the street. They also need more time to rest once they get home. If they come down with a cold or a fever, they may have to go to bed and stay there an extra day or so. The changes of season may also become more difficult for them.

A major contributing factor to all this is the deterioration of the mechanisms responsible for regulating our blood pressure, oxygen supply, and body temperature. In old age these mechanisms tend to work less vigorously and efficiently. A person's physical equilibrium depends upon their functioning during every moment of life—during every activity, from sitting over coffee at breakfast to running for a bus. One result of such a physical decline is that an elderly person's equilibrium comes to hang in an ever more precarious and provisional balance.

Some elderly are reminded of this loss on a daily basis. They may escape it when they are watching television, reading a newspaper, or napping because their bodies are then essentially at rest and the demands placed upon them minimal. The mechanisms have only to maintain this state. It is not a stressful task, so an aged person is likely to feel as little discomfort or anxiety at such times as would we.

When the levels of activity become more strenuous, however, it is another matter. An aging body, no less than a younger one, reacts to the exercise involved in climbing a flight of stairs by boosting the heartbeat, blood pressure, and oxygen intake. But the wide range of endurance and precision younger persons possess has been lost. In old age it may take much less stress for individuals to feel they have pushed themselves to their physical limits.

As these limitations become permanently narrower, a punishing exhaustion comes to be more and more a part of your parent's life. When walking up a stairway, your father's body may not be able to adjust smoothly. His heart may race full tilt so that one flight induces the same pounding breathlessness in him that a younger person would feel after skipping up two or three floors. The most obvious means he has of compensating for this loss and avoiding painful discomfort is by taking things slower. Dad may also scale down the overall sorts of exertion he is normally able or willing to undertake. There is nothing "wrong" with this. After all, if his current activities are more or less sedentary, his comfort and his ability to participate and enjoy are comparable to your own.

A son or daughter who sees that exercise has become a problem for a parent can respond by planning activities in which little more than walking from the house to the car is involved. When strolling, you can consciously set a more leisurely pace.

Not all parents, though, will readily admit or adjust to this loss. While some fathers may not have the physical strength of the past, they may still continue an artificially high level of activity, pushing themselves beyond their limits. Often, on what would be an otherwise casual jaunt, it is Dad who sets the fast pace. This may be his way of saying that old age hasn't gotten to *him*, so if you want to keep up, you'd better hurry! Perhaps he will pay a price later on in the evening through fatigue or other distress. Nevertheless, his need to *feel* that he hasn't slowed down has prevailed. We often must learn to accept such psychological needs even when they tend to interfere with our parents' physical health.

A complex array of bodily mechanisms works to keep the body normal under a variety of circumstances. Exertion is just one. We depend upon such mechanisms for protection during harsh, extreme weather. They also ward off infection and disease. When the body is damaged—when, say, a wrist is fractured—they work to repair it. They provide us with a wide, comfortable margin of safety for everyday life, much of which we take for granted.

Another result of the narrowing physical limits in old age is the loss of the wide margin of safety provided by our bodily mechanisms. With changes in the body's capacity to adjust to heat and cold, a person may begin to develop new reactions to weather conditions. For instance, the outdoors may begin to feel different to an elderly person. Some of the forms these changes may take can be dramatic and upsetting. We would not fault middle-aged sons or daughters for any initial shock they might feel were they to see their father hunched in an overcoat among his cohorts on a park bench in mid-July. It appears to be a crazy stunt designed to attract attention. In reality it is simply an advanced stage of a common biological change.

One of the most important benefits of the wide margin of safety younger persons enjoy is that it permits us to take a fair number of physical risks. Stepping out into a very frigid morning, we may discover fairly soon that we should have put on an extra sweater. We get where we are going with a shudder and a curse and then warm up as soon as we can. In short, we know—although we surely don't put it to ourselves this way—that our bodies will make up the difference by making us shiver, by stepping up our metabolism, and by providing the needed extra warmth.

Once we get to work, we may find that the flu is going around. Again we go on about our business because we know that our bodies are resilient enough to ward off a viral infection. And if worse comes to worse, we might be ill for a day or two.

But our aging parents' bodies may no longer possess the resources to permit them to take risks of this sort. Their resistance has diminished considerably, so they are less able to avoid infection and illness. If they do not bundle up properly in very cold weather, their bodies may well be incapable of making up the difference. Once they catch a cold, the mechanisms, which have all they can do to maintain a stable condition, are then placed under an extra burden. And this, of course, is handled less efficiently. Bringing the infection under control again takes longer, and sometimes it simply cannot be done. This is one of the reasons that it takes more time for the elderly to recuperate from an illness and that a cold or a fever may easily turn into something more serious.

Often in old age, ailments become more problematic because the health has declined to a point where the capacity to take the simplest medicines disappears. A doctor, for example, may be unable to prescribe aspirin because it will irritate your mother's stomach. Many medicines that younger people may use safely cause discomfort or distressing side effects in the aged and make treatment of some illnesses in the elderly more difficult.

Many elderly parents make up for this overall decline in ways that are familiar to us all. Some move to milder climates. Others discuss and prepare for weather conditions with the same preoccupation a general might bring to waging war. There are times when all their concern and elaborate precautions seem irritating and excessive to their children. Often this is just common sense on your parents' part—a reaction to a physical experience their children have never known. It may be carried to potentially harmful extremes, though, and used as a cover for emotional problems they prefer to conceal. This becomes especially common if your parents' physical disabilities contribute to their refusal or unwillingness to get out of the house and around on their own.

ACCIDENTS

Your parents' tendency to stay at home develops from more than a growing susceptibility to colds or shortness of breath. As part of their overall physical decline, aging people begin to lose the sharp reflexes and coordination they once had. This often means that they cannot react as quickly to avoid accidents. They may see a car approach or feel themselves about to slip on wet pavement yet be unable to avoid the danger.

Muscles and bones have also deteriorated. Even if your parents initiated a regular exercise program, they would never be able to restore the physical strength they once had. A man in his twenties who has been confined to a wheelchair for years can build massive muscles in his shoulders, chest, and arms. An elderly person cannot. Bones change because they are living tissue formed through the secretion of hormones and affected by the stresses and strains of physical activity. In old age the body simply cannot endure the level of exercise that it once could. Besides, the body now produces hormones and calcium in smaller quantities. As a result the ribs, spine, pelvis, arms, and legs of an elderly person tend to become lighter, thinner, and more brittle. A seventy-year-old man's skeletal structure may, in fact, weigh 30 percent less than it did during his middle years.

As our elderly parents' limbs become less supple and dependable, they become more vulnerable to fractures and breaks. In fact parents in their seventies are about five times more likely to meet with this problem than their children. This is not because the elderly become more absentminded or careless. Almost one fourth of parents who suffer fractured necks or spinal disks were doing nothing more dangerous than opening a window or sneezing. Your father may have tripped on a bottom step twice in the past year and then gone on his way with nothing more than a skinned palm. But the third time he tripped, the bone was ready to break, so his hip was fractured. Since his body cannot produce the amount of hormones and cells necessary for a smooth recovery, he may be laid up for some time.

This is the main reason that an elderly parent's mishaps can so often have serious consequences. Other changes, however, contribute not only to the possibility of accidents but to new restrictions on the freedom of movement a parent has enjoyed within and outside the house.

The sense of balance can worsen as the part of the brain that manages this function begins to deteriorate in old age. When this happens, a person may begin to have dizzy spells. There is a simple test a person can make to assess whether this change has set in. It involves the ability to stand erect with the eyes closed. Most parents either disregard this loss or put up with it and carry on. When the phone rings, for example, your mother may feel the same intensity of dizziness as she stands to answer it that you might if you stooped over to look at a low shelf of records or books.

There may be several reasons that your mother does not mention this loss to you. She may have taken the attitude that dizziness is just one more thing a self-respecting person has to put up with without complaint during old age. Talking or worrying about it won't make it go away. From her point of view, were she to become consumed by something as common and everyday as temporary dizziness, she might conceivably be confined to a sitting position all her life. Besides, if she does complain, you might suggest that she undergo the discomfort, expense, and inconvenience of a medical examination. Who knows what such an examination might find? And so she simply answers the phone and listens until the dizziness passes.

Such a problem becomes dangerous, however, when a parent tries to maneuver on stairways and curbs. Landings and cellar steps often have inadequate handrails and poor lighting. A dizzy spell that comes on as Mom is climbing the stairs can bring on a dangerous backward fall. Looking down a single flight of stairs may give her the same nauseous sense of vertigo you experience as you peer down from a high-rise balcony.

ARTHRITIS

Another change is one of the oldest and most common ailments of mankind—arthritis. Medical research has not been able to determine precisely why it develops. This painful swelling of the joints can stiffen fingers, backs, elbows, legs, arteries, and spines. Most people feel their first bout with it during middle age and watch it become more pervasive with age.

Usually an elderly parent knows the full extent of his or her affliction. An exception to this, however, occurs when arthritis narrows the arteries that convey blood to the brain. When Dad's head is turned sharply upward or sideways—which happens when he replaces a ceiling light bulb standing on a ladder or when he puts the groceries away on a top shelf or when he looks quickly around while driving the car—blood can be cut off from the brain. This can induce dizziness, fainting, and a fall.

More often, however, arthritis is a chronic, constant condition that stands between Dad and a multitude of small actions the rest of us perform without a thought. It is a companion that can greet him as he climbs out of bed, as he tries to shave, as he lifts the coffeepot, or as he tries to grasp a spoon.

In addition to the physical pain of arthritis, there is the powerful message that your parent has become useless and incompetent. How else would you describe someone, as the reasoning goes, who cannot even turn a doorknob or bend down to pick up the morning newspaper without painful effort?

Some doctors believe that arthritis becomes more painful and spreads faster if the elderly are under great emotional strain. A study found that if a group of deeply troubled elderly overcame their fears, anxieties, and grief, their arthritis subsided and became less painful.

EMOTIONAL REACTIONS

Unfortunately, our society tends to condemn psychosomatic problems. Emotional problems can, in fact, be just as serious and paralyzing as physical ones. Yet we would probably tell our mother, who has an emotional problem, that it's all in her head in order to dismiss the complaint altogether. Everyone understands and accepts someone who is laid up with a broken leg. But if the only way a parent's emotional difficulties can surface is through something like arthritis, the common tendency is to label her a nag or a complainer. Rather than urge her to seek counseling or psychotherapy, which have proved especially helpful for the elderly, we may hold her psychosomatic behavior against her.

From a parent's point of view it may be much easier and less painful to use arthritis as a convenient symbol of problems too disturbing to probe, let alone express. In this instance Mom herself may be unaware that she is covering up.

It would be misleading, though, to consider the word *arthritis* a code word for unspoken emotional problems. A nagging backache may be a reminder to your parents that they are growing old. But it is first and foremost a physical problem that can be as confining as it is uncomfortable. In this sense it can snowball the feeling of discouragement that your parents may have had in the first place. Like the rest of us, aged parents have days when they feel terribly blue for no apparent reason. Having to lug this physical burden along with a draining mood can be intolerable. You may call to find out how your father is doing and hear him answer that his arthritis is killing him. It may just be that, with everything else on his mind, he was just not up to handling this persistent companion that afternoon.

MOBILITY

Taken together, these physical developments can turn your elderly parents' attempts at getting around in the world into a highly calculated risk. Around the house they are more vulnerable to accidental falls from tripping over extension cords and slipping on waxed floors. It is often wisest, in fact, to run such cords along the walls and cover the floors with carpets. To prevent other bad accidents, grab rails may have to be installed along stairways and in the shower.

Venturing outdoors can be no less difficult. During winter Dad may have to ask himself beforehand whether he will be able to dress warmly enough to avoid contracting an illness. Will he be able to maneuver safely over snow-covered steps and icy sidewalks? A cane or walker is not much insurance. Reaching his destination can become a real accomplishment. After all, some motorists become angry and impatient if they have to wait for an elderly person to cross the street before the light turns. The bustle of pedestrians on the sidewalks is another pressure. An aged person is viewed as a nearly stationary object to be quickly outmaneuvered. All this can make one feel jostled, harassed, and threatened.

If your parents have gone out to run errands, the return trip adds the burden of purchases that must be brought back in tow to this same list of pressures and difficulties.

The most far-reaching problems, however, do not arise from potential accidents but from how deeply these changes cut into your parents' normal activities and freedom of movement. Drastic change is hard at any age but especially so for the elderly. If your father used to spend his recreation time tending a garden or enjoying sports, his losses may leave him feeling dispossessed. A mother may have always derived a strong, quiet pride as well as self-respect from running a clean household and cooking nourishing meals from scratch. Her physical losses and disabilities can remove such important satisfactions from her life.

DRIVING

There is one activity, though, which once given up can impose dramatic and permanent restrictions overnight. That is driving an automobile. In our society there are few privileges so closely associated with independence, competence, and adulthood as the driver's license. A car is so much a part of our lives that most of us consider any time when the machine is in the shop for repairs as a real hardship. Important as is the independence and mobility a car provides your parents, you must remember also that they may have been enjoying this independence and mobility uninterruptedly for most of their adult lives.

The question of just when Dad should relinquish his license is a knotty one. Everyone ages at a different rate. Your father may have the kidneys of someone ten years his junior and the heart of someone four years older. He may have the reflexes of a younger man and the coordination of an older one. In some states the aged are required by law to submit to driver's tests on a regular— sometimes yearly—basis. In many cases, though, it is a decision that must be reached by parents and the family with advice from the physician. In some instances a parent may be able to drive during normal daylight conditions and simply give up nighttime, long-distance, or particularly hazardous driving. The following case may be typical of a problem that confronts many parents and their children.

Ellen Anderson found herself in a bind. She suspected that her eighty-two-year-old father was becoming a danger to himself and others every time he touched the ignition key. Her father's driving had become an ongoing source of anxiety for her, and yet she could hardly bring herself to talk to him about it. Every so often the phone would ring, and she could not help imagining it was bringing news of an accident he had gotten into. He had always been a safe, cautious driver, but she suspected that he now drove too slowly for conditions and could no longer react quickly enough to yellow lights as well as to the assorted maniacs on the road. Sometimes she would bring herself to ask if the traffic had been particularly bothersome lately.

Her father would either shake his head or answer no and change the subject. On the two occasions she insisted upon driving instead of riding along as his passenger, her father curtly vetoed the idea. Nevertheless, whenever they approached an intersection or a slow-moving car, she braced for a collision. Nor was it easy to know if the sudden stops he made were due to his declining attention span. Were cars passing him because he had slowed down or because everyone generally ignores the speed limits?

Mr. Anderson had always been a fairly obstinate person, and she did not want to be blamed for calling him incompetent. She knew, too, that without a car he would be less likely to get out of his apartment. At his age long walks and waits for buses and trains could not be taken in stride so easily. The abuse from foul weather would get to him. And above all, a Saturday night movie or trip to see what few friends he had in the suburbs would be out of the question if he had to rely on public transportation.

To tell the truth, if her father had to give up driving, he might naturally want others to pick up the slack for him. This was no problem if his friends and he went out together, but she knew that the new responsibility would most likely, and most often, fall upon her. She disliked the idea of becoming his chauffeur or errand girl about as much as she relished being the villain who stood silently by while he injured himself or someone else.

When Mr. Anderson had to take his driver's test, he failed and his license was revoked. When Ellen heard the news, part of her was genuinely relieved. But she was quite surprised to see how hard he took it. He was inconsolable for days. It was one of the few times she had ever seen him weep openly. At first she spoke to him sympathetically, but she soon found herself becoming impatient and short tempered. After all, it was only a car, and he had not been so upset even when his brother died.

Actually her father's response was as natural as her own. He had watched all his small losses accumulate over the years. The effort he had made to cope physically and emotionally had been a private one he never discussed with her. He was afraid his losses would lead to a loss of liberty and a personal helplessness. The prospect was so frightening that he had covered up and denied the possibility. But there was no denying it now. The loss of his license made his changes dramatically plain to him and everyone else.

If Mr. Anderson was an obstinate man, this was partially a result of a personal pride that he never asked anyone for anything. Now, though, he was forced to surrender a good measure of his independence. If his daughter viewed his behavior in a harsh light, it was because he had acted at odds with deeply ingrained social conventions. We are expected to deeply mourn a death, especially one within the family, no matter how insignificant or rancorous the lifelong relationship may have been. It is the rare child who can appreciate how deeply the loss of a license and the freedom and competence it represents can hit a parent.

INCONTINENCE

It was mentioned earlier how much strength our muscles may have lost by the time we reach old age. We have seen how this loss can make getting around all the more difficult. There are several sets of muscles, though, that can alter a parent's life and never be discussed at all—the muscles related to control of the bowel and the bladder. If they deteriorate, our parents may have to urinate or defecate more frequently. Worst of all, they may soil themselves during the night or if they find themselves in public places where no toilet facilities are readily accessible.

Everyone's childhood includes some buried shameful memories of wetting the bed or soiling themselves in grade school. Gaining control of our bodily functions was one of the first skills we mastered in life. The message that this is now lost can be devastating to our parents. All those early childhood feelings may be reawakened. Although this loss is no more our parents' fault than the twenty-four-hour flu, the odor and the discomfort can be an overpowering signal that they have lost a fundamental autonomy, the control over their very being. A bodily function that we all manage privately and quietly throughout our lives now becomes a public embarrassment.

As a parent attempts to cope with this change, he or she may seem to become increasingly antisocial. It takes no special insight or knowledge to see how such a behavior change can result from this special physical problem. The particular activities a parent suddenly drops may be a tip-off. If Mom or Dad has enjoyed auctions, picnics, or sports contests for years but now seems abruptly to have lost all interest in them, you might be able to restore that enthusiasm by making it a point to find aisle seats and make regular trips to the washroom on your own initiative, nonchalantly suggesting that your parent come along. In planning joint activities, precautions might be taken to see that toilet facilities are easily accessible.

Such physical changes often leave an elderly parent deeply discouraged. Just as there are some parents who have few, if any, of these problems, so will there be others who are so inflexibly self-reliant that they neither solicit nor accept assistance from you. Becoming dependent upon others for assistance may be absolutely unacceptable to your parent, who either refuses to be a burden or obligation to others or fears the possibility of being refused or being abandoned. This potentially terrifying situation is therefore to be avoided at all costs. As a rule, the degree of self-reliance your parents maintained in the past will be extended into their reactions in old age.

MENTAL FUNCTIONING

A common side effect of all these physical declines is that some aged people become so cautious that they wind up being overprotective of themselves. This becomes a source of real concern when they reach the point of becoming shut-ins. They may then no longer leave the house to take the morning walk that they not only enjoy but that the doctor ordered as crucial exercise. They may drop out of a church social group because "there is disease everywhere," because "flu bugs turn into pneumonia," and so on.

If your parents become socially inactive and withdrawn, a debilitating depression may result. Ultimately this emotional despair itself can overshadow whatever other serious physical problems exist. That is, the emotional damage caused by despair can be far more serious than the physical restrictions themselves, and it may finally become the real reason a parent refuses to leave the house. Physical changes then become simply an excuse. Since these are real ailments, it can be very difficult for you to argue or convince your parents to get out of the house and participate in social activities for their own good.

No matter how many of these losses some elderly parents may have encountered, their children will often describe them as "alert as they ever were." It is another way of saying that, no matter what has already happened, the worst catastrophe of all, senility, has not occurred—yet.

Along with cancer, changes in the brain seem to be feared above all other ailments. A middle-aged son or daughter may see his or her parents no longer taking an active part in the world. The parents look older and seem more fragile. Since most of their faculties have evidently slowed down, the children conclude that the intelligence must too. It is true that a decline in brain function does affect a portion of the elderly—but only a small portion. We know that most of the serious mental functioning problems seen in older persons are a result of Alzheimer's Disease. Strokes, diet, certain medications, alcohol, stress, and other factors may also produce symptoms of mental deterioration. But not all unusual behavior that you may observe in your parents means Alzheimer's Disease or "senility." Senility, in fact, has been a blanket word inappropriately applied to changes of all kinds and no longer seems to be an accurate or useful term. Here it will be enough to describe the most common minor changes of old age and to point out how needless many of our preconceived fears truly are.

Although our understanding of the brain's workings is still in the beginning stages, we do know that during the latter half of life, several thousand brain cells die each day. They are not replaced, and by age seventy-five a person's brain may weigh less than it once did. At first glance this may sound disturbing. The fact is, however, that the human brain has far more cells than it needs to perform at normal capacity.

A recent medical case history bears this out. A man who suffered all his life from severe epileptic seizures submitted to brain surgery as a last resort. A portion of his brain was removed, and today he is leading a normal life with virtually all his faculties and intelligence intact. Only now he no longer suffers from epilepsy.

Scientists have also found that certain aspects of human memory pass their peak relatively early in life. But this, too, should be taken with a grain of salt. Our memory of numbers, for example, begins to decline at age twenty-seven. This may be of some importance to a professor of mathematics engaged in original research, but the rest of us have little cause for concern. The same may be said for design memory, which slows after age twenty-three. In fact, well-educated, highly trained people who live into their mid-seventies have been found to retain just about all their faculties. It is true that when young people are pitted against the elderly in intelligence tests, the younger group scores higher. But that is often because they are racing against the clock. Given more time, and in some cases larger print, the elderly do just as well.

Elderly people tend to meet new situations and evaluate problems on the basis of their past experiences. What they should do and how they should react depend on what has worked for them or been expected of them in the past. "You can't teach an old dog new tricks" is another way of saying that the expensive lessons of trial and error accumulate. In old age there is a lifetime to fall back on, and new information just may not find a fresh place on which to leave an impression.

This is one reason, though not the only one, that the elderly are less able to process and retain new information. Other reasons have to do with the problems of memory loss in old age and the tendency of our parents to reminisce about events in the remote past. These important topics will be examined in detail later in the book.

CHOOSING A PHYSICIAN

As an aged mother's health problems multiply, her anxieties concerning them also mount, and her need for security, reassurance, and guidance is also likely to increase. Your mother may turn to you, of course. And she may also turn to her friends.

Their influence may be beneficial. The frequent conversations your parents and their friends have about who just went into the hospital, who was discharged, who came down with an illness, who got over a malady—all these concerns often seem morbid and stifling to their children. But the parents know others whose concerns and preoccupations are like their own. More than that, the kinds of fears and terrors our parents may harbor can now be shared and understood. Even by listening passively, our parents can find out how others have coped and can learn that their own feelings are neither odd nor unique. On the other hand, these conversations also remind them of the many serious problems that may await them. The list can be long and threatening.

At this point the one person they may turn to more than ever before is their physician. The doctor takes on an ever greater role in the lives of elderly people as more frequent treatment becomes necessary. He or she can be seen as the most powerful and effective figure in prolonging our parents' lives.

Medical science unquestionably has developed the knowledge and technology to combat a vast array of problems that once led to incapacity and death. From a strictly scientific point of view, it has been miraculous, and the elderly have benefited along with the rest of us. In practice, though, neither doctors nor the health-care system in the United States adequately meets the needs of the elderly.

Financially, the problems are self-evident. Most elderly people take a drop in income upon retirement. Medicare, Social Security benefits, and a pension are often inadequate to cover medical bills. Health costs have soared and will continue to do so. A major illness can wipe out savings, and in some instances the elderly may even become reluctant to visit a doctor and seek the care they need because they just can't afford it. In addition, many doctors do not want to treat Medicare patients because they often cannot collect their full fee or because they object to the red tape and requirements the federal program demands.

The nature of medical practice itself has changed, and this has created problems for the elderly. The house call, for example, is now a thing of the past. As the aged become less mobile, and getting around becomes more painful and difficult, good health care is harder to attain.

Not so long ago someone who was sick could simply drive or walk over to his or her neighborhood physician. For the most part this can no longer be done. Complex, expensive machinery and laboratory equipment are now an inseparable part of modern medicine. Individual doctors cannot afford to purchase all or most of the advanced equipment, so they often practice in large medical centers. By their nature these places are impersonal, bustling, and complicated. They can be confusing, intimidating places for elderly persons to enter and navigate through. In reaction to this, the aged sometimes stay away altogether.

Aged people often live in the run-down, poorer section of a city. A good percentage also live in small towns and rural areas. Doctors, on the other hand, prefer by and large to practice in splendid downtown or suburban locations. If an aged patient has trouble driving or has an emergency, the doctor may be practically inaccessible.

But there are other, perhaps more subtle, ways in which physicians are disappointingly out of reach. There has been a national shortage of doctors in the United States; this shortage does not appear to be winding down. Until the situation changes (and there is some reason to believe that the medical profession may have kept its numbers artificially low), there will be no compelling economic motives for doctors to make themselves more available.

As it is, waiting rooms are busy, crowded places in which old people are often not permitted to "waste the doctor's time" discussing their anxieties. The physician-patient relationship often becomes impersonal, and since more and more doctors have become specialists, their interest often extends into fewer and fewer of an aged person's problems.

Many times the interest does not extend very far at all. Doctors usually do not like to treat the elderly, for often there are no cures for the ailments of aged persons. A doctor has been trained to expect good results and sound recoveries from his treatment. The aged usually grow worse, not better, and so cannot give physicians the satisfaction of curing them. For the aged the physician can often do nothing more than prescribe medication that is more symbolic than helpful. As a result the elderly often run the risk of becoming overmedicated.

Sentimentality aside, the passing of the general practitioner and family doctor has been a severe loss for the elderly. In him, or her, they had someone who provided a comfortable and reassuring personal relationship. Our parents did not have to hesitate to enumerate a series of questions or symptoms, both real and imagined. The doctor had treated them for much of their lives and had their trust and confidence just as surely as he had a grasp of their medical history.

Unlike the specialist, the family doctor could dispense general advice, such as what kinds of exercise, diet, and health precautions our parents should take. He was also more likely to see our parents' physical problems in the context of their everyday lives. An aging father might ask if the arthritis in his arms or the numbness in his legs would prevent him from tending a garden or talking an airplane flight to visit his family. He would really be asking about the threatened social and emotional losses. A young specialist has been trained to answer strictly in terms of whether the muscles or legs will perform. The family physician is more prone to be sensitive to the underlying concerns of the patient. The younger specialist is more likely to answer questions about diet in terms of minerals and nutrients. The more experienced and sensitive doctor might shape his or her answer in terms of your father's budget as well as his ability to pick the food up, cart it home, and prepare it by himself.

It is true that the old-fashioned family physician may not have known as much as a specialist about the most up-to-date medical techniques and procedures. In this respect the treatment offered by him, or her, may suffer in comparison. But a parent may have developed a relationship with the old physician that, in the long run, more than made up for such deficits. The young man or woman who replaces the family doctor may never be able to inspire the confidence or command the cooperation of an aged parent.

Finding a doctor who is sympathetic to the aged is an important, often difficult job. There are a number of things you can do to make sure this is accomplished. Your own physician, or perhaps your friends, may know of such a person and be able to refer you. But you should go with your parent on his or her initial visit to make sure he or she receives proper treatment and respect. If a doctor gives your parents only cursory attention and a placebo or if he or she handles your father and mother as though they were hardly more than bundles of bones, you ought to quickly seek service elsewhere. When you first arrive, it is a good idea to see if there are other aged people in the waiting room. You are perfectly within your rights to ask the doctor if much of his or her practice includes the elderly. Since surveys have found that many elderly people consider their doctor the most important person in their life, it can be quite dangerous to be overly restrained in this area.

But your doctor may not be acceptable to your mother or father. It is even possible that your mother's health may be at risk if she refuses health care in order to control her own affairs.

Bertha Whitney had not seen a doctor from the time her husband died over twenty years ago. She had two reasons for this. One, she blamed the doctors and the hospital for his death and vowed they'd never get their hands on her. Secondly, she was the kind of person who begrudged spending money. While her husband had left her well provided for, she was nevertheless determined that doctors wouldn't get any of her money. Her health had been good over the years and she managed whatever problems came along, through self-medication, old family remedies and some unwelcome intervention from her only child, Roseann.

Roseann was lately becoming frantic. Bertha's body had gradually become bloated. She was having trouble breathing and, clearly, something awful was happening. For several months, Roseann engaged in arguments with her mother— insisting that she see Roseann's doctor. After all, he was the top specialist at the city's leading hospital and there was no one better. She'd made appointments, arrange to take Bertha to see him—and each time, Bertha would angrily refuse. It was soon clear that Bertha, herself, was in great discomfort, but would not consider Roseann's doctor.

With every ring of the telephone, Roseann expected it to be a neighbor of her mother's calling with some horrible news. And then the phone rang. Her mother was on her way home to get a bag and go to the hospital. She had just seen her doctor and he was going to need to drain fluid from her body and she'd be in his hospital for a few days!

"Her doctor?" Roseann couldn't believe her ears. "I just couldn't stand the pain," Bertha explained, "but I also couldn't stand that doctor of yours you tried to make me see. There was a feature story in the neighborhood news last week about a doctor who gave a lecture and his picture was in the paper. He really was very handsome and I called him up and made my own appointment."

Roseann was sure he was some sort of quack, but in checking it out, she learned he was a reputable specialist in internal medicine. The hospital was not the fancy University teaching center where Roseann's doctor practiced, but a small community hospital that had a decent reputation. Bertha had the fluid drained, was put on medication, discharged with follow-up plans for her other ailments, and had her next appointment scheduled to see her "handsome" doctor. Roseann swallowed hard, crossed her fingers and hoped it'd be OK.

Bertha's doctor may not have been what her daughter wanted, but he was Bertha's own. She had not only needed a doctor. She needed to be in control of her own life. And she re-wrote, in her own way, that famous commercial of a few years back—"Daughter, please, I'd rather do it myself."

A solution more and more people are turning to is the neighborhood medical center or clinic. While at first sight such institutions might seem to be impersonal places, they have many advantages over the specialist's office your parents may be visiting now. Old people who move from doctor to doctor tend to accumulate a whole array of pills and capsules. Often a parent will wind up having several different medicines for each ailment, some of which may be toxic if taken in combination. In old age medicines tend to take on special meanings; they can be seen as a protection against death and, as such, have an almost magical significance. A medicine cabinet crammed with various plastic bottles may seem as valuable to a parent as the family jewels. It may be a good idea, we might add in passing, for either you or a visiting nurse periodically to go through your parents' collection and eliminate prescriptions that are of no real use or whose effectiveness has expired.

Neighborhood health centers and clinics may solve some of these problems. They can serve as a clearinghouse for your parents' medical background, and they keep in a central filing system your parents' complete medical history and drug profile. Since they are located right in the neighborhood, they are usually quite adept at and sympathetic in handling aged people. In addition, your parents may feel more secure knowing help for emergencies and questions is within easy walking distance. If your parents need regular check-ups and care, they will probably get to know the staff. If they need the services of several specialists, they may find them housed under one roof and in easy access for consultation about their health problems.

We have discussed the physical problems associated with aging. In the next chapter we shall see how the aging process affects personality.

III

The Emotional
Problems of Aging

5

How Does Aging Affect Personality?

Toward the end of Marcel Proust's novel *Remembrance of Things Past*, the narrator attends a reception where he sees again an old nobleman, the Duc de Guermantes, whom he had known decades ago. As the now elderly gentleman struggles to rise from the chair in which he had been sitting, the narrator is startled by the evidence of the duke's physical decline. The tottering progress of his old acquaintance is compared to the waverings of men perched on giant stilts as tall as church steeples that grow taller and more perilous with the years. And the narrator compares all men to giants who straddle simultaneously epochs in their lives widely separated by time.

Proust's poetic comparison conveys a very special truth that applies to all of us. The narrator of his novel perceives clearly—like something literally visible—a social dimension that is within each individual.

Proust is profoundly correct in his observation that while the social experiences and needs of individuals may seem invisible, they are as real as the shape of their lips or the color of their eyes. A brief survey of individuals' social anatomy would include the personalities they have developed, the work they have done, the roles they have played within their families and communities, the friends and places they have known, and their memories of all these people, places, and things. You and your elderly parents—for that matter, all of us—carry a unique body of emotional experiences with us throughout our lives as surely as we do our tendons and our veins.

Although Proust's insight may not be difficult to grasp, for many of us it is not easy to accept. It may not normally occur to us that our aging parents' social identities, personal histories, and emotional needs are fully as much a part of them as are the physical aspects and needs of their bodies. We tend to make a distinction between these two spheres. Generally we consider the social emotional sphere to be less "real" than the physical sphere. Such a distinction often leads us to react one way to a father's irritability if it seems to center around his arthritis and another way if he becomes irritable "for no reason" during our daily phone call. Many sons and daughters may not realize what a costly distinction this is or just how it can make them unwitting victims of unnecessary stress.

As in the example just given, many sons and daughters may empathize with a parent's outburst because they see no reason to become agitated or resentful over their parent's arthritis. They usually do not take personally this malady and its accompanying distress. But since they are unused to analyzing a parent's emotional makeup in the same frame of reference, they often may react differently to their parent's psychological problems. Some sons and daughters will take an emotional outburst very personally indeed and feel that they are being asked to submit against their will to their parent's willful, never-ending stream of abuse. The parent's behavior is frequently seen with bitter resentment, but it is also viewed as something beyond change or control.

We have only to multiply these two contrasting reactions by the thousands of different situations in which they may appear to see just how dangerous this false dichotomy may be between our social-emotional sphere and our physical sphere. Everyone, to some extent, makes this error. But a willingness to modify some attitudes can enhance your ability to cope with your parent's emotional well-being and the impact it may have upon your life.

Much of what we understand of human psychology and emotion is still in the realm of theory, and we know much less about the workings of the mind than we know about those of the body. No one can x-ray an ego or a cluster of memories. We cannot examine the composition of your mother's personality the way a doctor can the nerves in her spine. We cannot hold a human need in our hands, discover the true weight of a grief by placing it upon a metal scale, or lance a depression with a sterilized scalpel.

These needs, however, exist and function within us all. They operate according to a set of laws and principles that is gradually becoming accessible to scientific understanding. Even so, some real obstacles keep us from seeing the causes and effects of emotional problems with the same clarity we can those of physical problems. An example follows.

> Richard Johnson's father had always been a placid, uncommunicative man. At the age of eighty-two he lost the sight of his left eye. Shortly afterward, Richard stopped by to visit his father. He had no more than opened the door when he realized that his father was feeling very low. Almost by instinct, Richard made a series of observations and arrived at a logical, accurate explanation of the situation. He knew his father had become listless and depressed as a result of the loss of sight in one eye. Perhaps Richard did not need a great deal of insight to connect the physical problem with an emotional response. If he had failed to grasp this cause and its effect, his father's difficult behavior would have seemed to have sprung from nowhere. In other words, Richard was able to accept his father's morose and at times hostile conduct because he understood the dynamics behind it.

This "method" of interpreting an elderly parent's conduct is not nearly so easy to apply when the behavior is a reaction to a social loss. The interpretation and acceptance of troubling behavior can be much more difficult to make because many times we haven't the faintest clue as to its sources. Our elderly parents themselves may not know why they feel and act the way they do.

> A year before the incident just described, Richard had arranged to have Sunday brunch with his father on a lovely spring morning. He had found his father depressed on this occasion too. But he had been unable to account for his father's bad mood because he had no way of knowing that on that particular day his father had been wrapped up in the memory of another spring when he had enjoyed the camaraderie of friends on a softball diamond. To Richard's father, that memory stood for a loss that was as real to him as his subsequent blindness. Yet Richard was never aware of the reason for this first fit of depression and could only be distressed at his father's unaccountable behavior.

A prime aim of this portion of the book is to increase your understanding of your elderly parents' social losses. In this way it is hoped that you will be better equipped to make reasonable connections and draw intelligent conclusions with greater frequency. Studies indicate that factors that cause the greatest amounts of stress in elderly people develop in response to important social losses in their lives. Some relief from this kind of stress can be given. But to do so, a middle-aged son or daughter should be aware of other gaps in our understanding that crop up when a wide distinction is maintained between a parent's physical and social existence.

Many times we operate under the assumption that a mother's physical condition and the problems it presents are beyond her conscious control, while her emotional makeup is well within her control. A woman may have been a manipulative mother all her life. But if the doctor confirms that her diabetes is indeed severe or that her heart clearly shows abnormal functioning, the sudden increase in the number of contacts she has with her children would probably be taken in stride. If she begins to telephone them several times a day around Christmas, her children will make allowances as long as the pains she complains of are physical in nature. If, instead, she calls without being able to claim a physical problem to justify her craving for attention, her children will probably find her actions utterly intrusive and exasperating.

The fact may well be, however, that this woman has no more control over her personality and behavior patterns than she does over what goes on inside her body. The human personality does not normally develop into something very different with the advent of old age. As a rule, our parents, just like ourselves, have traits that become more pronounced and firmly entrenched with the passage of time. A kind, nurturing mother will maintain her fine qualities into her seventies and eighties. A woman who was self-centered and thoughtless when her hair was brown will probably be just as unpleasant after her hair has whitened.

Many sons and daughters come to realize that their mother has been acting out the same familiar pattern throughout their entire relationship with her. When the relationship has been unsatisfactory, this insight, however, may be put to poor use. "My mother has always been self-centered, intrusive, and overly critical" is a statement that seems to inflame the grievances her children harbor and to provoke the aggravation they feel over her past and present behavior. Although this is a perfectly natural and understandable response, it would clearly be advantageous for all parties to be spared this sort of stress. Insight into the nature of such a mother's consistent, unchanging behavior might be used to find some detachment from it all. Ideally, a son and daughter might reach a point where it seems as futile to feel angry about their mother's personality quirks as about her rheumatism.

To understand in a general way how our elderly parents adjust to old age, we ought to have a general feeling for the social changes during this time of life.

Seen through the dimension of time, our elderly parents may be likened to Proust's giants. But how big they feel on earth may depend on the society in which they live. We are all familiar with the wizened figure of the aged Oriental patriarch. Although to Westerners he may have appeared frail enough to disintegrate in a breeze, he commanded enormous respect from the younger generations of his own country. In their eyes his accumulated wisdom and experience made him a powerful man. His vast inner world had earned him a special, comfortable replacement for whatever physical losses he had suffered.

In the United States such compensations exist, but they are harder to come by, and they are rarely of a scale that can nullify the deficits we associate with aging. Old age, especially in the United States, is a time not only of physical losses but of social ones as well. As people age, their bodies invariably deteriorate. The speed and severity of the losses they experience cannot be foretold, and in many respects those losses are unavoidable. Similarly, the older people become, the more inevitable it is that they will outlive and lose most of the people and roles that provided them with a sense of belonging, of being cared for—of who they were.

A mother who finds that she has lost her firm step may no longer have the freedom to walk across the street to buy the groceries. Her private world has constricted, in part, because she has lost the power to travel easily within it. As she loses her family under her roof at home, her close friends, her brothers, her sisters, or her husband, her emotional world becomes impoverished in a similar way. She has lost functions she always performed and depended upon. She has lost common bonds to the world she once knew. She has lost the recognition that the world once gave her. Such losses are often more painfully felt than physical ones. In almost every case, she may try to compensate for them, just as she might adopt a cane to aid her gait. Unlike the aged Oriental whose social world was enhanced by time, elderly people in this country generally experience old age as a gradual stripping away of their power.

As the social second skin is peeled back, our elderly parents' needs may become painfully exposed. Each of us has certain requirements that must be met so that we can adequately survive. Our parents need, for instance, enough food to eat. They need a dwelling to shield them from the elements. If they are deprived of sufficient food for two or three days, they are likely to become weak, dizzy, and listless. If they are denied food altogether, they will inevitably starve to death. If they live without shelter for several days, they most likely will come down with a cold or a fever. If they are forced to live outdoors indefinitely, their lives will unquestionably be shortened, and they will die of exposure. No one seriously doubts this. It is a self-apparent fact of the human condition.

Yet most of us are not wholly aware of the fact that our parents' lives depend almost as much on meeting their emotional requirements. All of us need to feel that we are worthwhile, attractive, and useful. We need compassion, intimacy, and companionship from the instant we enter the world to the moment we depart from it. If we live for a period of time feeling that we have no useful purpose, we are likely to feel fatigued and depressed. If we must face years in which we consider ourselves worthless and unloved, our lives, too, will be shortened, either from "natural" causes or, as is too often the case among the aged, by our own hand.

Some people may assume that our elderly parents' emotional needs decline just as their eyesight usually does. But this line of reasoning is equivalent to saying that our elderly parents' vision deteriorates because they are no longer interested in viewing the world. An elderly father usually does not come to need people less because most of his old cronies are no longer around. While some elderly do voluntarily disengage from the world as their social ties diminish, old age does not usually modify this basic social element of the human condition. It may be helpful to think of the roles our elderly parents have played and of the social relationships they have amassed as pieces of furniture and mementos they have collected and arranged in their home over the years. Every social loss may be likened to the removal of a couch, a dining-room table, or a bed. A place from which so much has been taken away must be desolate indeed.

Like the rest of us, the elderly react to their injuries. The difference is that for them social losses accumulate in the same manner that their physical condition declines. Like the aching back, the stiffened fingers, and the blurred vision, social losses come in rapid succession and in greater numbers than at any other period of life. An elderly person needs to recuperate, to adjust, and to readapt after each loss. When such losses coincide with physical problems, they may overwhelm the strongest of persons at any age. An elderly man may become so threatened by his vulnerability to weather conditions that he will begin to grow reclusive. If he then suffers the loss of some of the most important people in his life, a depression that often brings a loss of appetite and of sleep may snowball into a total withdrawal from life.

Studies using younger people as subjects found that prolonged isolation may induce overwhelming hallucinations as well as other radical psychological departures from reality. Fortunately, the majority of our elderly parents do not live under such ghastly conditions. But these studies demonstrate how powerful is the need for human contacts and relationships.

Elderly people have identities to maintain and social functions to perform. By and large they fulfill these needs, just as we do, within the sphere of their own social world. Even so, many of us are uninformed as to the actual scope of this invisible social world. When our father dies, for example, we know that a spouse, our mother, has lost a companion. But we may not be equally aware that our mother still has a strong need to love and to be loved.

Most of us have to educate ourselves about the social losses elderly parents are likely to encounter because our society has not properly understood this problem. We hold a funeral for a father and expect and accept the outpouring of grief by his survivors. But we hold no funerals for the loss of a job through retirement, the loss of a woman's mothering role, or the loss of her belief that she is somebody of importance in the world. Although we do not expect the grief over these losses to be deep and long-lasting, it often is. Statistically, the highest rate of suicide occurs among elderly men. Frequently this is associated with the loss they experience at retirement from their jobs. Elderly people often undergo a very rapid deterioration and are subject to a great amount of stress after the loss of their spouses.

Again, as was the case with the late-night phone calls about physical complaints, you need to try to interpret the real message behind your parents' responses to you and to their social losses. One of the most important principles to keep in mind in dealing with elderly parents is that their behavior is purposeful.

A mother who has been an accusing, disapproving influence in a daughter's life may not have been able to control her conduct or the effects it has had. But we can say with assurance that her conduct had the goal of fulfilling her needs. These needs may have seemed destructive, and the behavior may have been inept and self-defeating. But it was acted out for a reason—to achieve her personal goals or to meet her personal needs. In fact, this most likely explains what motivates your mother today. The accommodations a daughter has made to such a mother may have been unsatisfactory and painful. But the mother, too, has made an adjustment. She, too, has a reason, a purpose in responding as she does. The greater the degree to which we can acknowledge and scrutinize the pattern of our parents' hidden motives as well as our own, the more flexible we can become in establishing legitimate patterns of interaction.

The most important losses our elderly parents undergo are those of their spouses, relatives, friends, occupations, income, and positions in the community. We shall discuss these losses with an eye to showing how our parents experience them, how they try to make up for them, some of the common responses that aggravate or alarm their children, and some methods a son and daughter may employ to alleviate their parents' distress.

No surefire formula exists to enable us to predict how our parents will respond to the vicissitudes of old age. There is no surefire sign to tell us ahead of time who will cave in and who will pick themselves up and go on.

We might make the same assessment of anyone's ability to predict the emotional resources and strengths our elderly parents possess. As a rule, our elderly parents' patterns of response to the changes that occur late in life are much like those we observed when they were younger. If we think of a human personality as containing a repertoire of strategies used to meet the individual's immediate surroundings, we can have a better idea of how well, or how poorly, our parents are likely to cope.

A father who has been self-confident, self-reliant, kind, and mature will probably be well equipped to face the losses of old age and master, perhaps with some assistance, the depression that follows such losses. Parents who have generally been suspicious, irritable, and unforgiving and who have had a variety of conflicts and difficulties with other people in their lives will probably continue to experience difficulties in their old age. The feelings they have about themselves and the mechanisms they have used to meet life are poor. When new social losses begin to pile up, the self-defeating qualities that have made them miserable and unapproachable usually become more pronounced. And so, though some elderly parents may be unaware of it, they remain unable to help themselves and never truly understand why their children quite logically prefer to avoid them.

The combination of loss with the weakness that is part of old age subjects the personality to a rigorous, thorough testing. All of us have emotional frailties, an underbelly that we manage under normal conditions to keep well under control. A middle-aged son or daughter then can be quite naturally surprised when the stresses of old age exacerbate the darker corners of a parent's personality and throw it into unexpected, powerful relief.

There are losses that strike the most vital of nerves—losses that reawaken some unresolved conflict deeply buried in the past. It is not unreasonable to suppose that elderly persons who have always been moody and depressed feel so because they have had to drag a number of early frustrations and losses along with them throughout their lives. The load of additional frustrating experiences in old age may well make their already heavy burden unmanageable.

Although some of the most common strategies elderly parents use to cope with their problems are discussed here, you should realize that there are no hard-and-fast rules in this area. Each parent may develop and improvise his or her own coping styles. It is not always easy for a son or daughter to know when Dad is doing not only what is proper but what is best for him. This is especially so when his behavior seems unexpected or unconventional.

DEPRESSION

No matter what sort of adjustment your parents are able to make to old age, it would be hard to imagine that anyone comes to grips with the aging problem without experiencing some periods of depression.

Depression is a complicated form of emotional response. In some cases it can be a dangerous, destructive state of mind deeply rooted in our parents' earliest experiences of life. In other cases it serves a positive, healthy purpose for people confronted with immediate problems. It is not always easy for a son or daughter to distinguish between the two types of depression or to be able to recognize when a parent's depression can be modified and when it cannot.

Depression is often a mild, comprehensible method by which the human psyche struggles to cope with a traumatic situation. All of us are more familiar with some aspects of an elderly parent's depression than we might at first suspect, for this is the most common as well as the most natural response of all human beings when any significant loss has been suffered. For example, children who have been trundled off to summer camp or adolescents who experience unrequited love often react to their circumstances with grief and depression.

If your mother should fracture her leg, you would have no trouble understanding why her limb is covered by a plaster cast or why her daily activity has been abruptly scaled down. You would also realize that, while she has withdrawn from social contacts, this is only a temporary condition. Her body is steadily mending during her time of enforced idleness.

You should understand then that your parent's psyche has responded in a similar way to an emotional fracture. This is how the human psyche attempts to mend itself. Grief is work. Your mother may lose interest in the world around her and reduce her normal activities because a precious social element in her life has been taken from her. This procedure may be seen as an unconscious struggle of her mind to recognize and come to grips with the loss. All the old memories and meanings are dredged up and examined. It is a painful, time-consuming process. Your parent is struggling to resolve buried feelings of affection, remorse, anger, or guilt in order to make a final peace with the event. Only then can her mind accept the loss, and renounce it as inevitable and beyond recall. Only then can she get on with the affairs of her life.

Depression can be the most logical and appropriate reaction a person experiences in a loss—whether he or she is emotionally well-balanced or disturbed. Even so, the normal symptoms of this process may baffle, distress, or annoy you. Few sons and daughters are naturally able to watch impassively as their parents lose their appetite, their interest in their personal appearance, their ability to get a good night's rest, or their willingness to engage in social activities. You may realize that depression is simply weeping at the grave of a remembered loss. But that may not make you feel comfortable as you watch a parent who has fallen prone to fits of crying, listlessness, or irritability or to outbursts in which he or she proclaims his or her worthlessness, misery, and isolation. Perhaps a reasonable goal for you in such a case is to come to realize that such behavior will, in most instances, gradually pass away.

Normal grief usually terminates successfully. You may know, however, from your own encounters with your mother or father that this process is not always so neatly accomplished. Each elderly person has a different type of reaction, and each has a limited ability to cope with physical losses. Thus each person's response to an emotional loss will be different. Remember that these reactions are usually beyond the conscious control of your parents. Some may have the resources to bounce back from a major loss after a period of a few months. Others cannot. It may take some older people much longer to adjust to the loss of a spouse, while still others may never be able to fully accept it. More than one elderly widow, for example, has kept her dead husband's clothes hanging beside her own in the bedroom closet as if to deny that he is really gone.

The point is that we ought to appreciate and respect the importance of grief. We must realize that it may be necessary for a whole range of losses of which we ourselves know nothing. Moreover, while our parents often have many specific reasons for becoming depressed, they may feel low simply out of a vague grief over the general decline they perceive as coming with old age. Within limits, this is a reasonable, understandable feeling—one to which they are fully entitled.

Although grief and depression can go hand in hand, they are not synonymous. Depression becomes a severe problem when it wholly consumes a person's normal daily functioning for an indefinite period of time. Slipping into periodic states of depression may be normal and unavoidable, but drowning in a bottomless morass of it is not.

Middle-aged sons and daughters probably ask too much of themselves if they feel they ought to know precisely how much depression is acceptable and how much is not. This matter cannot be strictly quantified. Like mental health professionals, you need to use your own best judgment in approaching your parents' depression.

Sometimes, the loss of a job, a serious drop in income, the death of a sibling, or some other incident may touch off a wholly unpredictable, profound depression, which may catch even the healthiest of persons off balance. In these cases the normal feelings of grief and depression often assume the tremendous propulsion of an ancient, forgotten experience that may consist of unfathomable shame, outrage, or guilt. Its origin may lie in a sense of childhood rejection or resentment over a sibling's arrival on the family scene. Since these experiences, and your parent's reaction to them, occurred long ago, your mother may have coped with her feelings by covering them up or by turning her rage against herself. Your mother's self-laceration—seventy years later—is obviously a problem beyond her understanding or conscious control. A prudent son or daughter who recognizes this situation might recommend that such a parent seek professional counseling. And aged clients who have generally functioned well during their lives show rapid progress when treated for depression.

Given a choice, the elderly, like most of us, prefer not to be depressed. They would rather feel happy and energetic than enervated or punished by blue moods day after day. This might even be said of parents who appear to enjoy and even to cling to their unhappiness. It may be that on a subconscious level such parents refuse to acknowledge and accept a loss. It is also possible that the depression is a device they successfully cultivated years ago to get the attention and love they felt they could not receive in any other manner. Such depression may also fulfill some hidden need for punishment over old feelings of anger or guilt. Although such parents may become a strain on their children, there are ways in which substitute listeners can be found to temper their stubborn, unconscious behaviors. Such substitutes may be drawn from outside the family circle and will be described later in this chapter.

The total composite of your elderly parents' physical losses and remaining strengths can be likened to a piece of Swiss cheese. Although there are numerous holes, there remains a substance of health, future potential, and other positive points on which to build. In short, search again for the cheese and never mind about the holes. Your need to search for the abilities that have survived the losses applies to your parents' social losses as well as their physical ones. Strength and weakness have never been an either-or proposition, except in the most extreme circumstances. And there is something within almost all elderly parents—no matter how dimly felt or hamstrung it might be—that is struggling to let self-fulfillment find the upper hand. Here are some of the most common ways in which our elderly desperately attempt to fend off serious threats of depression.

Let's talk first of all an extremely trying situation for middle-aged sons and daughters. It concerns their regular contacts, often involuntary, with a parent whose only subject of conversation seems to be how miserable his or her life is. Many times they will be presented with an endless list of complaints that is impressive in its thoroughness and exhaustive in its attention to detail. A typical phone call to such a father may tell of his dissatisfaction with the breakfast food he has eaten, the poor fit of his old clothes, the nastiness of the weather, the insensitivity of the corner grocer or newsboy, the ingratitude of friends, and the disappointingly few calls he receives from his children—even from the one who just now has made the call to him! In reality it is probably not a three-cent hike in the price of bananas that has caused this man to be so angry. More likely it is a combination of his advancing infirmities, his lack of friends, and his inability to fill up happily his free time.

It would be unusual, to say the least, for an elderly parent to describe his unhappiness to you in the popular professional jargon: "You know, son, my identity continues to feel the ongoing assaults of a variety of social and physical losses for which I was largely unprepared and as yet have been unable to compensate for satisfactorily."

Although a parent feels the effects of such forces, it may be beyond his power to see them squarely for what they are, to face up to them, and to attempt to achieve a resolution of them in pure and simple terms. To do so in some cases would mean opening up a vulnerability that might well lead your father to a fit of overwhelming despair. So he copes instead by redirecting his anger into the petty, inconsequential aspects of his existence. This, of course, is not done with premeditation. The purpose of this behavior is simply to fend off his fears and frustrations. It may not make the complaints any the more pleasant for you to hear. But you ought to recognize that this may be the only available means he has to find a meager emotional release.

A second group of parents calls their children regularly to put on record how miserable they feel. Yet the mother's daily social routine could hardly be more crowded. Her sons and daughters may see her complaints as simply an attention-getting device and resent it. Such a mother may only have time to complain for a moment because she has not yet put on the makeup she will be wearing for the church luncheon she must go to shortly—an event at which she will serve not only coffee and tea but also some exquisite pastries she prepared the night before. She may promise to call with further complaints later in the day, after she and a male friend have finished shopping downtown. During her shopping expedition she may even pick up a present for you, which she will try to deliver that evening on her way home from the theater. Yet, she complains that she is miserable.

Most professionals who work with the aged feel that the emotional welfare of an elderly person may be fairly measured in terms of how well he or she functions on a day-to-day basis. A woman who feels good enough to stay as attractive as possible, to cultivate a group of friends, and to pursue even a limited social life fits this definition. She may feel moments of painful despair at intervals, but she has clearly found an effective way to cope.

The problem of loss and depression is in many ways bound up with the overall decline in the quality of life that usually occurs during old age. The vast majority of elderly, in comparing the present to the past, are deeply aware that their sources of gratification have diminished significantly. In large part the most objective observers would have to agree with them. In an infinite number of small but subtle ways, their current life has become deficient.

REMINISCENCES

Like everyone else, the elderly have a natural urge to restore their existence to what it once was—to make up for their losses. In and of itself, this is a healthy drive. It can take several forms, not all of which are constructive, however. One of the most natural and useful forms is reminiscence. The need to recall, recount, and relive the past is a necessary and invaluable activity for almost all aged persons. Many sons and daughters underestimate its importance. They regard the old stories and anecdotes as utterly trivial, tiresome, and irritating. They are perfectly entitled to feel resentful at having to "listen to the same old stuff four dozen times." At the same time, however, there are several reasons why elderly parents need to reminisce and should be encouraged to do so. This behavior serves quite definite and positive ends. One of the most important principles we have in dealing with our aged parents is to appreciate just how they are seeking fullfillment. We should then try to provide someone—not necessarily a son or daughter—who can help them reach it.

Earlier we described how middle-aged people often undergo a reorientation in which they begin to see themselves—perhaps for the first time—in terms of how much time they have left to live. This change usually involves the creation of a new perspective and new attitude toward one's own life. The future may no longer have the same limitless dimensions, but it does provide an element of uncertainty. That is, although the present job may amount to a waste of one's talents, there is still a chance to switch or retrain. If, in taking stock of ourselves, we see that a certain number of immaturities, maladjustments, or injustices have accumulated, it is nonetheless feasible and possible for us to set things right. The same might be said of our income, marriage, weight, and many other aspects of our lives.

For our aged parents, however, this kind of reorientation is far more firmly entrenched. It is no longer a novel and frightening concept but something taken for granted. The most important aspects of our elderly parents' lives—in fact their very lives—have already unfolded. A clean break—at least a clean break in the sense in which a middle-aged person conceives of it—is now out of the question. Basically there is neither time, opportunity, nor stamina to establish a fresh existence. Nevertheless, a life—all that has been done with it and all that has crystalized around it through time—must soon be relinquished. And as this understanding grows, our elderly parents often find that a need for self-evaluation and personal integrity has emerged.

This final crisis of life, however, has some unique features. Adolescents actively pursue the search for meaning, fulfillment, and a squared conscience, but they do so through participation in the outside world. In a sense they make themselves up as they go along. Our elderly parents' search, on the other hand, is conducted across the landscapes of their inner world. The task is no less demanding for the aged. The material they use is not what is about to be but an analysis of the experiences and responses they have already made. Although it does not take the form of physical exertion, the energy and attention they have to summon for this review of their lives make it a very active process indeed.

Throughout our lives we all reorganize and reinterpret our past to gain a more accurate sense of its meaning. In reality the collection of experiences that make up a lifetime only assumes a coherent pattern through our efforts to assign it one. An otherwise dull dinner party becomes fraught with significance, for example, because we see in retrospect that it was there that we met someone who later introduced us to our future spouse.

Psychologically, reminiscence in old age becomes mapmaking on a grand scale. To sum up life and put things in order, the elderly strive, however unconsciously, to judge whether their lives have been ethical, fulfilled, and worthy of appreciation. This effort may be seen as an attempt to make a final peace, to resolve their lives so that the gravest loss of all can be met with courage, faith, and resignation.

Of course this undertaking does not present itself to most people in such clear and structured terms. Nor do many aged fully realize that they are working toward an overall goal. There are no assurances that the task can be concluded successfully. In some respects this explains why the sheer repetition of many exhausting details is common in our parents' reminiscences. The whole process can be seen as another in an almost endless series of attempts to stumble upon the correct fit for a particularly disconcerting element in the vast, dimly understood puzzle of their lives.

Ideally our aging parents may gradually attain an almost imperturbable and accepting frame of mind. At the opposite extreme this process can be horribly painful and distressing. The memory of what cannot be changed or undone in the past may make unresolved feelings of guilt, the sense of a futile, wasted life, or past acts of cruelty and defiance into an unbearable burden for some elderly.

The memories of past events tend to overshadow the current day-to-day routines of many aged persons. The recollection of a meal in a Chinese restaurant twenty-four years ago, for example, may be more vivid and real than a visit of last week or even of yesterday. This may be partially attributed to the emptiness of an elderly person's current life. But often this keen awareness of the past is quite involuntary. We should remember that the swift uninterrupted workings of our memory belong to a region of the mind that, like our lungs or heart, operates without our control or direction.

Many middle-aged sons and daughters, like their parents themselves, are mystified by the consequences of this rather ordinary thought process. The misunderstandings may result in conflict, guilt, and unnecessary confusion, as the following account reveals.

Rosalyn Butler, a schoolteacher, decided to treat her eighty-year-old mother, Mrs. Roberts, to a Sunday excursion. She planned things carefully in advance with a view to affording the most pleasure to her mother. She made reservations at an old restaurant where her family had often eaten when she was growing up. She ordered her mother's favorite dish in advance and even arranged to have them seated at their favorite booth. Since her mother had not been in the restaurant for years, Rosalyn hoped it would be an evening of lovely reminiscence.

As soon as they arrived, however, her mother mentioned that the old maitre d' had been replaced. The decor, she added, was now soiled and frayed. Rosalyn could see that the whole atmosphere seemed to sadden her mother. When the meal arrived, Rosalyn was stunned and hurt to see her mother push it away, complaining that she was fatigued and had lost her appetite.

Rosalyn asked if there was something wrong with the food or if she herself had said something inappropriate. But her mother cut her short and hardly said a word for the duration of the meal. The daughter felt the stab of a very old wound. Once more she had failed to receive the acknowledgment or approval she had sought all her life. The evening was ruined, and the next few days along with it, because she had again placed herself in the hopeless position of seeking to become once again a daughter who deserved to be loved.

Rosalyn could not have known that her mother's reactions had little to do with any of these considerations. Mrs. Roberts, like her daughter, had made the connection between the present atmosphere of that restaurant and her memories of the past. But for her the connection was a painful one. The resemblance between this meal and the old family tradition was so intimate that by the time the meal arrived, she felt that she was standing at the graveside of a former, terribly precious time in her life. Her reminiscence prompted her to realize all at

once that she was no longer a young, attractive mother con-
tending with a boisterous brood. She could no longer enjoy the
ironic smile and nervous mannerisms of her late husband nor
the recognition and friendliness of the restaurant's old staff.

While middle-aged sons and daughters may assume that such
incidents as the one just described are serious blunders on their
part, or catastrophes to avoid in the future at all costs, the elderly
parents themselves will probably have no such reaction. Often they
neither hold their children responsible nor in any way regret the
event itself. A life in which vivid memories are the rule is inevitably
one in which grief plays a perfectly natural and understandable
role.

This sort of reaction tends to be stirred up most easily during
holidays like Easter, Thanksgiving, or Christmas. At such times our
culture puts a premium on the festivity and warmth that are supposed to result from a big family get-together. The reality may be
that, for many Americans, such gatherings are regarded as unavoidable chores. The expectations that surround those days, however,
have become deeply ingrained in almost all of us. Ironically, holidays often turn out to be times when people are made acutely
miserable as they compare their actual lives with what they would
like them to be. As any hospital emergency staff knows, such times
prompt higher than normal rates of admission for depression and
suicide attempts year after year.

Elderly people as a group may be particularly vulnerable to
such comparisons made at holiday time. In many instances the
holidays are even more painful because of the powerful memories
of the intimacy and happiness such celebrations once contained.
Present-day get-togethers then can sometimes be sources of great
stress for our elderly parents. Their memories may begin to well up
at the sounds of music, the grandchildren's tumult and singing, the
traditional foods, and the family yarns. A middle-aged son or
daughter who does not realize how natural and even healthy this is
may become quite disturbed or embarrassed when a parent's tears
"unaccountably" start to flow. In their confusion and uneasiness,
the offspring may ask if there is something wrong with the soup or
if the noise at the table is disturbing. More than likely, though, it
has meant a great deal to the parents to be present for the occasion.
They probably need and enjoy the momentary togetherness. The

weeping is in some ways a tribute to the richness of a family life they come more and more to treasure.

If reminiscenses were only a tool for the torturous process of a life review or a prod to aggravate the pain of various losses, perhaps it would be appropriate to characterize the need to remember as a major burden of old age.

Just as often, though, the purpose of reminiscence is to soothe, reassure, and invigorate. In low moments, our elderly parents may feel that they have become worthless and useless, people who are aching, tired, and full of pain. Their memories, however, remind them that once they were important individuals in the mainstream of life. Kurt Vonnegut, Jr., in his novel *Slaughterhouse Five* illuminates this aspect of life. He describes his protagonist, Billy Pilgrim, as having come unstuck in time. All the moments and events of his life exist simultaneously and forever. At various moments he literally reinhabits his position as a national celebrity at home, as a soldier on the battlefields of World War II, or as a visitor on the strange planet where he was locked in a cage with a movie starlet.

In many ways the intensity of our elderly parents' remembrances permits them to escape their present condition in just this manner. The moments in which they can describe their late spouse and friends, their old jobs and responsibilities, transport them into a different, more comforting universe. Like Billy Pilgrim, an elderly father recaptures what has been lost. The memory of a person, a sentiment, or an atmosphere becomes, in fact, a father's substitute for the lost objects themselves. The need to restore the losses has been temporarily fulfilled. Our parents become for a few moments what they once were.

As we all know from personal experience, memory tends to smooth over and obliterate the unhappiness we perhaps experienced at a particular time. It may be an instinct of self-preservation that leads the mind to picture the past with feelings of wistfulness. Our elderly parents' childhood may have been filled with poverty and deprivation. But the pleasure they take in recalling it may hardly be a bad thing at all. It is one of the surest, most dependable sources of pleasure and escape they have. Whatever it might truly have been like, it was a time when they were neither infirm, disillusioned, nor dependent, as they may well be now.

If part of this need is to recapture a sense of importance and to discover if life has been worthwhile, another part is to gain

appreciation and confirmation in the eyes of others. Surely this is
one reason why a sympathetic audience can be indispensable. If we
follow our elderly parents' monologues carefully, it is possible to
see how all these forces intermingle. As you read over the following
account, try to keep these points in mind.

Anthony Delano is a seventy-six-year-old ex-salesman who
treats his twenty-two-year-old granddaughter, Lisa, to a fancy
dinner once a month. He invariably makes the reservation in
his name, clearly taking the greatest pleasure in pretending that
she is his date for the evening as they walk to their table.
During the meal he reminisces nonstop. He orders a carafe of
wine, lectures on the history of the vintage, and tells about the
times when he used to enjoy it in great quantity.

This then leads Anthony to describe the saloon his father
owned in an old, poor, vanished neighborhood of Manhattan.
He goes on to describe the kind of wood the bar, chairs, and
tables were made of; the names of many of the steady, colorful
customers; and the duties he had as a small boy before and
during business hours. He tells how he used to go around to
the tables to replenish the pretzels and how the customers used
to dote on him, seat him on the bar, and tip him some pennies.
His father used to say that Anthony made a 10 percent difference in the "joint's" profits.

His father, however, was a stingy, brutal man who
abused his wife in front of the children and forced her to do
the most menial, degrading jobs in addition to her housework.
Although his mother took most of this abuse without protest,
Anthony recalls that by the end of the day she was very short-
tempered with her children. He remembers vividly how he and
his brother used to sneak out into the street after dinner to
avoid her angry blows. He often used to come home late, even
as a lad of seven.

During Anthony's early twenties, when he was living
away from home for the first time in a small town in New
Jersey, his best friend was a wonderful fellow named Gino,
who was always ready with a laugh. One day Gino decided to
propose to a girl he had known for some time, a real shrew
who later made his life miserable. Since Gino could not work
up enough courage to ask the question, Anthony and he decided to find out just how much wine it would take to get him
in shape to propose. To be on the safe side, they rounded up
another friend, a nice guy named Joe, who used to live not far
from the restaurant where Anthony was now sitting with his

granddaughter. (Here Anthony remarks sadly that he had heard recently that this man had moved into a nursing home.) At any rate all three of them went through almost two dozen bottles of that great wine. Along about four in the morning, Gino was so drunk he could barely breathe. But as luck would have it, they had managed to park their car in his future wife's driveway. And so Anthony and Joe picked Gino up, leaned him against the young lady's door, rang the bell three times, and drove off before she could open the door. Poor Gino, Anthony adds, never forgave either of them for the trick they had played on him.

When the salad is brought to the table, Anthony watches his granddaughter eat, since he can no longer take such rich salad dressing. Next, he recounts for her the special recipe his mother used for the huge salads she served on Mondays. This reminds him of his brother, Pete, whom his father had always liked better than he did Anthony. Pete had been a bright young fellow with a lot of potential who had never succeeded in making a living, while Anthony, by the time he retired, was more than just well-off. Talented as Pete was, he always landed in trouble and was usually broke. He used to borrow money from Anthony without paying it back. Anthony recalls saying that it was like throwing money down a sinkhole to lend it to Pete. But for all that, his father never changed his preference—the old buzzard!

Even so, Anthony recalls that when Pete came down with cancer, the family phoned Anthony, who took the next train out to Chicago to help him. It was Anthony who saw to it that the doctors who were caring for Pete gave him the best possible treatment. Doctors, as his granddaughter might know, cannot always be trusted. One of the doctors was condescending and uncommunicative, and Anthony had ordered him off the case. True, the man was an expert—one of the finest in the country. There was hell to pay from his mother and father. But after all, his brother was terminally ill and doped up on morphine. The least the family could expect was courtesy and respect from people they were paying good money to. That was how he had been brought up to treat others, and that is what he has always demanded in return. Then Anthony muses that maybe it was a little rash, chewing the doctor out like that. "Boy, did I give him a piece of my mind," he boasts, tapping his cane and wiping his lips.

When the main course arrives, Anthony scolds the waitress, pointing out that the food is no longer cooked with the same care as in the past. Anthony feels that, since the retirement of the restaurant's former chef, the meal he ordered for his granddaughter is no longer being prepared with the same fine ingredients.

Because of his granddaughter's protestations, Anthony finally relents on his insistence that the meal be sent back. By the time the dessert is served, Anthony mumbles something about his inability to exercise his bum legs during a spell of hot weather. Fortunately, this particular evening has been cool and pleasant, so he can comfortably maintain his circulation without feeling any pain.

At the end of the meal, Anthony pays the check with a flourish, leaves a sizable tip, and apologizes to his granddaughter for prattling on and on with his boring, useless old stories.

As you probably noted, from start to finish Anthony reveals some of the most pressing issues on his mind. He begins by restoring the feeling he once had of being a handsome squire of young women, a dashing and sexually attractive figure. Then he becomes a man of the world who appreciates gourmet food and wine. Savoring the sight of an intimate glass of wine with a young woman, he enjoys vicariously the pleasures of a vintage although his doctor has forbidden him to drink. Having temporarily compensated for this physical loss, he transports himself back to his childhood, when he was an admired center of attention, something he can no longer claim to be. He enjoys again the camaraderie and banter of tall, powerful men and even receives the approval of his father, who never cared much for him at all. The simple bar in the rundown neighborhood lives again and is transformed into a warm, comfortable home that he may never have known in reality.

An old wound, the resentment over his father's treatment of his mother, is reopened, and the villain is properly punished and condemned. Anthony's heart is again permitted to go out to a mother from whom he has been separated by death for many decades.

Another series of physical losses is noted and temporarily banished as Anthony recalls the years when he could stay out until all hours and come home more exhilarated than exhausted. The strangeness and the poignancy of being independent and on his own for the first time becomes a welcome antidote to his present situation, in which he feels isolated and stagnant. He may see very few people—let alone intimates—these days, but during the meal he is able to speak of the camaraderie of two young devil-may-care men who shared with him the night air and risks of impromptu adventures.

The risks Anthony runs now are of a far grimmer nature, and, unlike his memories of youth, his unconscious feelings of self-assurance and invulnerability have vanished. The readiness for practical joking has gone the way of an endless supply of stamina and finesse while inebriated.

Confronted with still another food he is no longer permitted, Anthony relishes instead the memory of the dish and the communal warmth he associated with it in the past. This second recollection of his family brings to mind some still unresolved conflicts over the deeper acceptance his brother enjoyed. The anger at this injustice, the hurt and the suspicion that his father's judgment may have been accurate, the disgust over his exploitation—all these feelings are gone over once again. The death of his brother occurred thirty years ago. But Anthony's grave misgivings over his own conduct at the hospital stubbornly resist one lasting and acceptable interpretation. His brother aside, nothing can take away the cleansing feeling of righteous indignation Anthony had in standing up to an imposing authority figure, the physician. Today Anthony has to take quite a different tack with doctors!

After a final flourish to demonstrate that he can still be an authoritative, demanding man, Anthony's imagination drifts back to earth, where he again becomes the man who has little worth admiring and whose physical infirmities have turned his world into a painful, confining place.

An elderly person's preoccupation with the past, then, may be a critical mechanism used to cope with old age. Although you may grow to recognize this, it does not logically follow that your insight therefore obligates you to become an enthralled audience. Perhaps it is *because* reminiscences bring so many of our elderly parents' psychological needs into play that adult children often feel an aversion to them. The demand for attention and appreciation may often be directed at sons and daughters who have their own storehouses of painful memories. This same mother and father may never have had the time or the interest to listen to their own children when they were small and when it mattered a great deal to the children. Such a parent may have been a disapproving, intrusive, manipulative influence. The emergence of a new psychological drive is hardly enough to transform our parents into lovable, enchanting storytellers in the eyes of people whom they may have abused for years. Though an aged person's reminiscence serves a useful therapeutic purpose, it may be seen as merely another burden to be borne by an unwilling listener.

Beyond that, the good old days may be a subject that our elderly parents find of the greatest immediate importance. Middle-aged sons and daughters may quite naturally feel that their present life and time hold that position. People in the prime of their lives can hardly be faulted for becoming irritated at parents who express nothing but disgust or contempt for the world of today, a place your parents may condemn as expensive, immoral, and cruel. People who are deeply involved in the immediate problems of their family, job, and community usually have a series of responsibilities and demands that absorb most of their time and attention. They may feel no urge to surrender the few spare moments they have to hear the same old stories repeated over a pot of coffee. Nor are they likely to be persuaded otherwise once they discover that their elderly parents see the present world as inadequate in large part because they no longer have a vital part to play in it.

It would largely be self-defeating for sons and daughters to force themselves to listen to their elderly parents for hours on end. They may be tempted to do so out of a belief that it will make them good and attentive offspring. But the most effective responses to elderly parents come from your ability to recognize what their fundamental needs really are. In this instance the need is not to test the loyalty and devotion of their children but to receive enthusiastic appreciation. The exact blood relationship of the people who provide this kind of gratification is of secondary importance. Clearly, the impatience and the irritation you may feel mounting inside you as the stories go on and the minutes drag by are hardly designed to satisfy your parents' needs or your own. The most natural and sensible thing is to accept your disqualification from the pool of available resources and begin to seek out others—in other words, substitute listeners.

A situation such as this is a classic example of a conflict between the generations. Twenty or thirty years from now you may feel the same pressing need your parents have to rehash the accomplishments and satisfactions of your own youth and middle age. For the time being, however, the demands your elderly parents bring may be incompatible with your own requirements. Since you both have legitimate needs, you can solve the problem best by identifying and seeking out substitutes.

In most cases ideal substitutes are readily at hand. Grandchildren often make the best audiences of all. There are several important reasons for this. Your own children have no long history of wounds and resentments that would dampen their enthusiasm in listening as it might your own. They hear these stories for the first time, and, like the narrator, are likely to have an open-ended, responsibility-free schedule that may make them available for longer periods of time.

Grandchildren normally have little awareness of the deeper reasons for an elderly person's reminiscences. Their innocence is invaluable because the curiosity and attentiveness they can communicate is spontaneous, sincere, and not at all self-conscious. In addition, the milieu and the experiences a grandparent wants to share are those that are available to your children only through movies, television, or books. The inexhaustible, petty details of the past are fascinating in a child's eye because they heighten the sense of a vanished, exotic culture. Grandparents often appear as heroic survivors with marvelous adventures to relate.

Grandchildren may find it impossible to imagine you, their parent, as someone small and dependent upon the wrinkled white-haired gentleman at the kitchen table. They may have no difficulty at all, on the other hand, visualizing the stories they hear and identifying themselves with the hero of it all.

All this, of course, fits your parents' bill of needs quite handsomely. By encouraging your children to spend an occasional evening or afternoon with your parents, you have successfully fulfilled the needs of two generations. There are, naturally, exceptions. Some children may have no interest in this sort of thing. If your parents are unpleasant people who dislike the company of children, it would be best to avoid such meetings.

On the whole, however, these exchanges can be educational as well as entertaining. The United States, we ought to remember, has a population of citizens almost all of whom claim two national identities. A large portion of the current generation of elderly was born and raised on another continent. Their stories often concern a country the grandchildren have never seen. All over America there has been a recent resurgence of interest among the young in learning more about their heritage and roots. Grandparents are a unique source of information and a font of family history that would otherwise be lost.

Just as your children will be personally enriched by absorbing family lore, so, too, will other groups of children who are directly related to you.

Some valuable programs have taken place in churches and synagogues that involve this sort of focus on reminiscence. Elderly members of the congregation are invited to meet with the children in the youth group. This is usually for the youngsters' benefit—to educate them through reminiscences about ethnic communities and customs that have largely died out today. But it is the elderly themselves, especially the men, who seem to benefit most from the experience. The audience is interested and responsive. For an afternoon a man's memories become something more than a reminder of what he once was and of all that he has lost. Instead he becomes someone who has a heritage to pass down to others. This is one way an elderly person comes to see "strengths" within himself he never suspected he had.

Unfortunately, there are relatively few such programs. You might be on the lookout for them, though, and might even propose that such events be started up in your own congregation or community.

In general the more your parents become wrapped up in their immediate affairs, the less they should need to dwell on the past. We have discussed reminiscences in detail to illustrate some of the general principles you ought to find helpful in many of your other dealings. Reminiscences are not simply a habit peculiar to your own parents that you find irritating and time-consuming. They are a normal, important outlet for persons trying to cope with the natural and inevitable emotional conflicts of old age.

Other substitutes that can be beneficial to your parents' situation and yours will be discussed in the chapter that follows.

6

Can Some Involvements Harm You or Your Parents?

Most of your parents have been quite content to lead lives independent of their children for the last twenty-five years. They have been
socially and financially self-sufficient for even longer. Some may be
emotionally flexible and resourceful enough to handle retirement,
the death of a spouse, and the losses of friends without asking for
much, if any, of your assistance. When they come to you for help,
it is usually with the unspoken understanding that they are turning
to you only temporarily. For their own integrity and self-respect
they intend to resume their independence as soon as possible.

The more losses your parents sustain, though, the more they
may need the support and encouragement of others. This may take
the form of demands that amount to requesting someone to help
rearrange the individual's whole existence. One of the first people a
parent turns to will usually be a son or a daughter.

But it does not always work that way. If a father's problems
become acute, some children rush in to provide solutions in the
form of their own personal efforts. This happens even when the
relationship has been a distant and bitter one, and a son may end
up paying a high emotional price for his involvement with his
father. No one should be expected to put up indefinitely with a
situation that brings intolerable strain. To avoid such strain while
still ensuring proper care for your parents, it is necessary to determine the basis for a reasonable assessment of what this renewed
contact with your parent can mean.

Many children make the mistake of thinking that their parents
become old the day the first Social Security check arrives or the day

a cane is first put into use. But your parents do not suddenly or officially turn old, any more than you suddenly become middle-aged on your fortieth birthday. Likewise, most elderly parents do not somehow grow into more serene and accepting people as they enter their seventies and eighties. The opposite may just as often occur. The personal characteristics you found aggravating and hurtful years ago have gradually become more apparent, for the difficulties of old age tend to drain our parents' strengths and intensify their weaknesses.

Just as your parents will remain about the same persons they always were, so, too, will remain your feelings about them and the manner in which you and they got along in the past. As a young person you may have quarreled with Dad about sex or religion, or with Mom about ways to rear your own children. Don't expect that Dad and Mom have come around in the meantime to your viewpoint on these topics. Of course, people do change and mature throughout life. But as a rule, there is just not much your parents can do, or will want to do, about how they feel and behave on matters of importance to them. It is unrealistic and unreasonable of you to expect anything different from them.

In its own fashion the relationship you and your parents have constructed has become just as set in its ways. Depending upon your situation, this may be a source of delight, indifference, or dissatisfaction. Your mother does not know consciously why she continues to criticize the tie you wear or the car you drive. She cannot control herself. Nor can you control the way you get worked up over her remarks. It is *because* it was your mother who made the comment that you are tempted to respond with a familiar sense of resentment. When Mom tells you the coffee you made this morning was weak, she may have only intended to make an innoc-uous observation. But you may feel that she has conveyed in a petty way, as she always has, that almost everything you do is wrong as far as she is concerned. People do not consciously recall all the times they felt a parent's disapproval when they react this way. It is the essence of the feelings and the incidents, however, that accumulates. Just about any provocation may serve to trigger the old reactions.

It is then crucial to understand and respect what the history of your dealings with your parents has meant to you over the years.

This reality determines how directly involved and helpful you are capable of being. Recognizing your own unavoidable "limitations" is a major first step to finding ways to get the same job done.

Your feelings, whatever they are, are absolutely legitimate reasons to curb fresh contact with your parents. The truth is that if the relationship has been a troubled one over the years, middle-aged children often find it impossible to see their parents' real needs objectively. A study by Dr. Bertha Simos found that middle-aged offspring could riot talk about the problems their parents were having today without explaining at every turn the way Mom or Dad had been over the years. To describe a mother who was friendless, a daughter would explain that Mom had always rejected her children as well as the people in the neighborhood. What was the use, therefore, of doing anything to help her? A daughter who had no patience for her father's present physical troubles told the interviewer that Dad had never paid any attention to her problems when she was small. Why should he expect better treatment from her now?

Without your being aware of it, the decision as to how directly involved you should become with your elderly parents has already been made. One clue is the gut-level feelings you have as you talk to your mother over the phone or when you go out with her to dinner. If you feel only guilt and a sense of obligation, further contacts with her will probably intensify those feelings. An occasional Sunday visit to her home may be pleasant, but you recognize that this is as much of her company as you care to have. To start cooking her dinner every evening after she can no longer get out of the house would quickly become a chore you would deeply resent.

Another tip-off is the amount of time and attention you have devoted to your parents over the last twenty-five years when there were no big problems to meet. This fact alone should tell you just how important a part your parents have normally played in your life.

You should also be able to recall which side has initiated most of the contacts. Perhaps your folks have made most of the phone calls or extended most of the invitations to pay a visit. More than likely this means that it is more important for them to keep in touch with you than for you to keep in touch with them. If, on the other hand, it was you who pursued their company—even if only out of a feeling of guilt—then being in touch is something that chiefly satisfied your personal needs.

The kinds of relationships between aging parents and their adult children range between the ends of a continuum. At one end of the continuum are children who are constantly in touch with their mother, purely out of love and a concern for her welfare. They exchange family news and advice on everyday problems and have a wide range of things to share. A fund of love, trust, and respect has accumulated over the years, and this allows them to stay involved without second thoughts. Since they have always been in close touch, they learn about whatever mounting problems their mother may face simply through the course of their regular conversations.

This level of concern and affection spurs these sons and daughters to give their parents all-out support, and it often sustains them through even the grimmest circumstances. For example, it may become necessary to place a mother in a nursing home. In time she may become bedridden, physically unpleasant to view, and enfeebled to the point where she can only complain about poor food, lonely surroundings, and an indifferent nursing staff. She may even become so confused that she no longer recognizes people, including family members who come to visit her. Yet her children visit her as often as possible because they are comforted by her presence. Just seeing her is sufficient for them because the memories they have of her are rich enough to transcend her present condition.

Such tributes to love are rare and extraordinary. But no mother's magic brought them about. Concern and love can never be demanded, nor should they be. They can only come as the fruit of a healthy and deeply caring parental relationship.

If you visit any nursing home, you will understand how unusual such close relationships are in life. A stranger visiting a nursing home may hear elderly parents describe how ungrateful and insensitive their children are. As proof, the parents may point out that their son or daughter has not even seen them for months. They may recall ruefully the old proverb that a parent always manages to find room for twelve children, while twelve children never seem to find room for one parent.

The stranger may be very upset by his experience and reflect that the world must be a cold, inhuman place, since so many people apparently have turned their backs upon these pathetic, harmless, endearing men and women. The observer has no way of knowing, though, that some of these old people always made their own children feel unloved or unwanted. It is this troubled kind of relationship between parents and children that lies at the opposite end of the continuum.

Often the apparent neglect of a parent in a home for the aged or in an apartment is due to a multitude of causes. A father may have provided a homelife that was a battleground and a scene of threats, punishments, tantrums, and slamming doors. His children, who are now absent, have just as many memories as anyone else. And they remember how punitive, unforgiving, and rejecting their father was. Such a father may now tell a stranger that his son is a disappointment to him, an inadequate fellow who never lived up to his responsibilities. This latest lack of concern, in the father's eyes, is only the most recent example of many such displays in the past. But this pathetic-looking old man probably hammered into his son's head all his life a single message—that the son was no good, a disappointment to his father, and that nothing he ever did came up to snuff.

Needless to say, treatment like this can cripple the son's chances for a mature, fulfilling life. The absence of the son during his father's old age may really be a triumph of self-preservation over the deep feelings of inadequacy the father managed to instill in the son as he was growing to manhood. There are, in fact, instances of children openly gloating over an elderly parent's physical and emotional problems. From the son's or daughter's point of view, for example, the miserable old man is finally getting what he deserves. "Because of the awful treatment he gave to Mom, my brothers, and myself," one son may say, "he's just now getting a taste of his own medicine."

Most relationships between parents and children, of course, fall somewhere between these two extremes. Interest in and concern for one another are rarely an all-or-nothing affair.

It must be emphasized, however, that you should not ignore your basic feelings. Difficult as it may be in practice, it is important to prepare ahead of time for what the scope of your involvement can comfortably be. You need to sort out and face up to the complicated feelings you have. The nearer this point comes to being settled in your mind, the more clearly you will be able to decide how to handle the needs of your parents as they come up. It should also be easier for you to accept the advantages of finding substitutes without feeling that you are guilty of neglect.

If there has been a lapse of many years during which you had little regular contact with your parents, you may have forgotten the reasons. As you became more involved with your own family and career over the years, your memory tended to shove the old disappointments and resentments far from your mind. You may then mistakenly conclude that all those incidents are now just water over the dam—forgiven and forgotten.

Memories never really disappear though. Fresh contacts may awaken them. If your relationship had been precious to you, chances are that you would never have gotten out of touch in the first place. The history of your past relationship does not dissolve the day your parents meet some sudden catastrophe. New contact always serves as a reminder of what has been in the past.

> Susan Erskinwick used to fly to Arizona to visit her parents twice a year. She called them regularly on the phone, talking warmly and at length with her mother.
>
> After her mother died, Susan invited her father, Steven Smith, to come and live with her. It was not long, though, before the incidents of the new daily routine became colored by past memories. Her father was a reformed alcoholic who recently had given up drinking. One Saturday morning he urgently requested Susan to drive him to his doctor's office. Although Susan agreed, she felt resentful. When had he ever given up his free time for her when she was younger? On the way to the doctor's, she heard her father draw a quick breath as she sped through a yellow light. Susan had to bite her lower lip to keep from telling him to keep his petty criticisms to himself, especially since it was she who was making the sacrifice for him in the first place.
>
> Finally Mr. Smith's impatience, ill temper, and grumbling—qualities his wife had always managed somehow to keep in check while she was alive—made Susan's homelife unbearable. Her father, too, realized after six months that he had made a mistake in coming to live at Susan's home. He returned to Arizona, and he and Susan were in touch by phone on Wednesdays, holidays, anniversaries, and birthdays. Their conversations were brief and superficial, however, and soon Susan found that she was too busy to call or visit Arizona as in the past. Years later, after her husband urged Susan to fly out

and see Dad while there was still time, she realized how much
of her interest in her parents had faded when her mother died.

In Susan's case her relationship with her father always had
been rather superficial. It was unrealistic of her to assume that,
because her father had become needy or dependent, she would, or
even could, suddenly shed her old feelings of ambivalence toward
him. It was a mistake for her to try to look after him personally.

If Mr. Smith had been a totally punitive, unloving man (as is
sometimes the case), Susan's problems would have been far greater.
The ugly incidents they had experienced together and then avoided
in the past would have been brought back home with full force.

If you try to look after your elderly parents, there is another
important question you must ask yourself: "What effects will my
new responsibiliies have on my own immediate family?" The demands some parents make are so great that you may find yourself
having to choose between your obligations to them and your obligations to your spouse and children. If that issue has never been
wholly resolved in your mind, an enfeebled parent can mean a
major psychological conflict for you. As a general rule, you ought
not enter into arrangements such as cooking Mama's dinner for her
every evening or moving her into your home if such arrangements
will probably bring fresh tensions into your family life. You may
not only be confronted with contradictory responsibilities toward
your parent, children, and spouse, but you will also probably discover that you have forfeited the needed time you once had all to
yourself.

If your spouse resents the time and energy spent away from
the house in order to care for your father, for example, your new
involvement is probably a mistake. Your spouse may understand
that your father is sick and lonely and that there does not appear to
be anyone but you to brighten his Sunday mornings. But your
spouse has every right to feel irritated if the pleasant time he or she
customarily spends alone with you and the children has been
spoiled because of a father-in-law's troubles.

All decisions like the one to care for your father should really
be made only after a complete discussion with your spouse.

A husband or wife can be helpful in a variety of ways. He or
she is usually far more detached from the situation than you are
and can see more clearly whether your parent's demands are rea-

sonable. He or she can also give useful advice about whatever guilt feelings you may have and is in an excellent position to point out whether you are tormenting yourself needlessly.

In addition, your spouse may have strong personal feelings about your parent—either positive or negative. He or she may have always enjoyed your mother's company, for example, and would welcome any new involvement, even to the point of spending as much time and energy on Mama as yourself. On the other hand, he or she may have always been indifferent or hostile to her. This often happens if a mother has opposed her child's marriage in the first place. Under these circumstances you might find yourself caught between a parent you can't adequately help and a spouse who resents whatever time and energy you do devote to your parent. If this type of situation starts to shape up, you would be advised to seek some professional advice and move toward some alternate plan.

Many middle-aged sons and daughters would probably prefer not to involve themselves in their parents' lives but feel too uncomfortable and guilty to say no. For various reasons, they cannot justify to themselves a refusal to care for their aging parents simply because they feel a natural, proper desire to live their own independent and burden-free lives. They may then take on extra responsibilities for Mama, for instance, because they believe it is "the right thing to do." Too often, however, they may fail to see why their good intentions are really quite misguided.

It is usually a mistake to start running errands and paying frequent visits to a parent only because you believe no one else can truly provide Mama with the help she needs. To assume that you are indispensable is not only factually incorrect but often a clue to the fact that you may harbor some painful, threatening feelings about a parent that are too difficult to examine or question. On some inner level you may feel that you will pay a terrible price for saying no. Old childhood worries may be reawakened: Perhaps your mother will no longer love or approve of you; perhaps she will punish or abandon you. You may secretly feel angry at her but cannot bear to express your anger for fear of her reaction.

These are all inappropriate reasons for allowing your parent to suddenly play a greater part in your life than in the past. All you are really doing is knuckling under to your own fears. If you force yourself to take on a whole set of new responsibilities you basically do not want, you may only be adding an extra burden to your life.

One of the most serious errors sons and daughters commit is to rearrange their own lives for their parents out of a sense of guilt. The new responsibilities will inevitably turn into bitterly resented obligations. The right question to ask yourself is not, "How much do I owe my mother?" or, "Does saying, 'no,' make me callous and ungrateful?" Rather, it is, "Do I have a genuine wish to be with my parent once again?" If so, what emotional price might you have to pay as a result?

If new commitments turn into fresh strains, a son may fail to grasp that the problems that arise are as much within himself as with the aging process of his parents. The man who complains about how much trouble he feels compelled to go to for his mother privately knows that his interest in his mother's daily welfare is rather limited. He would prefer to continue to live as he has been, without taking on an added burden. He would probably do better to act upon his true feelings and arrange for a relative or friend—perhaps even hire an outsider—to visit his mother regularly, run the necessary errands, and be available if a need should arise.

Other sons and daughters become even more heavily involved in a parent's daily welfare for inappropriate reasons. These people rush in to assume total responsibility for a mother's well being even when she could otherwise function pretty well on her own. Such individuals, in fact, are terribly uncomfortable with the notion that their parent can get along without them. It would hurt their feelings to know that their mother might prefer people from outside the family to give her the assistance she needs, or that she might feel like less of a burden with outsiders and at the same time enjoy the stimulation of seeing new faces. Behind their actions are a number of fears. They may be afraid that their parent really doesn't love or need them at all. They may also be frightened that they will soon lose their parent through illness or accident. They believe in some magical way that by constant neamess they can prevent their parent from being taken from them.

We tend to underestimate just how deep are the wounds and attachments we still feel in connection with our parents. Somehow grown people are not supposed to wish that a once remote, unaffectionate father will accept them warmly at last. They are not supposed to carry around the hurt suspicion that Dad did not love them years ago because, in fact, perhaps they did not deserve to be loved. Old feelings are very powerful and can stimulate middle-aged sons and daughters to seek closer contact with a parent. If your relationship with Dad has always been strained, trying to do a lot for him now will probably not make up for everything that has been missing all these years. Sometimes a mellowing comes in old age, and parents want to make up for old hurts in the relationships with their children. Both of you may find yourselves trying to come closer together and succeeding in some ways. But a potential also exists for further strains and conflicts as your parents' needs and demands become greater. Basically, people remain much as they have always been. Greatly increasing your contacts and involvement with them is no assurance that Mom and Dad or you will be at all different from your old selves.

Obligations undertaken for these reasons are usually discharged by going through the motions. You might undertake the obligations because you think you owe it to Mama, but the situation may actually worsen your relationship with her. A parent you encourage to phone several times a day to complain about her ills may drive you to the point of even welcoming the day when she has become so depressed and withdrawn that she no longer speaks to anyone. Unhappy as she might then be, at least you could be pleased at finally being left alone. If you find yourself catering to a parent's every demand in the belief that, if you give in just one more time, he or she will be satisfied, you may ultimately reach the realization that nothing will ever be enough for Dad. You may then decide that you prefer to give him much less—even nothing at all— simply to rescue yourself and your family from a grasping old man.

One of the reasons some people have such a hard time in this kind of relationship is that they have been trained by their parents to respond in only this fashion. Today a mother may tell her son that only he can give her the attention and care she needs in order to survive. She may claim that if her son turns his back on her, she will suffer terribly and die. Now Mom may actually believe what she says. And if her son does one day find the courage to withdraw from the relationship, she would probably feel hurt and angry. But the demands she places upon her son do him very serious damage, which is just as much a matter for consideration as her bruised feelings. Whether either of them realizes it or not, Mom has been trying to manipulate her son's emotions in an attempt to center his life primarily on her. In point of fact, mothers who beam this sort of message today have probably been doing so for years.

At this point in our discussion, we might reasonably ask what has happened to all the other middle-aged children in the family.

After all, many elderly parents have a number of sons and daughters whom they might call upon for assistance. Doesn't each of them have a role to play and a contribution to make? Wouldn't any middle-aged person who faces the prospect of an additional responsibility for a declining parent naturally ask himself or herself where a brother or a sister fits into the picture?

The question is a legitimate one. This should not provide—but frequently does—bottled-up aggravations and resentment. Often elderly parents come to rely exclusively on only one of their children. This sort of relationship normally develops informally over many years. There may be any number of reasons why it comes to pass. Other members of the family may be living in different parts of the country. They may be unable or unwilling to rearrange their lives to assume major new responsibilities. Eventually the designated child, usually a daughter, comes to be seen by Mother as well as the rest of the family as the "caretaker"—the one Mother automatically depends upon to take her shopping or to the doctor, to keep her company, or to help with the housekeeping chores.

There are, of course, a few caretakers who find their new responsibilities genuinely rewarding. But more commonly the caretaker feels overwhelmed and overworked, put upon and abandoned by her siblings. If a brother or sister comes to assume that she is not only responsible but accountable for the mother's daily welfare, the caretaker may bitterly resent the situation.

It is true that all those brothers and sisters are around and might be able to provide valuable help. Unfortunately, the reasons they never seem to be willing to assume their fair share are not entirely their fault. We ought to recognize that a caretaker many times finds herself in that role because it fulfills some of her own basic needs as well. These needs should be examined, however, if they lead to obligations that come to be viewed mainly as burdens.

The fact is that some people have come to see their lives as a series of martyrdoms and victimizations. Self-sacrifice is somehow associated with being the most giving, the most sensitive, the most noble, and the kindest of people. Uncomfortable as the situation they find themselves in may be, it is nevertheless the one in which they feel most at home. Being the only one Mother turns to can carry several emotional payoffs. A daughter might see her new duties as tangible proof that she is the most concerned, loving, and considerate member of her family. Her mother's dependence is felt to be a clear sign that she is the most important, most beloved, and favorite child. Thus a caretaker may come to view herself as the most competent and indispensable person in her family.

Unquestionably, a small percentage of middle-aged sons and daughters are simply indifferent to their parents' well-being. For the most part, however, your brothers and sisters have a concern for your mother comparable to your own. Phone conversations and visits with a parent, as we have seen, naturally stir up old memories and conflicts, old longings and guilts within you. The contacts your mother has with her other children, which you may not witness, undoubtedly stir up the same kinds of feelings within them.

Too often, a caretaker fails to realize that she has indirectly chosen to place herself in that position. She may not see it that way. She probably does not tell her parent, or anyone else, that she has always been the first one to volunteer her energies simply because she feels too guilty to say no or because she is convinced—perhaps sometimes inaccurately—that no one else is sufficiently concerned.

Over the years this attitude snowballs into a self-fulfilling prophecy. A mother learns that she can always depend on her daughter, and eventually she comes to depend upon her always. The middle-aged person's siblings get the impression that their mother prefers the services and the company of their sister to their own. They begin to defer to what appears to be their mother's and sister's wishes. The caretaker interprets the diminished involvement as proof of her siblings' indifference and insensitivity. A daughter might truly wish that her brother would drive her parent to the hospital each Saturday morning. She might wonder why her sister cannot take over the housekeeping chores once a week. But since she assumes her siblings are always too busy or unconcerned, she doesn't even bother to ask them. The duties become hers by default.

In far too many instances this situation is rectified only when the caretaker simply cannot cope with the strain any longer, or when her husband (if she is married) finally objects strenuously to the disruption his wife's devotion has brought into his family life. When caretakers come to a social agency for help, one of the first questions asked is whether there are any brothers and sisters. More often than not, when the worker contacts the other family members, he or she finds that they had no idea their sister was overburdened. They had assumed she enjoyed the contact with their parent. Usually we find that the siblings are more than willing to help out in some way.

The scope of their assistance may not be all-encompassing, but that hardly makes the help useless. A brother may not have the time to spend on nightly visits. But he may be able to contribute comfortably to his mother's financial support. He may also be willing to hire an accountant to handle his mother's financial affairs. A sister may not be able to contribute monetarily, but she may have no objections whatsoever to occasionally driving her mother to the doctor or taking her grocery shopping. A second brother, who lives out of town, can be mobilized to phone once a week and come on a visit a few extra times a year. You may enjoy visiting with your mother but feel very uncomfortable complaining to your mother's landlord about the heat or haggling with the Social Security office about the late check. You may well have a brother, however, who considers locking horns with service people his forte.

In the eyes of a caretaker, each of these smaller tasks might not seem to compensate for the total effort that she puts forth. But each can give much needed relief. In the eyes of a parent, the very variety of inputs serves as a morale booster. It demonstrates that her children are all thinking about her and are all concerned. Beyond that, a parent benefits a great deal by having the rent paid and the finances in competent hands, by having the Social Security check expedited, and by having her long-lost son up to visit more often.

The utilization of brothers and sisters illustrates several important principles. It is an effective, healthy way of enlisting substitutes for the caretaker. It provides you and your parent with additional options and resources. It enhances your parent's ability to live on her own, causing little change in her daily routine and life-style. Last but not least, it permits you to have a much healthier control over your own involvement.

Generally you should involve your brothers and sisters as much as possible. There are some families, although they are in the minority, who meet regularly on their own to discuss their parents' problems and to divvy up the responsibilities. It is a well-functioning, self-aware family that realizes they are all in this together and are all working in the best interests of their parents.

When families are not so closely knit, another strategy often proves effective. The family physician or a social worker can often approach middle-aged brothers and sisters. He or she is an objective party who understands the problems without being hampered by or caught up in the family history. Such a professional is often able to stimulate efforts in a brother whom everyone else has written off long ago.

Let's go back and take a second look at a case we discussed earlier in this chapter. You'll recall how annoyed Susan Erskinwick became while taking her father, Mr. Smith, to the doctor's office. Mr. Smith's silent but felt reflection on her driving ability was correctly interpreted by Susan as a criticism of her as a person. Susan reacted as a daughter to a father. While she had a genuine desire to see that he was taken care of, her feelings about him became a real handicap. But after all, what her father needed was not some reassurance of his daughter's devotion but a quick, safe means of transportation. Susan did not feel comfortable enough with her relationship to her father or her understandable wish to spend Saturday morning differently. If she had, she might well have arranged for her father to take a taxi to the doctor's office. Cabdrivers not only know their way around town but are also immune to passengers who go in for backseat driving.

In many ways we continue to view the aged people who raised us through the eyes of a son or daughter. This is a perfectly normal, yet significant limitation. If you find substitutes to help out your aged father, you are helping him to lead as well-rounded a life as you yourself do. We are not always aware of just how much an aged parent benefits from being placed in all sorts of different contexts that have nothing to do with his or her family.

> Brenda Harrison, a successful business executive, one day came to a realization of the value of such contexts. In doing so, she saved herself an enormous amount of aggravation.
>
> Brenda had always felt that her father treated his wife and children in an insensitive, selfish way. After her mother died, Brenda spent a few months trying to help her father out with the cooking and the cleaning of his apartment. It was not an easy chore. Her father refused to lift a finger to help and kept criticizing her efforts to be useful. Yet Brenda noticed that whenever the two of them stopped at the corner grocery store, her father became a paragon of courtesy, self-restraint, and tact. Several employees, in fact complimented her privately on what a charming father she had. She could barely restrain

herself from describing what he was "really" like. She also felt jealous over the kindness he only showed to outsiders.

One afternoon Brenda was on the phone to her sister, complaining about the two different sides of her father's personality. It suddenly occurred to her that the ugly half only came out when he was playing the role of "Dad." She quickly decided to arrange for someone else to come in to cook and clean for her father—someone for whom he could play the role of a dapper, elderly gentleman. The money she spent for the housekeeper was insignificant compared to benefits he received from having his household needs met in a way less conflict-ridden for both him and Brenda herself. Her subsequent contacts with him, while not as frequent, were under conditions of less tension and strain. They could get together for family gatherings, holidays, or fun occasions that allowed an expression of the more comfortable and pleasant side of their relationship.

In summary, then, we ought not presume that greater involvement with an elderly parent is necessarily in everyone's best self-interest. It can be, when the relationship has always been a warm, intimate, and generous one. When it has not, a guiding principle is to find other people and other social outlets that gratify a parent's needs.

Adult children who find themselves assuming a new and major role in a parent's life ought to remember that they are, in fact, presenting themselves as substitutes for the whole range of social and physical losses the parent has suffered. Just as you would automatically check to see that a particular senior center is a legitimate, professional organization before advising your father to participate in its activities, so, too, should you evaluate your own qualifications to be all things to one person.

Ways that you can help your parents cope with their social losses will be considered in the next chapter.

7

How Can You Help Your Parents Cope with Social Losses?

Many of the emotional problems the elderly face come about because the roles that gave their lives meaning and importance have been taken from them. We may feel that we perform all sorts of roles in life only because we are obliged to do so. In reality, however, we depend upon our roles to preserve our emotional well-being.

Suppose someone asked you to tell who you are and why you got out of bed this morning. You would probably answer by describing yourself, your job, your marriage, and your children. We each play dozens of roles in our lifetime. We play a surprisingly large number every day. By turns we are spouse and worker, parent and child, customer and commuter, friend and citizen.

THE MOTHERING ROLE

Although the roles of women have greatly expanded for members of our own generation, most of our mothers saw themselves primarily as wives and mothers. Your mother's work, in fact, was primarily the raising of you and your brothers and sisters. Her sense of who she is today is bound up with what her children have become, what your father did for a living, and where she resided as an active homemaker. We are accustomed to thinking of our mother as someone who gave selflessly to us. We needed our mother to fondle us when we were young, to provide us with love and warmth in a well-run household, to be there when we returned from school, and to listen to our problems and complaints. We ought to realize, though, that a mother depends just as deeply, although in a far different way, upon her children. In important ways the woman who raised you is someone who needs to be a mother in order to have a sense of personal identity. After all, for more than twenty years the meaning of her life was defined by her keeping house, caring for her husband, and guiding the lives of her children.

Of course life did not change drastically overnight for Mom the day the last of her children left home. In most cases she still had a good deal to live for. There was probably a great sense of relief that the burden and responsibility of child raising was over. She no longer would have to contend with the annoyance of adolescents who would not make their beds or clean up after themselves and who often complained about the quantity or quality of the desserts she prepared for them.

By this time your father probably had a secure income, and it seemed as if Mom and Dad were about to enjoy together a new start in life. Your mother's health was good and would remain so for many years. Although her children were out of the house, they still kept in regular contact. They might call on their parents from time to time for emotional support, a favorite recipe, advice, or even for a loan. On holidays and other festive occasions they probably came over for dinner, at which time Mom could act like a mother once more. Her friends were still living nearby, and her place in the community was solid.

By the time your mother reached her seventies or eighties, however, her life had changed a great deal. Her old neighborhood may have deteriorated, and members of different ethnic groups may have moved into it. Her friends may have disappeared, her husband may have died, and her health has probably gotten worse. Some of her children may now be spread all across the country, while others live in distant suburbs. And by now her kids have become middle-aged adults with careers, children, and community interests of their own. They have long since become full-fledged, self-reliant adults who are content to lead satisfying lives without a mother's help. They may also be so caught up in their responsibilities and the demands upon their time that they have very little energy to spare for their aging parent.

Many elderly women are quite comfortable with all these

changes. From the start they intended to raise children who would be secure and self-confident enough to be pushed out of the nest and to enjoy full, independent lives. They know that this is the natural order of things. Instead of feeling that they have been abandoned or forgotten, they see their children's autonomy as a true measure of their own success. Often these women accept the fact that their job as mother has ended, and they begin to search for other new and meaningful roles.

Some elderly women, however, have a much more difficult time letting go. Their sense of who they are and their purpose in living is still totally bound up with being a mother. The loss they feel of the importance they once held in the lives of their children is too painful to accept. They refuse to admit that inevitable changes have occurred, and they still struggle to be a mother to their forty-, fifty-, and sixty-year-old sons and daughters.

Alice Henderson, an eighty-one-year-old grandmother of seven, has become a real problem to her two children. She lives fairly near her daughters and drops in to see them regularly. When she does, she acts as if she were still the central figure in her children's lives—the one to whom they look for direction and support. She has no hesitation, therefore, about criticizing a mess in the bedroom or instructing them how to cook the meat or how to raise their children. She belittles their husbands and questions their choice of friends. Whenever her daughters are faced with a decision, Alice makes it clear that neither of them can possibly know what to do without her advice. She runs all sorts of errands for them both—"knocking herself out," as she says, for her children, who have never asked her to do so.

When Alice finally goes home, she becomes terribly hurt if her daughters do not call her for a day or two. Each time she fails to hear from them promptly, she asks why they have not gotten in touch with her sooner. She then complains that her daughters do not see enough of each other, that they neglect her, and that they do not appreciate how difficult it was to bring them into the world and care for them. After all, she stayed in the house for days on end when they were small or sick. Now that she herself has become old and aching, she feels that they should care for her just as she had once cared for them. If her daughters invite her over on a Saturday evening, Alice usually sighs and tells them that she is too tired to go out.

These practices nearly drive her children out of their minds, for they deeply resent her insistence on running their lives, and their feelings are perfectly understandable. It may be appropriate for a mother to supervise the life of a seven-year-old girl but certainly not that of a normal, healthy adult in her fifties.

Short of turning themselves into little children who need a strong, assertive mother, Alice's daughters can never totally satisfy Alice. At bottom Alice and women like her are angry at the world because they desperately want to keep their children dependent on them. Alice sets up situations that remind her of the old days, when her daughters needed her and when she was in direct control of their lives. By making her daughters feel guilty, she forces them to make her the center of their attention. Thus, for a short while, she can still enjoy the influence she once had.

Many middle-aged people wind up bearing the brunt of the needs of a mother like Alice Henderson. They come to think of her as self-centered and manipulative. She does, indeed, have a painful effect upon her children. But she is probably unaware of what she puts her sons and daughters through. This is important to remember. While she *is* trying to control her children's lives, she does not do so to be malicious. She simply needs to be a mother to someone, to feel she is still worthwhile and needed. She may take out her needs on her grown sons and daughters. But she really has as little conscious control over her behavior as she does over her blood pressure.

A common and appropriate response to the recognition of a serious emotional problem in a young person is to seek treatment from a psychiatrist. An elderly person suffering a similar trauma may also benefit from formal psychiatric treatment. But more often another remedy may be found, which would probably be cheaper, more effective, and less distressing. In the case of an elderly woman trying to come to terms with her distress over the loss of her mothering role, sitting for many meetings with a therapist may not be the most effective solution.

Such women can often be helped when their daily activities are enriched or rearranged. They need to find fresh situations and people as substitutes for their children, who no longer need mothering. Many of these women have useful skills. The more ways they find to use them properly, the less need they should have to intrude into the lives of their offspring.

There are several ways in which you might try to keep your mother occupied. If she enjoys mending or knitting, you might bring her your family's sewing needs. You could ask your friends if they have any work of this kind that your mother might handle. There is no reason you couldn't ask her to knit sweaters or afghans you do not desperately need. There may be a special pastry or soup she makes better than anyone else. If so, she might enjoy preparing some of these dishes for your family on a regular basis or whenever she comes over for dinner. Your mother may no longer have the stamina to whip up a full-course holiday dinner for a dozen people, but she probably still has great satisfaction in cooking some of the foods that have always been family favorites.

You might also keep in mind that grandchildren can often provide your mother with an opportunity to feel like a homemaker again. She might enjoy baby-sitting. You might also arrange for your children to spend an occasional Sunday afternoon at her home.

Of course not all elderly parents will leap at the chance to do these things. Some women never enjoyed working in the kitchen or raising children, and they might feel put upon or used if you were to bring your mending or your children to them. You know your own situation best. As long as you are not asking for her help in such a way as to take advantage of her, you are doing the right thing.

Another way in which an elderly woman may fulfill her mothering need is by keeping a pet. A widow who lives alone often may become quite devoted to a cat, a dog, or a bird. She may be able to build a new life around a pet, just as she once built her life around her husband and children. Moreover, she will have found a dependent, childlike companion whose whole world centers around her. She may pamper it with special treats and talk to it all day— coaxing it, complaining about it, and consoling it in turn. She will find in it a companion who will never criticize or reject her and who enjoys all the cuddling and care she wants to lavish on it. When her pet dies, she may be grief-stricken and mourn its death almost with the same intensity we normally associate with the loss of a husband or a child.

Unfortunately, an elderly woman's children often do not understand how rewarding her relationship with her pet is. Nor do they realize that its loss may represent for her the loss of all her dear ones. Instead of finding their mother's grief pathetic and ridiculous, they should respect it and accept her behavior. They may even want to present her with a new pet as a substitute. A replacement of this sort may be just as good for an eighty-year-old as for an eight-year-old. One word of caution is in order: It is advisable to find out in advance how your mother would feel having a pet to take care of.

Still another outlet for women who enjoy mothering is the organization. At the church women's club or Golden Agers chapter, elderly women may take pride in providing the cookies and cakes for social events. Instead of serving a cup of after-dinner coffee just to their husbands, they will be able to pour coffee or tea and prepare sweets for several dozen persons. These organizations offer an opportunity for planning, entertaining, leadership, and other roles that can be important new roles for Mother to play.

Some homes for the aged run special programs for outside volunteers who are invited to provide services to residents on a regular basis. The volunteers write letters, assist with meals, listen to complaints, and provide real companionship for the residents of the home. Surprisingly, a great number of these volunteers are in their seventies or eighties. They are people who are not very far removed from membership in the home themselves, and they come to assist those who are more disabled and in need.

> Flora Schwartz, a seventy-nine-year-old widow, is a volunteer at a large home for the aged. She organizes group singing and talent shows. Much of her activity outside the home during the week is dedicated to making sure that the next program will be even more successful than the last one. If asked why she goes to the home, she will answer that she is a member of the staff. She has explained to her children that she is in no way identified with "those old fogies." She considers herself a sprightly, active woman who enjoys the company of people of all ages.

Perhaps her children feel that Flora is kidding herself, but she appears most comfortable when she believes that she is "mothering" residents of the home. It does not matter that her clientele happen to be ten years her senior. If this is the way she has to see herself in order to find gratification in her efforts, she should be respected and encouraged.

RETIREMENT AND THE OCCUPATIONAL ROLE

During the colonial period, a man might introduce himself to a stranger simply as George Pruitt, one of the Pruitts of Newberry, South Carolina. This information would tell enough about his background so that another colonist would know a great deal about his social status, education, income, and possibly even his character. The position the Pruitt family held in their town would enable anyone to determine just how to act toward a Pruitt.

This is obviously no longer possible today. If someone introduces himself to you as Martin Mueller, one of the Muellers from Cleveland, it would mean absolutely nothing to you. But if he told you that he made his living as an insurance salesman, the pieces of information you need to know about his background would quickly begin to fall into place.

This contrast helps point out just how important a man's occupation is in his own eyes. Martin Mueller may see himself as a successful, respected salesman up to the day he retires. From then on he may face a serious emotional crisis in which he sees himself as just another arthritic old man who lives in Cleveland and has nothing much to do. The discovery that on retirement one becomes lonely and no longer feels significant as a person contributes to the alarmingly high rate of suicide among men over age sixty-five. This does not contradict the fact that many elderly people relish the opportunity to leave their jobs. They may have plans for fishing, traveling, or simply sitting around the house and taking it easy at last. But many others do not make the transition to retirement nearly as comfortably.

There are several reasons for this. We mentioned in an opening chapter how important it is for middle-aged people to begin to look for ways to redirect their energies and interests. A hardnosed rationale lay behind that piece of advice. One of the most difficult emotional shifts a man must make is from seeing himself as a worker to seeing himself as a retiree. This, of course, applies to working women as well. Since many men and women can realistically anticipate spending ten to twenty years as a retiree, it makes sense to plan for the retirement years well in advance.

Most people, of course, do not do so. In the United States old age is generally expected to be a gray time of life designed as a kind of waiting period until death arrives. Many men really dread the idea of their own old age and retirement so much that they cannot face the prospect rationally, if at all.

Our culture has so stressed the importance of work and productivity that a man's identity is bound up in what he does for a living. While most men enjoy their leisure hours and welcome the chance to enjoy their annual recreation, the return to his job is even more important to a man's overall life satisfaction than going on vacation. While younger people may view retirement as an idyllic state of permanent vacation, older men forced to retire before they are ready to do so view it mainly as evidence of their own unworthiness.

For most American men recreation is not just a lost art; it is not considered an art at all. We may pay lip service to retirees, congratulating them on having earned the right to gratify themselves in other ways. But in reality we tend to look at them as useless people, who are just too old to do anything worthwhile anymore. The money many live on comes from Social Security. Although this is money they have earned themselves, some of us look upon retirees as people living off charity and as burdens on our society.

The elderly make up over 11 percent of the population of the United States, and this figure will continue to grow. As it does, our attitudes toward the aged may gradually become more enlightened. Private and governmental institutions may also begin to respond in more concrete and constructive ways to their needs. The next generation of the aged—ourselves—should be better educated, more secure financially, and more demanding politically than the current one. In the meantime small changes have already taken place. Mandatory retirement has shifted from sixty-five to seventy. Federal and state governments have designed a number of programs that allow elderly men to contribute their occupational skills.

We ought to keep in mind that age sixty-five has become the date most of us associate with the first day of old age. But there has never been any absolute or scientific rule to justify the figure, which was chosen in the mid 1930s when the Social Security program was launched. The federal bureaucracy had to find an age at which it could start issuing benefits. Congress selected the age of sixty-five because it was the average life expectancy of most Americans at the time. But today millions of people live longer—into their seventies, eighties, and even nineties. Yet the figure of sixty-five still lives on in our minds, assuming an authority and importance it was never intended to have originally.

Despite these facts many elderly fathers look upon themselves and their retirement as our society does today. Many emotional problems and behavior patterns that confuse and irritate you may be due to your father's struggle to cope with all that has gone out of his life since he retired.

It really doesn't matter whether or not a man enjoyed the work he did for forty years. In fact, he built his existence around it. It was his job that routed him out of bed and forced him to get dressed each morning. It gave him a place to go and people to see all day. It demanded the biggest part of his time and energy. And it not only defined his importance in the world but also permitted him to feel that he was successfully providing for his family. If a man believes that he is what he does for a living, the day he retires may leave him feeling that he no longer exists at all. He has lost any reason to get up and go out of the house five days a week. There are no more familiar people who count on seeing him during the day. His family does not depend on his energy or skills anymore. Social Security benefits and pension funds will provide for his family whether he rises at the crack of dawn or sleeps until noon. For many elderly men the need to work goes far beyond any thought of a paycheck.

> Peter Hutchinson is a seventy-six-year-old man who in the 1930s turned a small department store into a giant business. It made him a millionaire many times over before he was fifty. If he chose to do so, Peter could spend his retirement in ways that the rest of us can merely fantasize about. Yet every morning he puts on his shirt and tie and takes his place in the office at a desk assigned to the chairman emeritus. Ed, his middle-aged son, actually runs the business and makes all the important decisions. His father's presence is really in no way essential to the company's day-to-day operations. In fact there was a time several years ago when Ed was very close to asking his father to leave altogether, for Peter's way of doing business had long since become obsolete. The decisions he insisted upon making were actually cutting into the firm's profits. But Ed finally came to the conclusion that his father's sense of well-being was so bound up with the company that it was better to respect his father's feelings and accept what small business losses might result from what he did.

Few elderly men, of course, are presidents of family-run businesses. Those who held blue-collar jobs may be able to drum up some handyman work for themselves around the house and neighborhood. They may no longer be able to pull their weight at the steel mill, but they can still paint a fence, fix a sink, repair an auto. If they have developed arthritis or some other physical problem, however, such work may be impossible for them. Frustration in such cases can be punishing. White-collar workers—accountants, clerks, or salesmen—may have just as much difficulty upon retirement. Their skills cannot be applied outside the job at all. While baby-sitting for the grandchildren might gratify some elderly wives, it is not normally something from which many men can take satisfaction.

It is not unusual for men who have recently retired to go through a period of depression. They may sit around the house not knowing what to do with all the time on their hands. Their wives, on the other hand, may not be used to having them around the house and underfoot for twenty-four hours each day. They may have their own routines and needs for privacy that their husbands disregard or criticize.

There are some men who genuinely lose interest in the people and things they once enjoyed. This can be perfectly normal. Well-intentioned children should not force them into activity for its own sake. It is only when a father's new indifference becomes part of a general pattern of listlessness, depression, or withdrawal from the world around him that his disengagement really means emotional trouble.

There are several things you can do to help your father handle his retirement successfully. If you have a warm and comfortable relationship with him, you will get an accurate idea of how your dad is coping simply through your normal conversations. If, for any number of legitimate reasons, you have lost touch with your parents, serious problems may come to your attention only on the day one of your parents phones you in dismay to report them.

It is almost always a good idea to sit down with your father at some point to discuss what both of you can do to make sure that he makes a satisfying adjustment. After he retires, your elderly father ought to be able to find things to do that will enable him to feel good about himself. He should be able to tell you in fairly specific terms how he would like to spend his time. This may mean cultivating talents your father has never used in the past.

Michael Benson found at the age of seventy that he couldn't practice dentistry any longer. He had always been a fine story-teller and possessed a deep, resonant singing voice. His children encouraged him to join a senior citizens organization where he could participate in the theater group they ran. Gradually Michael made the transition from seeing himself as a dentist without a practice to a skillful man of the stage. Along the way he became involved in producing, directing, and stage management. The theater, in other words, provided him with a new occupation and a new life.

But his dedication eventually began to worry his children. Although Michael had been living with a weak heart for about fifteen years, he threw himself into his new activity like a man twenty years younger. Whenever his daughter told him he ought to take it a little slower so that he might be around longer, Michael would brush her off. And in a situation like this, both are correct. His daughter had a sincere, realistic concern for her father's health, and she had every right to share it with him. There was indeed a good chance that Michael might shorten his life if he kept up his pace of activity. But it is just as true that if he had permitted his health to be his number one priority, he would probably have wound up sitting around his apartment bored and miserable. That situation could also shorten his life. What his daughter had to accept finally was the fact that people need to decide for themselves how to live their own lives.

For the elderly who have so many limitations in their lives already, this right is especially important. The choice Michael made was to live as full a life as he could, regardless of the consequences, rather than to lead an empty and miserable existence simply to survive as long as possible.

As far as Michael was concerned, pleasure was a necessary part of life. And, by the time he reached age seventy, the sacrifice of several months of life, or even of a year or two, was one he was willing to make. This attitude, in fact, was one his eighty-three-year-old brother, Sam, had cleared with him.

Sam was a diabetic who lived in a nursing home. Diabetics, of course, are forbidden a large number of foods, most of which they crave as no one else can. Sam and others with his condition were waging a constant guerrilla war with the nurses over their right to eat cake, pastrami, and other foods that were like poison for them.

When Michael visited his brother, Sam would ask him to smuggle in a corned beef sandwich the next time he came. At first Michael told his brother he could not do so because it would make him an accomplice in shortening his life. He reminded Sam that the nurses had a medically valid reason for denying him things that were bad for him and that they really had his best interests in mind. Michael then realized that he was sounding just like his own daughter. So he stopped his lecture and asked Sam instead how much mustard and pickle he wanted on the corned beef.

The concept of pleasure is a good idea for you to accept. Once you have accepted this concept, you can encourage your parents to strive for a kind of balance in their lives. It is better to urge your father to get up early and go fishing in the cold morning air, if that is what he enjoys, than to tell him he must not fish at all for fear of catching a cold. The same holds true of his desire to stay up late playing cards with some neighbors or to walk out in nasty weather to a bingo game.

Some men have a number of mechanical skills. They may know how to repair a car, fix a toaster, build a bookcase, install a light fixture, or do other similar jobs. If your father is one of these people, you might ask him to do whatever odd jobs are needed around your own home. If he enjoys this kind of work, you might also ask your neighbors and friends if they, too, would like to take advantage of his skills. Your father might take longer on the job than some younger worker, but the results should be about the same and would certainly be much less expensive. The money he receives would not only come in handy but would also give him the important satisfaction of feeling his skills are still as valuable as they once were. In his own eyes he would not so much have become obsolete as he would have "scaled down" his pace. He might tell you (with some luck) that nowadays he can only take on "so many" new jobs. And while you might feel that he is really only getting this kind of work as a favor, he still sees himself as a working man. We ought not to smile at that. Such a father is making a real effort to hang in there and feel that he is still someone of importance. And to a large degree he is succeeding.

The amount of handiwork such elderly men do is not as important for their well-being as simply having the opportunity to do it on a regular basis. The majority of our aged are women. Even if these women know how to change a light fuse, they often feel embarrassed about doing it because that is supposed to be a man's work. If you think your father might approve, you could encourage him to make arrangements to stop in at a retirement home or a Golden Agers club once a week. In this setting he would not be seen as just an old man looking for something to occupy his time. He would become the skillful, helpful man who knows how to handle all the tasks that mystify members of the opposite sex. In his own eyes he would become the "man in charge of things" at the club or the home.

The majority of elderly fathers, of course, would search for other sorts of work. Many men who held white-collar jobs have limited mechanical skills. The ones who do have such skills usually do not find such tasks particularly fulfilling. By the time many working-class fathers retire, they may be so hampered by arthritis or other physical problems that fixing, gardening, or construction work of any kind is practically out of the question for them.

In trying to understand and help your father, though, it is important to appreciate the other features of his job that were just as personally rewarding, if not more so, than being paid for something he produced. The ritual of getting up early, putting on a suit, and arriving at some place at a specific time may mean a great deal. It represents in his own mind the kind of personal sacrifice a man makes to earn his self-respect. Assuming personal responsibility for the proper management of an organization is something your father may equate with his definition of manhood. Being a part of the group he has grown close to in the office may have gratified him in a way he never expected his particular line of work could. Five days a week for years your father lunched with his associates, sharing business and family matters. He probably got together with many of them at other times, having them over to dinner or meeting them to play cards or bowl.

When your father retires, he loses the chance to earn a paycheck. But he can struggle quite hard to keep other parts of the work experience in his life. Like all people, your father needs to feel he is a part of things. There are ways you can encourage him to do that. A first step toward that goal, though, is coming to accept the efforts he may already be making.

Andrew Matthews worked in a downtown St. Louis bank for thirty-eight years. Since his retirement, he meets a group of his former colleagues twice a week for lunch in the old restaurant across the street from the bank. On those days, he gets up at the time he always used to, puts on a suit, travels forty-five minutes by bus, spends an hour and a half at the meal, and then returns home.

As far as Andrew is concerned, the meeting was his job for the day. He went down to work to talk about important issues, and he returned home to read the paper in the evening. In reality, he has been put out to pasture, and the bank's stability in no way depends upon his trips. But Andrew has managed to consider himself in many important ways as still a part of the bank and its operations. His children would be making a mistake to see his behavior as just a way to kill time. It may seem to them like a great deal of time and effort just to shoot the breeze over a tuna salad sandwich. It would surely be insensitive, if not cruel, to point out to Andrew what he is "really" doing. If meeting his friends downtown makes him feel that he is back on the job, he has succeeded in minimizing his losses.

Some unions—notably those for clothing workers—have established programs for retirees. They set aside an area at the union's headquarters where elderly members can assemble every morning. They may play cards, have lunch together, and argue about union politics or the state of the world. They undoubtedly reminisce at length about the old days. All these activities, which many sons and daughters want no part of, do elderly fathers and mothers a great deal of good.

Another way aged fathers try to hold themselves together is by becoming deeply involved with a religious or social organization. A father who starts attending Mass or minyan every morning is not simply looking for a diversion. Nor is the service the aged's equivalent of a Saturday night party. The elderly man is meeting with his peers to fulfill his obligations to his faith. The same is true, in a more easily comprehensible way, of an elderly father's work on the board of his church or synagogue.

You may see your father become terribly worked up over the latest financial statement. He may examine every expenditure, no matter how trivial it might seem. Heated arguments have taken place about a broken window that might have been replaced for a few dollars less if only someone had been more diligent and shopped around. Every meeting of the Elks, the congregation financial committee, or the condominium residents association has both new and old business on its agenda. The items pertaining to each may sound to us like topics of discussion for a social gathering. But as far as the aged men in attendance are concerned, they are literally conducting business, just as they once did when they were employed. This, too, is a satisfying and appropriate attitude for them to assume.

At some point in our childhood, most of us can recall how much we admired our father for providing our family with a home as well as clothes, food, and spending money. At the time this made him a powerful man of the world in our eyes. When we grew a little older, we had other memories of him. We listened to him complain about how tough it was to earn a living and how we ought to show a little more appreciation for all he had done and was still doing for us.

By now all of us have expressed the same complaint ourselves at one time or another. But we ought not lose sight of how crucial the ability to provide has been for an elderly father's private estimation of his stature. It meant that other people depended upon him, that he was a self-reliant person who always paid his own way. When your dad begins to live on Social Security and pension money, he loses that source of pride. He becomes a recipient for the first time in perhaps forty years. Many men find their new role demoralizing and belittling. Unfortunately, some of the things they do to dismiss the unpleasant picture they have of themselves may disturb their children a great deal.

Bill O'Brien, a seventy-six-year-old retired steelworker, has a couple of habits that always set his daughter Cathy's nerves on edge. The money Bill receives from Social Security and his pension fund barely meet his expenses, and his family knows it. Yet every month Bill converts his entire income into small bills—one-dollar, two dollar, and five-dollar denominations—and carries them around in a wallet that sticks out of his back pocket. At the slightest opportunity he removes his wallet and displays it to all who care to see. Whenever he stops by to see his daughter, he calls his grandson out of the bedroom and presents him with a five-dollar bill. This is far more money than the boy is used to seeing, as well as a gift he really does not need.

Since Bill usually makes these gestures in Cathy's presence, her exasperation has become a part of the ritual. To avoid a scene, she instructs her son, who often feels too embarrassed and uncomfortable to accept the gift, to thank his grandfather and to return to his room. She then bawls her father out. Not only is he spoiling the boy, but Bill knows very well that he cannot afford to give money away. Besides, it is madness to carry around every penny he has to his name in his back pocket. Suppose it falls out while he's riding a bus. Any hoodlum on the street may consider Bill easy pickings. And what he does is embarrassing to her. Is he trying to tell her that she can't provide for her son herself?

What Cathy does not tell her father is that his presents make her feel guilty, for she believes that somehow she should be contributing to his support. In all honesty she can't afford to do so. Moreover, Bill has never hinted that he expects any help from her. All the same she interprets his generosity to her son as a none-too-subtle reminder of how much she really owes him. Cathy also resents the control over her life these gifts seem to give her father. How can she possibly explain that she's too busy to phone as often as he expects or to drive him to the pharmacy or a friend's house in the suburbs? After all, look at all he does for her own child!

Worst of all, Cathy suspects that her father may be trying to buy love and attention. Of course, some elderly fathers use their money this way because they don't believe their families will care for them otherwise. But most of the malicious, manipulative motives Cathy sees in her father's actions are really products of her own imagination. Her feelings are perfectly understandable. The truth is that she has never been very close or comfortable with her dad. Since she feels guilty about her relationship in the first place, she assumes that he is consciously playing on her weakness.

On the other hand, Bill is only trying to experience again the satisfaction of being someone who can provide for those who depend on him. Perhaps he can't afford to hand out dollars and cents the way he does. But the sacrifice is worth it to him because it enables him to feel once more that he is somebody. For a few moments he is no longer the person who depends upon the generosity of the government or a union.

The solution to Cathy's problem might be to allow her father to give presents to his grandson. Then at a later date she might return an equivalent amount to him in a form he would find acceptable. For example, she might take him out to dinner every so often or present him with a fishing rod or several bottles of wine.

Such gestures would put the money back into his pocket while leaving his dignity intact.

The above illustration shows the need for a father to continue in his role as a provider and just how this need is experienced by his daughter. There are other ways in which the elderly can fulfill their need to give to others. One way is through social organizations. As we all know, social organizations fulfill a number of needs. One of the most important of these is the opportunity they offer the elderly to help others. This may come in the form of fund-raising drives for such worthy causes as orphanages, the March of Dimes, or a cancer research institute.

One home for the aged in Chicago holds a dinner every year for a sectarian welfare organization that funds many agencies, including the home itself. While virtually all of the home's residents are entirely dependent on some form of public aid, during the dinner there is always a tumultuous swirl of people writing out their own checks and pledging five or ten dollars to the cause. With pride and satisfaction they are giving to those less fortunate than they are—to the neediest in our society. Ultimately a portion of the money raised finds its way back to the home because, in fact, it is the residents themselves who can be included among the neediest of all.

WIDOWHOOD AND WIDOWERHOOD

The loss of a mate through death is probably the most devastating blow an elderly parent has to endure. In studies of human reactions to stress, the death of a spouse ranks highest among all the possible stresses of old age. And it is not uncommon for the surviving partner to be so grief-stricken that he or she soon withers away and dies.

In fact research has shown that during middle age the most pressing concern many women have is for the physical health of their husbands. Professionals believe that such women may unconsciously be anticipating their own widowhood. A woman's life span may be five or ten years longer than a man's. The facts of human biology together with the pressures of our society produce this result. The male body simply may not have been designed to survive as long as the female body. Thus many women can realistically expect to live the last decade of their lives as widows.

The extent of grief a surviving spouse feels as well as the way he or she copes with that grief will vary from individual to individual. There is no standard way or best way to mourn this sort of loss. Some of our parents may go through an intense period of depression and withdrawal and then gradually work their way out of both within six months or a year. Others may need much more time, while some may never come to accept the death at all.

Still others may not appear to their children to be grieving at the time of the funeral. This often happens with a wife who has nursed her spouse through a long terminal illness. She has probably done her mourning as she watched her husband slowly approach his death. When he passes away, much of her grief "work" has already been done. She may quite understandably see her loss as a blessed release from the suffering that had afflicted them both for so long.

Unfortunately, many sons and daughters have a preconceived notion of how their parents ought to respond. They need to feel that their mother and father were a deeply loving, devoted couple This is a perfectly human and understandable wish. But it is unfair to feel that the absence of visible grieving means that a close relationship never existed between them.

> Lisa Booth could neither forgive nor understand the conduct of her sixty-eight-year-old father, Henry, after her mother's death. Lisa's mother had died of breast cancer. Through the lengthy ordeal her father could not have been more kind or helpful. He bore the brunt of all his wife's bitterness and anger without so much as a complaint. During the final months Lisa's mother was at home, Henry assumed the responsibility for all his wife's needs, never so much as suggesting that he might be able to use a nurse if even for the most unpleasant tasks. Yet after his wife died, he showed almost no sign of sorrow and was able to receive visitors calmly.
>
> After the funeral he quickly sold or disposed of many of the household furnishings and his wife's personal effects. He then moved to a Florida condominium where he and his wife had intended to spend their years of retirement. On his annual trip back to his old home, he told Lisa for the first time of the complaints he had about his marriage. Since Lisa had always been closer to her mother, she was mystified by her father's statements and resentful of them.
>
> It took time for Lisa to sort out her feelings about her

father and about her parents' marriage. Two memories in particular became important to her. One was her father's statement that he prided himself most on the fact that her mother had never wanted for anything. The other memory was of a conversation Lisa had had with her mother two years before the mother's death. They had been talking over the phone about their respective plans for the weekend, and Lisa had asked her mother why she and Dad didn't socialize more with other couples. Her mother had answered casually that the two of them were all the company they really needed.

Unfortunately, Lisa failed to remember that her father always reacted to crises in the same manner. Henry was an inarticulate, uneducated man who had never known how to demonstrate his emotions. As a young girl, Lisa had thought that this meant that her father was an unfeeling man who wished to remain remote from and uninvolved with his children. Nor could Lisa understand that some part of her father was angry that through death his wife had left him. But we can seldom express such selfish feelings openly. Instead his feelings came out in the form of petty complaints for "mistreatment" he had allegedly received decades ago from his wife. Lisa took the complaints at face value and felt terribly wounded. Even so, it would have made a great deal of difference to Lisa if her father had openly expressed sorrow at the funeral. If he had done so, she probably would not later have reached the uneasy conclusion that her parents' marriage had been unhappy.

It is important to keep several things in mind when you try to help your parent through this kind of crisis. Many middle-aged sons and daughters have the mistaken impression that the most painful days their surviving parent endures occur immediately after the death of the spouse. And, of course, death does come as a powerful shock. But the brunt of the shock is usually absorbed by the bustle, the arrangements, and the press of visitors. But several weeks or even months later, when everyone has gone away and left your parent quite alone, the full weight of his or her loss sinks in. This is just the point, unfortunately, at which many children assume that their parent's grief has truly healed.

Just as there is no one best way for a parent to handle his or her grief, there is no standard role you should assume in these circumstances. Some parents genuinely prefer solitude and quiet. Others need to keep as socially active as possible. A principle that ought to guide you both is that every elderly parent should decide for himself or herself the atmosphere in which he or she would be most comfortable. The appropriate thing for you to do depends largely upon the special needs of your parent.

With the best intentions in the world, some children make the mistake of assuming that they alone know what is best, say, for Mama. They decide that what she needs most is a frantic schedule to take her mind off her problems. They rush in to suggest that she immediately sell her house or vacate her apartment and move in with them. Or they may insist on her joining them in a round of movies, dinners, parties, and gatherings of friends. If Mama says she really feels too distressed to throw herself into all this social activity, they dismiss her objections because they believe she must not be left to sit alone feeling bereft.

But being alone for a while may be precisely what Mama needs to accomplish the painful task of healing herself and adjusting to her new life. Children who prevent her from withdrawing, though they do not realize it, are forcing her to postpone her own recuperation from her loss. The activity they create for her can actually do more harm than good.

At the other extreme we find children who leave a widowed parent totally alone. Sometimes a parent insists on this, and the children feel they are meeting her real wishes by obeying her. Grieving does require time by oneself to reflect and remember, as most of us recognize. But the stricken widow needs also to discover that other people need her, want her, and will give her a reason to continue her life. The concerned son or daughter should carefully try to distinguish a natural reaction of grief from a self-destructive decision to lie down and die.

It frequently helps if you offer your mother a number of different ways of spending her time. You might suggest that perhaps she would enjoy a Sunday drive, an afternoon visit with her grandchildren, or preparing a soup for dinner at your house. Your goal should be to strike a balance between forcing her into counterproductive activities and standing passively by as she sinks back into her grief.

In practical terms the death of a spouse carries a variety of losses for the survivor. Our parents lose a companion who knows them backwards and forwards and who has shared an almost infinite variety of memories and experiences with them. They lose not only the most important relationship in their lives but often suddenly find themselves thrust out of their old social circle. The world of their friends consisted of married couples. Now that your parent has become single again, he or she can no longer go out to dinner or the movies on a couple basis. Old married friends may seek your parent out once or twice out of courtesy or concern. But soon the invitations become fewer, and those that are received are often sent out of a sense of duty. There is no rational reason behind all this. Nevertheless, a single person often becomes a fifth wheel in the eyes of his or her friends, and this situation usually becomes more and more uncomfortable for everyone. Your mother may eventually turn down all invitations. Whatever pleasure she might receive from the companionship is outweighed by the pain of being reminded that her husband is no longer with her.

In some respects elderly fathers suffer different sorts of losses than their female counterparts. A man no longer has someone to protect and provide for. He has lost the one who cooked and cared for him, who kept in touch with members of their family and friends, and who largely handled their social arrangements. Now he may not know how to keep house, cook nourishing meals, or create a social life for himself.

These are all fundamental human needs. A parent should be encouraged to make the effort to put as much back into his or her life as possible. And that effort may include after a while seeking companionship with members of the opposite sex. But children often have a difficult time adjusting to their mother's new social activity. They do not want her to rush out and replace their father with someone else. If she should show interest in an elderly gentleman, her children may think that she has forgotten about their father. Some go so far as to suggest that she is somehow desecrating her marriage and behaving shamefully before their very eyes.

Loneliness can be a severe problem for the elderly, and your mother's reasons for cultivating a new companionship may be quite different from what you suppose them to be. She may simply need someone to provide her with company, security, and the opportunity to feel that she is still a desirable woman and a useful homemaker. Marriage, in fact, may not even be one of her goals.

In trying to help your mother in the most appropriate way, you have to examine carefully your own reasons for any uneasiness you may feel about her interest in male companionship. You are really asking the impossible of your parent if you somehow make her feel that by spending time with other men, she is breaking up the family or erasing the memory of your father. If she caves in to the guilt and the disapproval she feels in you, she may then be forced to lead an empty life out of consideration for your unreasonable anxieties.

If loneliness leads to depression, a more serious problem can result. You might inadvertently pay a steep price for the isolation you have encouraged, for you may create a situation where you have discouraged her from seeking opportunities for an independent life. She may then ultimately come to depend solely upon you for her emotional and social needs. Your mother may begin to phone you every day, claiming that unless you call more often, invite her to dinner on Thursdays, or include her in your Saturday night plans, she will have nothing to live for. This development may make you feel angry and burdened, yet you may have largely caused the problem yourself.

Neither you nor your mother ought to feel that since no one can ever take her partner's place, there is no point in cultivating the companionship of other men. An elderly woman like anyone else has a natural desire to be considered attractive. And there are ways in which you can encourage your mother to meet other men. If a middle-aged male friend were recently divorced, we would probably feel little hesitation in arranging a date for him with a single woman of our acquaintance. Peculiar as it may make you feel at first, there is really nothing wrong with arranging for your widowed parent to meet another single elderly person.

The singles' world an aged parent inhabits differs markedly from that of other generations. There are far fewer men than women. This scarcity puts males in the position of being in greater demand. A curious role reversal often takes place. For the first time in their lives, elderly widowers are in the uncomfortable position of being wooed and pursued the way young women normally are. Aged widows may feel they must become as aggressive as men were taught to be.

Michael Stevenson is a seventy-nine-year-old widower who lives in a retirement hotel. He has no interest in remarriage, but his stories about his environment sometimes startle his children. Women in the hotel call him up regularly, inviting him to dinner and even out to the movies. They offer to treat him to meals. They insist that he accompany them as their escort to various functions, at their own expense. They call him up regularly to go walking or window-shopping. His children, then, are as surprised as he is that elderly women may come to act in much the manner traditionally associated with males. Although Michael and his family understand intellectually that women ought to have the same social prerogatives as men, the behavior nevertheless leaves the elderly gentleman surprised and uneasy.

Decades ago your parents probably arranged their dates by phone or by meeting at Saturday night parties. Today the younger generations have outlets such as singles bars and discotheques that are obviously unavailable to your widowed parents.

Your mother is probably no longer invited to rounds of parties. Her physical problems may make getting around town a major undertaking. The days when she could hop into the car and stop over at a friend's house in the suburbs may be over.

As a result group activities in the neighborhood provide the most comfortable and important gatherings for the elderly. Senior citizens clubs, church clubs, and Golden Ager groups all have programs where single persons can mix. Such programs may involve an excursion on a chartered bus to a museum, for example, or may simply be an evening of bingo or a Sunday brunch and a lecture. Such activities place your mother in a congenial and natural setting. She has a reason now to fix her hair and dress in a way that makes her feel that she is an attractive woman who can still appeal to men. Here she can be in the company of members of the opposite sex without the pressure that goes along with the aggressive pursuit of a dating situation. Although to her sons and daughters these activities may seem purely group affairs, your parent can still legitimately have the small but precious satisfaction that she is on something like a date.

She may also receive the same kinds of psychological rewards from being in a situation where men and women mix in an informal way every day. Your mother may live in a housing project where people congregate three times a day in the dining area. Although she may not consciously tell herself she is enjoying a date at every meal, these meetings may have the same effect upon her.

In some ways an elderly woman may also see her doctor as a man who will show her some form of sexual attention. There are many complex reasons behind your mother's reliance upon her physician. She has a bona fide need for medical care, for reassurance about her health, and for someone she can depend upon to look after her. But she may also vaguely fantasize that her routine examinations are mildly sexual encounters. There is nothing wrong or unnatural about her need to see things this way. Elderly widows commonly have had to go without another man showing sexual interest in them for years. The encounter is a socially acceptable way for her to have a form of intimate contact with a man. For some women this fantasy can be useful and therapeutic.

Her physician, of course, views her office visit only in professional terms. As part of his responsibiliies, he will check for cancer and listen to her heartbeat with a stethoscope. In the woman's eyes, though, she may see the doctor as a man who is showing a personal interest in her physical being—in herself.

This sexual motivation may partially explain why some aged women look upon a trip to the doctor's office as a special social event. They will get dressed up and devote an entire day's energies to traveling to and from his office for a forty-five-minute meeting. Sometimes you may reflect that there may seem to be no physical complication that could justify all that time and effort.

Middle-aged children might be offended and embarrassed at the thought that their mother is seeking out some sort of an X-rated gratification through her physician. Yet if these visits provide her with a rational emotional satisfaction whose effects linger on for several days or a week, they may well be worth the extra fifteen or twenty dollars to you both. It would be cruel, no matter how troubled you may be by your mother's behavior, to confront her with her real reasons for spending the day downtown. The more understanding you can bring to how painful her unfulfilled needs may be, the less uncomfortable you should become over her efforts to meet them.

SOCIAL RELATIONSHIPS

Brothers and sisters—your uncles and aunts—often start to play a more important part in your elderly parents' lives. During old age a father may strengthen the close relationship he has always had with his younger brother. Your mother may never have been able to tolerate her older sister. Perhaps they have lived hundreds of miles apart for decades and all but forgotten each other. Yet now your mother may insist on making regular visits and keeping in constant contact over the phone.

Jane Williams was amazed at the reconciliation between her eighty-one-year-old father, Morris, and his seventy-eight-year-old brother, Lawrence. Forty years ago they had argued over a loan, and the grudge both of them formed at the time had been nurtured and preserved for most of their lives. Jane had heard the story hundreds of times but by now had only a dim idea of what must have actually taken place. She had learned from personal experience, though, that trying to negotiate a peace between them was impossible. In fact part of her own upbringing had included a basic resentment of her uncle.

As a result she did not quite understand why within the last few years her father insisted that Lawrence be invited for dinner and taken along on family outings. She was happy for them and their new closeness, but she also discovered that her uncle Lawrence was a crude, boring man whose company she could not stand.

There were several powerful reasons that drew the brothers together. They now shared many of the same emotional and physical problems of old age. They also shared a common family past, which was precious to them both. They felt a need to recall and reminisce about the old neighborhood, the meals their mother used to prepare, and the way their father used to kid them at the dinner table. Who else of their friends would understand all this?

Sometimes elderly brothers and sisters decide to live together after leading wholly separate lives for decades. This may provide them with the companionship and warmth they would be unable to find in any other way. The aged may also be troubled by the death of a brother or sister in a far different way than that of a spouse, for they share a common genetic inheritance. When a brother dies of cancer or when a sister becomes disoriented, our parents cannot help but worry that the same problem may someday affect them too.

To feel that you are part of a larger community is a basic human need. The stresses of isolation can result in mental illness no matter what a person's age may be. The social relationships people need to ensure an emotionally healthy life may be roughly divided into three categories: civic organizations, family, and friends. Isolation can often be a problem for the aged because they have suffered losses in all these categories almost simultaneously. The elderly play a less important role in their communities. This is not simply because they have retired from a job or withdrawn from life. Community organizations themselves are more interested in younger people. The aged may have greater experience and be more adept at some kinds of problem solving. But the new ideas, the enthusiasm, and especially the sheer energy of youth are usually seen as more desirable than the contributions of elderly people.

The main problem with family life is that the longer people live, the more likely it is that the people they always looked up to or depended on for support and guidance are now dead. Flora Schwartz, in introducing the Golden Ager talent show for her middle-aged audience, put the problem well: "Be generous with your applause," she told them. "After all, every member of my troupe is an orphan."

Elderly people have also survived the deaths of many of their friends. When we ourselves lose friends, it is usually because they have to move out of town, and we may still retain minimal contact with them. We also have other social outlets that make it possible for new people to come into our lives. For the elderly, however, this is not easily the case. They may also be vulnerable to the same kind of guilt that afflicts survivors of wars and the death camps. A soldier or a former inmate may feel guilty at having been spared while all those who were near him were lost. On an unconscious level the aged, like soldiers, can atone for their guilt by destroying themselves or by succumbing to depression, or what the army has come to call shell shock.

A son or daughter can play a special part in the lives of their elderly parents but cannot really make up for the loss of old poker-playing or fishing buddies. Sometimes a father may try to make a buddy out of his son or son-in-law. But this is almost always mutually frustrating because the two persons are not friends and peers. Nor do they have the same interests, problems, or needs.

The aged do not get together with their friends the same way the middle-aged do with theirs. They cannot so easily jump into a car and travel across town to a party or a dinner. Instead they usually meet and socialize within the neighborhood, at places within easy walking distance. Neighborhood social centers, churches, and social work agencies all run programs that are huge successes with the elderly. A Sunday morning breakfast at which there is a speaker may attract enthusiastic crowds. The meal and the speaker's topic may be of interest. But the main attraction is the opportunity to rub shoulders with other human beings. It may be the only opportunity some elderly persons have for such interaction during the whole week. It is important to see that your parents participate in these activities as well as the Saturday night bridge party they may have enjoyed in the past. If transportation is an obstacle for you, make some inquiries. You may discover that some of these organizations run pickup and shuttle services.

In the next part of the book, we will consider how you can further help your parents as their losses and problems—both physical and emotional—become more acute.

IV

The Waning of Independence

8

What Can You Do to Prolong Your Parents' Independence?

Every day social agencies that serve the needs of the aged receive calls from middle-aged people who need help for their parents. Many of the callers are concerned about housing. The agencies serve as referral centers linking aged clients to various programs and residential settings. "What housing arrangements can you recommend for my father [mother]?" people ask anxiously. In most instances their parent is widowed and has been living alone for some time. Often the children feel caught on the horns of a hard-to-resolve dilemma. Here are three typical cases:

Mel Rosen was appalled by his eighty-four-year-old mother's situation. He was a successful businessman who lived in a prosperous suburb of Chicago. Every other Sunday he made the long, inconvenient drive to his mother's neighborhood, where he himself had been raised. The area was now quite run-down. His mother was one of the few old-time residents who still lived there despite a high increase in the crime rate over the years. She no longer went out much and lived in constant fear and danger. Out of fear of the neighborhood boys, she kept her door double-locked at all times and still worried for her safety. Not long ago an elderly woman she knew who lived a few doors away had been robbed as she was having dinner at home.

Mrs. Rosen's apartment was no longer the clean, well kept place Mel remembered from long ago. Its absentee owners were not conscientious about upkeep and repairs. Mel was

163

anxious to move his mother to a modern, airy condominium near his own home because he was afraid for her safety and was disturbed and embarrassed by her living conditions. Such a move would spare him much aggravation and inconvenience and rescue his mother from the deplorable conditions she faced each day.

Yet Mel's mother would not consider relocating. She had precious memories of her neighborhood, and no place else would ever be home for her. She had never needed or requested outside assistance. After all, she still did her own cooking as well as the housework and chores. She reminded her son firmly that she had never taken a penny from him, and she had no desire to do so now. She was able to handle her own expenses but could not afford to move into an expensive condominium. Her savings were secure, if small, but she did not want to throw them away on a down payment or a higher rent. Her money was her nest egg, reserved for emergencies and as a legacy for her children.

Mrs. Rosen pointed out that she still had a few friends in the old neighborhood whom she didn't want to give up in order to live in some dehumanized, concrete block where she wouldn't know a soul. She also preferred her "old beat-up chairs and tables," as her son called them, to the brand-new furniture he wanted to buy for her. In short, the old neighborhood was where she had spent her life, and there was where she intended to end her days.

Mel had never known his mother to be obstinate or irrational. But her attitude on this particular topic struck him as incomprehensible, if not downright crazy. He discussed his problem with a social worker at the housing agency and was advised that his mother would have to call the agency herself before a representative would even raise the question of her moving. Mel, of course, was somewhat peeved at this news, but he passed it on to his mother anyway. Discovering that his mother had not made the slightest effort to call the agency, he made contact several weeks later with the same social worker. This time he insisted on the agency's cooperation in his effort to uproot Mrs. Rosen. But his request was politely refused.

The second case involved Janet Miller's seventy-eight-year-old father, who was living in a safe, well-kept community. He, too, enjoyed his apartment and had no plans to move. He had serious arthritic problems, though, which made it difficult for him to cook his meals, clean his apartment, and cart groceries back from the store. Whenever Janet visited her father, she found herself wanting to straighten up the place and do the shopping. Her father refused all her help, however, insisting that he managed perfectly well without her. He pointed out that he had never lodged a single complaint to anyone. It was insulting, he told her, to have his own child trying to run his private affairs and treating him as if he had become incompetent before his time. Janet could not reason with him. She did not see how he could possibly live the self-reliant existence that went with his attitude. She also called the agency to request their help in having him moved to a safe situation. But the agency replied that her father would have to express some interest of his own in the move before an agency member would even discuss with him the possibility of the move.

The last case had to do with Albert Markson, who was very concerned about his aged mother. After his father's death Albert's mother seemed to be in a state of collapse. For the last year or so she had not been able to make any decisions, no matter how petty, without consulting her son. Should a plumber be called to fix a dripping faucet? Would it be all right to fry a chicken for dinner, or should it be broiled? Did Albert think it too chilly for her to go shopping, and did he think it all right for her to go out today?

There were also late-night phone calls about physical irregularities that turned out to be of minor importance. Albert had never known his mother to be helpless or dependent in the past and wondered if he ought to invite her to move in with his family. The people next door to Albert had given their father an upstairs bedroom last year, and everything seemed to work out splendidly. Albert, however, suffered periodically from migraine headaches and was afraid that his mother's presence in his home might turn his problem into a chronic condition. His wife had never felt comfortable with her mother-in-law, and Albert did not know how to raise the possibility of such a move with her. The house was not large, and he knew that with the addition of his parent, they all would seem to be living on top of each other. Thus he basically did not want such an arrangement. Since his neighbors seemed to have done effortlessly the right and proper thing, he wondered if he wasn't an insensitive, ungrateful son.

The real issue, for all these sons and daughters, is more than just housing. At stake is making sure that elderly parents can thrive in the most suitable environment one can find for them. And *that* question touches upon some of the most basic principles that have been developed as a result of work with the aged. The problem generally arises when our parents can no longer function as they did thirty years or so ago.

The most intelligent and realistic solution to your particular situation has to be an approximate balance between your parents' needs and your own. To do this, an understanding of the general philosophy of caring for the elderly as well as ways of implementing it should prove useful.

As our awareness of the problem has grown, there has been a change in our whole approach to the elderly who face serious difficulties in their daily lives. Not too long ago, aged parents who could no longer cook their own dinner or administer a daily insulin injection that they needed had only two alternatives.

The first was to move into the household of one of their children. Many families paid a stiff price—emotionally, physically, and financially—for this new responsibility. But since it was a question of a parent's survival, they felt they had no choice, and they were largely correct. So they bore the strain that the move often involved with as much stoicism as they could muster.

The other possibility was to place a parent in a state hospital or a home for the aged. There he or she would have housing, protection, and food as well as nurses who provided around-the-clock minimal care. The institutions were usually impersonal and depressing places—little more than dumping grounds for people waiting to die. On the other hand, a parent would be guaranteed regular meals and daily medical attention. It seemed to be a place where all a person's needs could be safely and efficiently met.

But both these solutions created new problems of their own. Back in the sixties Dr. Margaret Blenkner published research findings of an unsettling nature as the result of her studies of two groups of elderly people and their children. One group had been given only the usually available services for the aged. The other group, the so-called experimental group, was provided with counseling by a social worker and subsequent protective services.

When Dr. Blenkner compared the outcomes of the two groups, she discovered that there were virtually no differences between the experimental and control groups except for two interesting aspects. The children of the experimental group whose parents had received the special services indicated far more relief and satisfaction than did the children of the group of aged who had received no special services. The other significant difference between the two groups was in the mortality rate. The death rate for the elderly recipients of the special services was *significantly higher* than the rate for those who had not been given additional attention.

Blenkner made a careful study of the reasons for this startling and disturbing finding. It turned out that the social workers and the children of the experimental group had assumed a greater role in the lives of their aging parents and were actively instrumental in placing them in institutions. The higher death rate, therefore, was traced to a higher rate of institutional placement. Considerable statistical evidence has been accumulated that shows a connection between the relocation and institutionalizing of the aged and an increase in their death rate.

There are many lessons that might be drawn from this experiment. A prime lesson is that uprooting elderly people from an old, familiar environment and placing them in a totally strange situation appears to inflict an increased amount of stress upon them. Although no one can predict just how much individuals can endure, stress of this kind generally cannot be avoided whenever people are moved to a home for the aged, a condominium, or a family bungalow. The elderly need a sense of security and hope like all of us. For them, however, security and hope become ever scarcer and more precious commodities. Placement in an institution provides for their obvious physical needs, it is true. But it also can rob the aged of any sense of a future in life to look forward to. Hopelessness may then prove to be as fatal to our aged parents as any chronic disease of a physical nature.

There are, of course, many advantages to new settings. But children should be aware of the serious risks involved in the decision to move parents. Ways to ameliorate the impact of drastic change will be discussed in the following chapter. But here we want to point out some of the reasons that continuity is so inportant for elderly people and why changes are so hazardous.

The aged are less flexible—physically and emotionally—than they once were. Their ability to bounce back and adapt to change has dwindled. They have been weakened and made vulnerable by the physical and social problems previously discussed. The changes they are now experiencing are painful and frightening to them. Disabilities, retirement, the death of a spouse, and the deaths of friends are all punishing blows. They are also reminders that their world has been seriously fractured and that their life is drawing to a close. As a reaction, the elderly cling to a sense of continuity.

Change so often implies a further unmooring of themselves from the life they have known that they tend to resist it.

If you become alarmed by an increase in street crime or the deteriorating schools of your neighborhood, you would probably feel little hesitation in canceling your lease or putting your house up for sale. Elderly persons have complex needs to retain as much familiarity as possible in their lives and may not find the choice nearly so clear-cut. The higher mortality rates for those who have been transplanted are a disturbing proof of how serious a problem uprooting is.

For most of us, the unpleasant aspects of moving include packing our household effects and shipping them to our new address and getting used to new surroundings. We endure such inconveniences because the new location offers us opportunities we consider more attractive. We may have left old friends, but we expect to enjoy meeting new people in the fresh setting. Our old apartment or house was adequate. But the new one will be roomier and located in a more congenial atmosphere. The old job may have been fine. But the new one brings more stimulation, including higher pay and a feeling that we have entered a new phase of life.

Our elderly parents, on the other hand, experience a move quite differently. They do not leave to find a more stimulating group of friends, a job with greater responsibility and a higher salary, or a more pleasant environment for their children. Their world has been steadily shrinking. For them it is not simply one more change of mailing address. Instead, moving is experienced as a major loss, one more in an ever expanding list of losses. They have to leave behind the familiarity, security, and sense of belonging that the old neighborhood gave them. They lose direct touch with the private memories so intimately bound up with the sights and sounds of their neighbors, shops, and parks. They also lose the old friends and shopkeepers they have known—people they will see rarely, if at all, once they settle into their new residences.

Often the overriding concern for members of the older generation is to preserve their links to the past. Adult children should be careful not to confuse their own perspectives and values with those of their parents, for readjustment to another setting can be a slow, draining, and frightening ordeal for the aged.

When parents are moved totally against their will or consent, the consequences are almost always disastrous. People who are forced into nursing homes deteriorate rapidly. They are constantly unhappy and never accept what they regard as a betrayal by their families. Sometimes they can be found wandering the streets in an effort to return to their old neighborhood.

The Blenkner study has also taught us how dangerous it is for us to confuse what is best for our parents with what is mainly best for ourselves. It is not always easy to tell the difference between the two points of view, and those of us who make such a mistake often do so with the best of intentions. Mel Rosen, for example, felt that his life would be a lot simpler if his mother lived nearer to him. Once he knew his mother was out of danger from muggings and robberies, a very nagging headache would be removed. If he were to examine his feelings carefully, however, he would find that the high-pressure selling job he tried to do on his mother was largely motivated by the ongoing burden her living conditions represented for *him.*

Some recent crime reports indicate that the elderly, surprisingly enough, are not the victims of violence in any greater proportion than the general population. They do, however, worry and complain about the danger of crime a great deal more than other people and indeed are vulnerable. Their concern is legitimate, of course, but sometimes they sense danger where there is none. A group of adolescents on the street may represent to them a delinquent street gang. A stranger strolling down the block in the evening may be assumed to be a burglar on the prowl.

> Since Mel Rosen's mother still functions as she always has and does not want to move, she will simply have to put up with her fears and the relatively higher risks. In her case there is no perfect solution, and she has chosen the lesser of two evils. Mel is far from satisfied with the situation. He has learned recently from a business associate, who is confronted with a similar problem with his parents, that escort services are available. For a fee an agency will ensure an elderly parent's transportation, protection, and assistance. Mrs. Rosen has said that she would be happy to make use of that resource. So Mel has come to accept her decision and has adjusted to it as best he can.

In cases like that of the Rosens, the parent's wishes should always be solicited and respected. There are times, of course, when a move simply cannot be avoided. This often happens when a family or the community in which a parent lives can no longer give assistance in time of need. But a slow revolution has been taking place in this country. It has begun to supply the elderly with other options beyond an offspring's household or an institution. Our emphasis should be on ways to minimize or postpone drastic changes as long as possible. No crime has been committed when a parent relocates to a senior citizen housing development or an institution. But moving in general—especially removal to homes for the aged—should be viewed as a last resort. When there simply is no other choice, no one should feel guilty about placing a parent in an institution. The tragedy lies in institutionalizing your parents despite the fact that resources and substitutes are available that would permit them to remain on their own for a few more days, months, or years. Every week your parents can successfully cope by themselves—no matter how many small forms of outside assistance they need—can rightfully be considered a victory for them and their family.

It is obviously impossible to predict when something will go wrong in your parents' lives. But just as you prepared for the problems of your own children's adolescence by reading books on the subject or talking to friends about it, so, too, you should prepare for your parents' old age. The first step perhaps might be to sit down with your spouse and discuss just how much direct personal involvement your family can handle. At the same time, you ought to find out what options, programs, and arrangements exist in the community where your parents live. These efforts should greatly enhance your ability to act effectively when the need arises.

Just as each of our aged parents is unique, so, too, is the total complex of their new needs. It will require creativity and determination—on the part of yourselves and of your parents—to come up with a tailor-made program of substitutes for the losses they may sustain. If a mother, for example, functions well on the whole but can no longer cook her own meals, she may best be helped by joining a lunch program at a local community center. If a father requires a daily injection of insulin but can function normally in every other way, a visiting nurse's services would enable him to keep living on his own.

In trying to get an overall picture of your parents' assets and liabilities, you ought to have a general idea of how well they have coped in the past. We all develop our own individual styles and strategies. The range of possibilities is a wide one, and, like the idiosyncrasies and quirks of your parents, their possibilities for dealing with them also carry over into the seventies and eighties.

The parents who handle old age with the greatest success are usually the ones who handled their own needs with aplomb and self-assurance in their earlier years. They enjoyed a good deal of experience in fending for themselves, neither needing nor asking for much assistance. Fortitude and resourcefulness enabled them to deal well with crises and tragedies and to build a family and a career. No one had to direct or supervise them in the past, and they tend to bounce back pretty well from the blows and losses of old age. Today they probably don't need anyone to counsel them on how to seek out new companionship or food services. They evaluate their own problems and then systematically take the proper steps to solve them. In some cases they continue, even into their seventies and eighties, to be the ones their children turn to for emotional support and guidance.

There are other parents who stand at the opposite end of the spectrum. Having little confidence in their own judgment, they do not view themselves as competent or capable and depend on others for the strength and encouragement to survive. Throughout their lives they have responded to crises as well as to the normal difficulties of life in an anxious or helpless way. Without the strong, steadying influence of others upon them, they feel hopeless, lost, and alone.

Human beings, of course, are complicated mixtures of weaknesses and strengths. Even so, elderly persons, like all of us, roughly fall somewhere between these two somewhat oversimplified descriptions of problem-solving styles. You should try to understand your parents' styles of coping with problems, since this will show you how you can best approach and help them if the need should arise.

Some parents may never require any help at all. Intruding into their affairs or feeling rejected because they do not depend upon you would be both unnecessary and misguided. Other parents may need a tremendous amount of daily attention and emotional support, which may well need to be supplemented by the professional services of social agencies.

Elderly people face similar physical and social problems of aging, and they can usually benefit from the use of outside resources. Your efforts on your parents' behalf will be most effective, however, when you can clearly distinguish their "objective" needs from the way they go about trying to meet them. In many cases you may only really begin to discover what their individual coping styles are when they become either widows or widowers.

In the preceding chapter we examined several broad aspects of problems caused by the loss of one's spouse. That same loss may rob the surviving husband or wife of the only source of his or her strategies for coping with life's difficulties. Prior to the death of one of your parents, you probably had only the vaguest notion of how your mother and father conducted their private lives. Your relationship was hardly on an adult basis when you were growing up at home. After you left to establish your own independent household, your relationship with your parents undoubtedly changed. You kept in touch through letters, phone calls, and occasional visits. But the intimacies of your respective lives were probably never shared.

The marriage relationship is a constant matching and trading of one partner's strengths and assets with the other's weaknesses and foibles. Each partner comes to rely upon the other for a myriad of decisions, actions, and emotional expressions that are part of our daily lives. One may tend to dominate, and the other may tend to be passive and dependent, but each needs the other to meet important needs.

In an infinite number of ways, each partner complements the other's temperament, flaws, and needs. Husband and wife are able to achieve emotional equilibrium for themselves through their mutual cooperation. One of your parents probably was able to handle the nasty neighbor who may have complained about the children. He or she knew when to call the plumber and how to manage the finances and probably decided which movie to see on a Saturday evening. Of course, there were times when the roles were reversed. But after a while both partners came to rely upon each other in regular, predictable fashion.

For the better part of thirty, forty, or fifty years, the surviving parent has enjoyed the sense of safety and protection that the marriage afforded. The intuitive knowledge that a partner was always there held in check whatever loneliness and day-to-day anxieties might come along. That parent has grown accustomed to this sort of arrangement. It is the way he or she has functioned best. Widowhood, however, strips away an indispensable element from life. It forces the survivors into a life of independence under stressful circumstances at a time when there is no long future full of possibilities ahead. The survivor may be ill equipped or unprepared for the new demands of an independent life, for this is an experience he or she may not ever have known in the past.

Sons and daughters may be needlessly distressed or disappointed if they believe that their widowed mother should somehow find great new reservoirs of strength that will turn her for the first time into a self-reliant being. This seldom happens. More often she will grope, however unconsciously and instinctively, to find another figure like her husband who can enable her to function as she always has. It is important to remember, though, that she has not lost her ability to cope. In fact she is making an effort to cope by trying to reestablish a constancy and continuity in her life.

This is not always the way things appear to a son who may suddenly find himself called upon to fill his father's shoes. He ought to recognize that he never can, nor should he try to, assume that kind of responsibility.

> As Albert Markson has come to understand this situation, he slowly is beginning to help his mother toward a combination of new supports and substitutes for her dead husband.
>
> Albert has recently decided to call a friend of his mother's, who is also a widow. This woman is quite happy to establish a "buddy" relationship with Mrs. Markson. Now every day at a prearranged time, they call each other to make sure they are alive and well. If there is no answer, they each have agreed to take it as a sign that something has gone wrong. Help in the form of a neighbor or a policeman will be sent for immediately.

Some parents do not have friends with whom they can enter into arrangements of this kind. For them, telephone reassurance programs may be the answer. These programs are often handled by social agencies, settlement houses, community centers, or private agencies. A parent's name is placed on a list, and he or she receives calls like the kind Albert's mother receives from her friend on as many days a week as necessary.

> Albert has also taken additional steps. He has planned with his mother actions to take in case of medical emergencies. The hospital near her home is a small one of no great reputation.

Another one some distance away, however, is large and well respected. When Albert telephoned to find out if any shuttle services were available, he learned he was in luck. Not only is there a stopping point within walking distance of Mrs. Markson's home, but the institution has a twenty-four-hour hot line for people in his mother's situation.

The two of them have also agreed to sit down every few months and review her circumstances. All this has given Mrs. Markson a sense of reassurance as well as the pleasures of human contacts. As a result the late-night phone calls to his home have lessened. Although it has required some salesmanship on Albert's part, he has also persuaded his mother to visit a senior center sponsored by the city's office on aging. It is located not far from her home. Although Mrs. Markson uses it primarily for social activities, such centers typically offer a variety of services. Her center, for example, offers referral and information services, counseling and social casework help, financial and legal services, meal programs, and access to home health care.

Janet Miller has also had to take a different approach with her father to achieve the same goals. He is one of the minority of elderly whose independence and self-reliance have been the hallmark of life. He seems stubborn and bullheaded to his daughter. She is right in feeling that he is refusing help he really needs. He claims he can manage by himself when he really cannot. The stumbling block, though, is that he simply won't accept assistance from his own child. It is a role reversal that would be too humiliating. His pride and self-esteem cannot tolerate it.

Once a daughter understands these feelings, she can proceed to help her father. There are usually several ways to make sure the necessary help is provided. Often it has to be given indirectly. Many fathers like Janet's will accept advice and services from someone outside the immediate family. Her father does not permit her to shop and deliver groceries to him. He does not have any objection, however, to having a grocery store take his order over the phone and send the groceries over with a delivery boy whom he can tip a quarter or two.

The smart daughter can preserve her father's dignity, conform to his way of doing things, and prolong his independence by arranging—without telling her parent what she is doing—for a neighbor, relative, or social worker to approach him and discuss his needs and problems privately.

At Janet's request a social worker from the agency that

she had contacted earlier paid a visit to Mr. Miller. She managed to check his refrigerator to find out if he was following a well-balanced diet.

There are many reasons why the elderly frequently suffer from inadequate nutrition. Often they have to live on a limited income and try to economize by cutting back on the quality or range of foods they buy. If they have physical ailments that make it difficult for them to prepare certain dishes, they may purchase ready-made or "junk" food. Some men have never learned to cook properly because that was never a part of their upbringing. As a result they may be forced to spend more money than they can afford at restaurants. But even more important than cost, a meal is really a social event. When people live alone, they often lose their interest in and desire for hearty meals. A woman may have considered it her responsibility to make sure her family had a full, well-balanced diet, and she no doubt went to great trouble to prepare substantial dinners. But as a widow living alone, she may have completely lost interest in preparing a tasty meal for herself.

After some discussion Janet's father admitted to the social worker that it was not only hard for him to shop but that he found cooking a real chore. He is still able to get out of the house on his own, so he agreed to join a congregate meals program being run in a nearby church. This service, and similar ones available across the United States, are federally subsidized and available to all aged persons, regardless of their income.

Five days a week Janet's father now takes his lunches and dinners in the church hall. This setup is quite different from the usual restaurant or cafeteria where people order their meals and consume them by themselves in a room full of strangers. At the hall he finds a group of regulars—elderly people who socialize and participate in birthday celebrations, singing activities, and a general round of camaraderie. Although Mr. Miller's attendance at the church meals is quite regular, at first Janet was disturbed to hear him complaining about the bland dishes and the irritating oldsters who "crammed the place," as he put it. But his complaints, like his refusal of Janet's help, are really his way of preserving his dignity. He has come to terms in some way with his losses. He has sought out a substitute.

His griping serves to show himself and those who know

him that he is still a capable, functioning, independent spirit. Since he is receiving the nutritional and social benefits of the congregate meals program, his complaints can really now be taken with the proverbial grain of salt.

Other elderly who are unable to leave their homes because of a variety of disabilities still need to maintain their old living arrangements. They can often do so by joining a home delivered meals program. This is a service that will deliver hot lunches (and sometimes suppers as well) to the homes of virtual shut-ins. This arrangement can be a boon to a son or daughter who would otherwise have to prepare a parent's meals personally or relocate him or her in a nursing home. In most cases the home delivered meals programs are federally funded and staffed by community volunteers. At present there are only a few of these reasonably priced, federally funded services across the country, but their number is expanding. Concerned middle-aged people in areas where such programs do not exist can help establish them locally. This aspect of aging as well as a model service plan for the elderly will be discussed in some detail later in the book.

As with the other substitutes mentioned, the home-delivered meals program enables the elderly to enjoy the benefits of regular contact with other people. The volunteers who go into the homes may have only a few minutes to spend with each of the clients on their routes. But they get to know all their clients and show them a measure of concern. This personal interest can be just as important to the elderly as the food they deliver.

Many communities also offer other services that help supplement an aged person's declining strengths. Chore services—staffed sometimes by retirees—handle the various tasks of repair and upkeep that are needed in all houses and apartments. For elderly people who haven't the physical stamina or the money to pay for fixing a leaky faucet, mowing a lawn, or taking down the storm windows, handymen supplied by these community chore service groups will do what is needed for a nominal sum.

Friendly visitors—often college students—will drop by the homes of elderly people on a regular basis to do odd jobs. Some volunteer their time, while others ask for a small fee. Retirees may perform similar duties, including running errands and picking up around the house. For the most part, though, friendly people like the students or retirees serve as companions. They break up the isolation and the monotony that often demoralize the hearts and spirits of the infirm. They can be invaluable for your parents, who may have few opportunities to talk about their private concerns.

Day-care centers for the elderly serve some of the same functions as the centers designed for young children. They are places that often operate in association with clinics, hospitals, and nursing homes. These centers are intended for elderly people afflicted with chronically disabling health conditions who do not yet require the twenty-four-hour-a-day supervision of a nursing home. The centers usually offer recreation and social work services, and many include nursing and rehabilitation service as well. A pickup and drop-off service is nearly always a part of the program. Some aged take advantage of day-care centers because they feel unsafe or lonely in their homes. More often, these centers are real boons for middle-aged children who need occasional relief from the demands of a parent who lives in their home. Or the center may provide relief for elderly spouses who are in good health but burdened by the constant care of an ill husband or wife.

Visiting nurses are often registered or licensed practical nurses whose services are normally prescribed by a person's physician. Such nurses can supervise and administer medication. Visiting nurses also assist in household nutritional planning. Middle-aged children may find them invaluable as counselors when a parent's medical and emotional problems seem overwhelming. A nurse can also function as a resource for referral to various other community services. A parent also benefits from the personal interest the nurse conveys about his or her welfare.

There are several ways you can learn about the range of services in your parents' community. Welfare, Medicaid, and Social Security offices usually know what services exist and where they are located. Physicians and clergymen may also prove useful. Most areas have information and referral services run by public or private agencies that have a comprehensive listing of programs for people of all ages. Perhaps the most helpful avenue of all, however, are the senior centers and family service agencies; some are sectarian, others nondenominational. They have professional staffs that should also be qualified to evaluate your parents' needs and to tell you just what care is necessary. The appendix at the back of this book lists a few of these resources.

Any number of overriding concerns may make a parent's relocation unavoidable. The advent of widowhood, however, does not necessarily have to force such a decision. Many well intentioned sons and daughters feel compelled, shortly after a parent has been left alone, to invite the surviving parent to live with them. Their motivation and offer may be generous, but they are often misguided. Although many parents would never consider moving in with one of their children, there are situations in which such arrangements work out satisfactorily.

Several questions must be thoroughly considered, however, before a final decision is made. Your first step should be to take a hard, objective look at the feelings you have had about your parent over the years. For a long time each of you has maintained separate households and life-styles. How much conflict might arise once your dealings are on an intimate, daily basis? If your parent has been an intrusive, critical, or demanding person, is there much chance you would be able to live together harmoniously? If your past visits to your parent's home were more duty calls than warm, comfortable get-togethers, a one-household situation could easily lead to a mounting strain. If, for whatever reasons, your offer comes from a sense of duty and responsibility rather than from a sincere, genuine impulse to have your parent with you, this new arrangement will probably create a lot of new problems for you both.

It is also essential for you to discuss the issue with your spouse and children. Adding another member to your household is quite different from adding a new wing to the house. Any reservations others have ought to be respected and carefully weighed. The amount of space you have available is also a real consideration. Cramped quarters are not only uncomfortable, but they often destroy the minimal privacy you and your family require.

A parent should also have his or her own circle of friends and own rounds of social activities. He or she should not be excessively dependent on your family for companionship, nor should your parent be made to constantly feel ill at ease or out of place in trying to fit in with your own acquaintances.

Once a parent has relocated to your home, it becomes increasingly difficult and painful to admit that a mistake has been made and to develop new arrangements. It is not by any means safe to assume that your mother or father would prefer to live in your household or would flourish there more than in any other setting. There are, of course, families where such an arrangement works out well. The relationship may be close and relatively free of discord. The pooling of financial resources can make life more comfortable for everyone. Space may not be a problem. Sometimes a mother can escape the isolation and loneliness of her old atmosphere and happily assume some house keeping chores. As a result she might free her daughter or daughter-in-law to pursue her own interests.

Just as often, though, in such a move there may be significant drawbacks that your mother or father may recognize now or shortly after the transition is attempted. Suppose your parent moves into a large house in a suburb populated by young and middle-aged adults with families. He or she may have simply swapped one location of loneliness and isolation for another. If your parent is one of the few elderly people in the neighborhood, there may be no one who can truly share his or her interests and concerns.

In many families both the husband and wife leave every morning for work. Their children spend the day at school. In the evening everyone has dinner together. Afterward, though, each member usually goes off in a different direction. The husband may have brought work home. The wife may have a community meeting to attend. A teenage daughter may divide her time between homework, conversations over the phone, long hours in front of a television set, and listening to popular music that drives everyone else in the house to distraction.

The result may well be that the elderly parent spends the days alone in a spacious, empty house and finds himself or herself just as alone in a busy household in the evening. Although your parent may find some comfort in the presence of the family members, it may seem lonely to sleep in a bed that somehow never seems to become his or her own.

If you are considering inviting your parent into your home, you would be wise to have him or her spend a week with you first as an experiment. The question you must always ask yourself is "What will be best for my parent?" Since the tastes and needs of individuals vary, there can be no one answer that is right for everyone. The wisest thing is for both of you to explore every possible option. Basing your decision on what did or did not work for a friend of yours, for your business partner, or for your next door neighbor is usually a mistake. If your experience parallels someone else's, this is often a mere coincidence. The family across the street may have a father who has prospered in a retirement hotel. That does not mean that your own mother hasn't every right to reject that possibility for herself because she wants to live among people of all ages. Perhaps your widower uncle and his widowed sister have set up a joint household and found that, even after fifty years of living apart, they still can't stand living in the same household. This does riot mean, however, that your own widowed mother and her widowed sister might not successfully live together.

There are some typical housing possibilities for your parents that merit your consideration. In the last few years the federal government has begun to construct sturdy, low-cost housing units for the elderly. The rental fee, while reduced, permits the aged to preserve their dignity by giving them the satisfaction of paying their own way. These complexes often have recreation and nutrition resources. Such projects are very popular, and there are far from enough of them. As the elderly population swells and our society begins to direct its efforts to provide adequate housing programs, we hope that many more of these units will be funded.

In such housing units, as in other buildings intended specifically for senior citizens, the bathrooms and kitchens have been designed and equipped for the special needs of the tenants. The residents of every floor normally elect a captain, who has the responsibility of knocking on everyone's door in the morning to make sure that all the residents are healthy and safe. In addition to these conveniences and safety measures, these residences help provide social opportunities that are important to the elderly.

In some places acceptance in these projects means waiting periods of five or six years. It may be a good idea to place your parent's name on such a list a year or so in advance of when you think it will be needed. By doing so, you may provide your parent with an opportunity that would otherwise have been out of reach.

Some parents have an aversion to this form of housing, for they feel it is an indignity to apply for public assistance of any kind. They do not feel comfortable declaring themselves to be old; neither do they feel happy with the idea of being lumped together, as they see it, with a bunch of other elderly people.

There are several different kinds of retirement hotels that offer the same kind of social advantages inherent in federal housing units. Some elderly people, however, may still dislike them for the reasons we have just mentioned. Since these hotels are privately owned and operated, their rents are usually higher than those for federal housing. Many of these private hotels provide recreational and medical services, but not all of them do so. Many have congregate-dining areas. The appeal for many elderly people is that they no longer have to bother preparing meals—a task that may have become for them difficult and time-consuming.

The meals are usually served at fixed hours. Some elderly may feel that this is a degree of regimentation that represents a loss of freedom painful to swallow. Some housing settings, however, supply the residents with a small refrigerator and kitchen, where they may store special snacks and do some minimal cooking of their own.

The range of retirement communities varies enormously in size, location, atmosphere, and expense. Your choice of one will probably depend on your parent's financial resources and personal tastes.

The death of a spouse leaves some elderly people—usually women—unprepared for the responsibility of handling their personal finances. They may never have had to assume the job of paying the bills and managing the investments. In some cases they have little idea what the family holdings amount to. They may be quite unaware of the federal supplementary income programs for the elderly as well as of Medicaid benefits. If they live on fixed incomes, they may have a tough time fighting inflation and the rising medical expenses that invariably accompany old age.

For all these reasons, the aged often become victims of swindlers, con men, or their own mismanagement. It is often a good idea for you to sit down on a regular basis with your parent and discuss his or her financial situation. If your mother is unwilling to share this information with you, she may be willing to talk to a worker in the local Social Security office who might give her advice.

There is another aspect of a parent's financial status that often causes emotional complications for their children and is seldom discussed openly. This is your parent's estate. The importance for most old people of providing a legacy cannot be overemphasized. Psychologist Erik Erikson calls the need to leave something of oneself behind a fundamental part of the final stage of a human being's emotional development. Social workers have discovered that the amount of material wealth involved has little bearing on the matter. Many residents of nursing homes who have only a few hundred dollars to their names are concerned whether their children will receive *without fail* their money on their death. They regard this as a matter of primary interest.

You should keep in mind the fact that the legacy transcends whatever current disappointments, resentments, or demands a parent may feel toward his or her offspring. An aged person's memory focuses on the past—on the infant, the adolescent, the young adult, and the self-reliant husband or wife that the son or daughter has been.

Often middle-aged people have more assets than their parents and may not need or care about the inheritance they will eventually receive. When the relationship between children and their parents has been unusually strong and close, the issue of who gets what seems practically irrelevant. Whatever is eventually bequeathed is either put away for a future emergency or used for some pressing financial need.

We have to recognize, however, that many relationships between children and their parents are not quite so problem-free. Some parents openly speak of their intentions. Others are secretive because they may suspect their children of being connivers. On a less conscious level, they may feel that they are only competent and authoritative as long as they retain an exclusive control over the details of their financial affairs.

Some parents have accumulated reasonably large sums of money in stocks, bank accounts, insurance policies, and property investments. This often has the effect of causing their middle-aged offspring to regard their parents as walking legacies. Such thoughts are painful and guilt-provoking. In spite of himself, a son may be unable to suppress the knowledge that he will be financially more secure after his parent's death. If the son is hard pressed by creditors and knows that his enfeebled mother is making no use of her financial resources, he may find it hard to banish his private thoughts. In time he may even come to resent his parent's continued existence, as though in an irrational way he believes that she is purposely denying him the financial relief he needs. His feelings may be aggravated by outside reminders of other people's inheritances. For example, he may have a poor cousin who suddenly was able to take an extended Florida vacation after her father's death.

The thought of a legacy may also contribute to a myriad of conflicting feelings of guilt a middle-aged person would normally feel over a parent who has become an ever increasing source of demands and obligations. The child may hope that the parent will completely solve all of the child's problems. A sudden and complete recovery of an ill parent is one way. Death is another. But in the meantime a daughter may believe that unless she gives in to her parent's demands, she will be punished by being disowned.

The anxiety over preserving a legacy may induce some people to submit to an otherwise intolerable amount of abuse. One cannot pass moral judgments on such cases. It should be pointed out, however, that the association commonly made between a parent's death and the financial benefits that can follow as a direct consequence is a normal thought. While it may make many people ashamed to admit they have such feelings, in reality there is nothing evil or even unusual about such a situation.

But it should also be pointed out that it is almost always a mistake to allow money to figure in such crucial decisions as to how much direct involvement you should have with your parent. Who, after all, can put a price upon the annoyance, humiliation, or strain with which the inheritance may have to be purchased?

Then, too, the loss of your personal integrity and the guilt you may feel after your parent dies and leaves a legacy may ruin the pleasure the money was supposedly to bring you in the first place. A man may buy a yacht with the assets of his inheritance and then find that the time he spends on the water is devoted to brooding over the deception he feels he brought off against his parent. Now that his parent is dead, there is no way to apologize or expiate the guilt he feels over his sham. The son may feel unconsciously that he has been rewarded under false pretenses and that he has stolen the money.

By way of contrast, other middle-aged people—often without being aware of the fact—may be angry with their parents for not accumulating enough financial assets over the years to leave something significant behind. These sons and daughters may find themselves reacting with irritation or indifference to their aged father. The son may have a complaint that is concealed even from his own consciousness. He may feel that his father had a responsibility and duty to provide for his son. Why didn't Dad act as he once did when the son was small by taking out a generous life insurance policy? It may seem to the son that the father has broken some unspoken pact. How can he expect his son to take care of him now in his old age after failing to provide for the son's inheritance? Often a son who decides not to put himself out for his father because there is nothing in it for him is reacting to some early childhood experience. His father's inability or "failure" to insure his son's prosperity may be associated in a son's mind with some lapse—real or imagined—of the father in the past.

Fortunately, comparatively few parents use their assets in a carrot-and-stick fashion to purchase favors and obedience from their offspring. Since many of their children are themselves at the height of their earning power, they may be quite immune to such tactics. Giving in would put sons and daughters back in the position they had when they were ten years old and had to negotiate for an allowance.

All the same, a parent's money can and sometimes does lead to bitter family disputes. A long-lost relative, for example, may suddenly appear and dote on an enfeebled parent by performing all sorts of services the children themselves may be unwilling or unable to undertake—all in the hope of getting a piece of the inheritance. A son's or daughter's resentment may run just as high when he or she suspects a private nurse or secretary of this same motivation. It amounts in the offspring's eyes to watching money being stolen out of his or her own pockets.

We must remember, though, that an aged person's world is often a shrunken one. An enfeebled old woman may have little contact with either her own family or with anyone else. The ones who become important to her may be the ones she *does* see—the ones who *do* make her life a little more comfortable. If we believe in the right of free will and that a person is morally entitled to distribute her material wealth in any way she chooses, the mother has committed no sin if she rewards someone who has been good to her in her final, most needy days.

One last aspect of our parents' financial background that can trouble the offspring occurs when they appear to have lost their sense of judgment. As stated earlier, the elderly are particularly vulnerable to the schemes of swindlers and con men. For more than monetary reasons it is painful to suspect that our parents cannot protect themselves any longer against thieves or their own misman-agement. Children may reluctantly have to request that a guardian be put in legal charge of their parents' money. This involves incom-petence proceedings and the certification of mental disorder by physicians. Sometimes such a step is unavoidable. It can only take place after individuals have been victimized by themselves or others. The American Bar Association can supply whatever background information you may feel you need on this specific topic.

In the following chapter we intend to take up some other important aspects of your parents' potential loss of independence, including (1) how to reply when your parents bring up the subject of their own death, (2) how to deal with disturbing new behaviors as a result of mental deterioration, (3) memory loss, (4) the possible effects of hospitalization on your parents, and (5) what to look for in a nursing home if you have to place your parents in one.

9

What About the End of Life—Hospitals and Nursing Homes?

Sigmund Freud observed in an essay entitled *Thoughts on War and Death* that it is absolutely impossible for human beings to imagine their own death. "Whenever we make the attempt to imagine it," he wrote, "we can perceive that we really survive as spectators."

Freud was referring to a fantasy all of us have had. We find ourselves in the middle of our own funeral service. We are there in two forms: as the dignified, insensible corpse and, at the same time, as an invisible observer. As the observer, we have a number of things on our mind. We watch carefully to see just how many of our friends and family have gathered to pay their respects. How much did we mean to those we knew? Are there any people there whom we never expected to see in attendance? Who are conspicuous by their absence? How grief-stricken are the mourners? Which ones are overwhelmed with guilt for the way they mistreated us during our lifetime? How are our spouse and children bearing up? Will we be missed or soon forgotten?

Most of us find ourselves only rarely caught up in such a daydream. What our life has meant to others, what things will be like after we are gone—these are questions we pose to ourselves only when we are living through a period of deep loneliness, personal rejection, or physical illness. Although we are aware of our mortality, this is not an issue that we dwell on frequently.

But, like most dreams, this fantasy of ours expresses some universal human concerns. In old age questions of this kind are immediate indeed. People in their late seventies or early eighties cannot help but be aware of their mortality on a daily basis. Sheer age is one reminder. Loneliness, loss, and physical illness—all of which now play a much larger role in life than ever before—are others. Finally, the elderly are deeply involved in the tasks of reminiscence and life review.

Most aged parents have a normal, legitimate need to share their private thoughts about death with their children. The subject usually comes up under circumstances of their own choosing. It may center around their legacy or funeral arrangements. Or it may be prompted by the need to express a final regret or a pledge of love.

Middle-aged children, quite understandably, often become uncomfortable with these conversations. But recently a series of books and articles have appeared that criticize this aversion. The authors of these publications commonly point out that we read about death every day in the newspapers and watch it simulated every evening on television. Nevertheless, we find it practically impossible to discuss the prospect of death in a candid, realistic fashion with those closest to us. Some maintain that our difficulties are unusual and abnormal, that they reflect all sorts of inadequacies in our values and ourselves. We smother our feelings about death, they tell us, in the kinds of taboos the Victorians placed upon sexuality.

We would agree, of course, that openness about death is healthy. But it simply is not true that other peoples in other eras of history have naturally or successfully cultivated a constant, overt interest in death as a topic of everyday concern. Human beings have never been capable of facing their own end or the end of their family and friends in an utterly forthright, unflinching way. This seems beyond the powers of ordinary human nature. The belief in life after death, after all, is a consolation as old as the human species.

Our parents may have lived long enough with the prospect of death to reach a basic acceptance of it. This is a good thing, and it is one of the outcomes of successful reminiscence and life review. But unless parents have reached an extraordinary age or have suffered from an extended and terminal illness, their children can hardly be expected to have achieved the same attitude. Most of us have been trained to consider it the height of insensitivity and even of cruelty to discuss someone's death face to face with him or her in the same tone we would use to explain what our children were currently up to in school. Earlier we mentioned some of the reasons that middle-aged adults block out from their consciousness or deny the inevitability of their parents' death. Practically every parent-child relationship is made up of powerful, dimly understood feelings of love, hate, grief, guilt, resentment, and compassion. These feelings often may live side by side in uneasy equilibrium. When a parent confronts you in conversation with the imminence of his or her death, it often serves as a painful reminder that this passing will upset our sense of balance.

For a variety of reasons, sons and daughters often cut short parents who initiate such discussions. They may abruptly tell them that they will "outlive us all," that their death is years away, and so on. Nevertheless, aged parents should have the opportunity to talk these matters out with their children when the time comes. They will surely let you know when they are ready. But it may well take a major effort on your part to overcome your initial reactions to the subject.

Your immediate emotions may also be put to the test if both your parents are alive and one of them has seriously deteriorated. It seldom happens that our mother and father decline at the same rate, at the same time, and with the same maladies. Every marriage is subject to stress when the normal equilibrium is upset. A sick child or a husband out of work may be serious trials during the earlier years. In old age the illness and infirmities of one of the partners may be the major challenge.

> Carl Gordon is a hardworking teacher who found himself drawn into an ever expanding maze of conflicting feelings after his mother broke her hip and could no longer assume the household chores, including the cooking. These responsibilities as well as her ongoing care fell upon his father.
>
> For the last twenty years or so, Carl had seen his parents mainly on holidays, birthdays, and other special occasions. His parents seemed to get along rather well, though Carl winced every time his mother dwelled with amusement upon her husband's idiosyncrasies. Carl remembered that his father had always been the more considerate and better-natured of the two. So he just attributed his mother's remarks to "the way things were between those two."
>
> Shortly after the accident, though, it became clear that his

parents had been on their best behavior during Carl's infre-
quent visits. Mr. Gordon began phoning his son to ventilate his
frustrations. As the weeks wore on, the calls became increasingly bitter and explicit. In Mr. Gordon's view, his wife had
always been bent on running his life. Now, because of the
difficulties with her hip, she absolutely ruled it! She had a
mother complex, he believed, and had never felt secure enough
to treat him with the respect a grown man is entitled to. Her
attempts to belittle him by telling stories at his expense in front
of others were a small but obvious example of her behavior.
Reminding him that she believed he could never handle everyday matters nearly as well as she could was another one. This
behavior was infuriating and insulting to him, and part of a
battle they had been fighting for forty years.

Since his wife's hip injury she had shown two new condescending attitudes. The first was a complete state of shock that
he was actually able to cope with the situation. What did she
take him for, he wanted to know. The second was that she had
dropped the pretense of just laughing at his peculiarities. Now
she was critical of the way he swept a floor, the way he
prepared a meal, and even of the way he walked the dog!

Mr. Gordon admitted to his son that he had married his
wife originally because she was good-looking, a fine cook, and
a very bright woman. Now she had changed into something
much less appealing—a tiresome bully. Who could live with
her, Mr. Gordon wanted to know. If things went on like this
much longer, he would file for divorce! At first Carl could not
believe his ears. He dismissed the idea of a divorce instantly.
But the longer he listened to his father, the more Carl began to
recall how overbearing, temperamental, and bossy his mother
had always been. Come to think of it, there were times when
he was growing up when he had wanted to stand up for his
father. Although Carl could not bring himself to say so out
loud, he wanted to show how much he sympathized with his
old father.

As Carl began to drop by his parents' house more frequently, he could see firsthand what the problem was. Fortunately, his mother was also becoming aware of the problem.
One afternoon she took Carl aside and sheepishly told him that
she did not know of anyone else but his father who would put
up with her. She added that there must be something wrong
with her husband for having done so all these years. She was
convinced of it, she said. And she had been telling Carl's father
that for decades! Carl's first thought was that his mother was

up to her old stunt of excusing her own behavior that she knew was intolerable by using an insincere, self-disparaging remark. Soon Carl's wife convinced her husband that by getting help for his mother, his father's problems would be alleviated as well.

And so a family conference was held, at which it was decided to hire a practical nurse to look after Mrs. Gordon. It was also agreed that Mr. Gordon should spend more of his time on activities that he found gratifying. He might visit with his wife as often as he wanted during the day, but the burden and the responsibility for her care were off his shoulders. As a result life in the senior Gordon household began to improve. The phone calls stopped. Whenever Carl and his family paid a visit to his parents, they found that the old ways of getting along had reappeared.

Not all families are able to make the kind of satisfying adjustment that the Gordons seemed to have managed. It is much more difficult to cope successfully and completely with a parent who has severely deteriorated. When an aged person's mental faculties alter drastically, the new behaviors that result might well upset anyone, even a close relative.

There is a wide range of mental disturbances, and scientists still do not know enough about their causes. These disturbances are generally referred to as dementias. Alzheimer's Disease constitutes about 70 percent of progressive dementia cases, while the remaining 30 percent of the cases may be a result of multiple strokes or other factors related to medication, diet, infection, or depression. Alzheimer's Disease is marked by physical changes in the brain and the dementia which results becomes progressively worse. Despite the extensive research going on, we still don't know what causes the disease nor is there any known cure for it.

The other dementias that result from strokes, diet, infections, medications and other causes can often be treated and recovery may be possible. A thorough diagnostic workup is needed to determine whether, indeed, it is Alzheimer's or something else. There, currently, is no specific means for diagnosing Alzheimer's Disease and only by ruling out other possibilities can the doctor conclude that troubling behaviors are a result of Alzheimer's.

The progress of the disease is usually gradual and minor confusion, thought problems, memory lapses, irritability and disorientation will be seen. At this time, your mother or dad may even be aware that they are not the same, that something is happening to them, and this may add anxiety to their already troubled world.

It soon becomes clear that your parents cannot live alone and there needs to be someone present at all times to protect them, often from themselves. Some families have employed a companion. Others have moved their mother or father into their own home and have been able to manage, but it takes a great deal of love and devotion and hard work. It's more than we can possibly go into in this brief overview, but there are a number of valuable books and other resources listed in the appendix.

Whether from Alzheimer's Disease, or from other causes, there are a variety of strange behaviors that researchers have observed in the more advanced stages of mental deterioration among the elderly.

1. incessant counting; the repetition of nonsense phrases; and talking to oneself
2. withdrawal; staring blankly off into space
3. paranoia; suspiciousness; hostility toward other human beings
4. wandering or walking aimlessly or in a disoriented way about the neighborhood
5. undressing or peeling off clothing in public places; forgetting to fully clothe oneself
6. screaming for no apparent reason
7. memory loss; no sense or inadequate sense of person, place, or time

These are usually not reversible conditions, and they become worse with time. Many children who witness problems of this kind in their aged parents become extremely upset. When the strain on the children becomes overwhelming, a nursing home may be the only form of relief available. If this happens to you, you should *not* regard it as a sign that you are a cruel, unloving son or daughter. It means just the opposite—that you do care for your parents and want to provide the best possible care. Placing parents in a nursing home under these circumstances is really only an admission that they are now best helped by other people who have the necessary technical resources to assist them.

Even when your parents' problems are beyond solution, your father and mother are benefited most if they have a constant source of patient, understanding companionship. Elderly persons will never receive the same level of attention and kindness in a nursing home that they would receive in a loving family environment. Such companionship is not always easy to arrange. But some middle-aged people manage to care for their severely deteriorated parents for years without sacrificing either their marriages or peace of mind. A mother's Alzheimer's Disease may leave her with the intellectual capacities of a child. Her offspring may have to set up their household as though they have a two-year-old living with them. Since they know that a young child may pick up and smash fragile objects or may wander outside in a burst of idle curiosity, they must remove all the crystal ware, glass ashtrays, and similar breakable things. They also must pad the sharp corners of their pieces of furniture and learn to keep the doors of the house always locked.

We mention these problems not to exaggerate their difficulty but to reemphasize the fact that a nursing home should be considered only after all other resources have been explored. It is a move that should be deferred for as many months or weeks as possible. Placement of parents in a nursing home is more lilkely to take place because something or someone in their environment can no longer keep them there rather than because of a dramatic change in their condition. Often placement can be deferred by doing something to support that sustaining environment and help it do its job better.

Perhaps the most common form of deterioration that afflicts the elderly is memory loss. In general this kind of mental loss begins in the middle or late sixties. Our memory function is usually divided into three main categories: (1) memory of persons (remembering people, matching names and faces, and remembering who is associated with whom), (2) memory of places (how to find one's way, street location, remembering where one is, a sense of which objects belong where), and (3) memory of time (distinguishing present, past, and future; anticipating when events will occur; remembering when meals, appointments, and other events occurred in the past or will occur in the future). Memory loss may occur in one or more of these major areas. For some aged, the mere changes in or loss of tissue as part of growing old is the chief factor in loss of memory. Little is certain about the precise relationship between brain changes and memory, but we do know that the memory loss is very real indeed.

Severe memory loss is one of the dominant features of Alzheimer's Disease, as we have already indicated. But most of us, as we get older, experience various periods of confusion or loss of memory and it doesn't mean we have Alzheimer's! Don't rush to conclude that your mother has Alzheimer's simply because she can't find her glasses or because she became lost on the way home from the store.

Emotional difficulties of old age also contribute to the problem. The elderly, as we know, rely upon reminiscence to temporarily escape their isolation, physical infirmities, and loneliness. The luncheon your father attended thirty years ago when he received a big promotion is something he may be able to recount to you in the minutest detail. Yet he may be unable to tell you what he ate for lunch yesterday.

Memory loss often begins with an inability to distinguish among the various people with whom one comes in contact. A father may not remember if it was the delivery boy or the laundryman who stopped by to see him yesterday afternoon. He may not recall whether the interview he had the day before was with a social worker or a doctor. As his loss becomes more advanced, he may also begin to have only a foggy notion 'of who his children are. He may confuse their names or forget their connection to him. Often an aged person does have some vague notion that he ought to recognize the people closest to him.

Children, however, sometimes react to such changes in their parents with annoyance and suspicion. It is painful to face the fact that their parents' faculties are slipping. It is, however, less painful to perceive such a loss as just a temporary lapse of memory. Children who feel that their parents may become a burden to them once this memory loss occurs may consciously refuse to face the problem. Instead they may try to convince themselves that their parents are pretending a memory loss in order to be irritating.

Another reason that the memory losses of parents often annoy their middle-aged offspring is that they may remind them of quite different memory lapses on the part of their adolescent sons and daughters. Your son and daughter may share the responsibility for walking the dog after supper or for washing the dishes. One evening you may walk into your home and see a mess the dog has left on the rug or a sink filled with dishes. When you ask your son for an explanation, he may simply shrug his shoulders and say, "Sorry, I forgot!"

"I forgot," for your son, is a catch phrase for any of the following excuses: "I was thinking about something else"; "I wasn't in the mood"; "My sister skipped her turn last week, so it was really her turn tonight"; "Chores give me a pain"; or "I'm sick of having people order me around."

A teenager's "memory loss" can be an aggravating act of inconsideration. A loss on the part of an elderly person, however, is more than likely connected to a biological change beyond his or her control. Unlike adolescents, aged people are embarrassed by their forgetfulness and will struggle to cover it up and conceal it.

Unfortunately, unthinking relatives inadvertently may expose our parents' weakness and leave them feeling humiliated. Some of these busybodies may even appoint themselves psychological investigators. To see how far the damage has gone with your father, Uncle Frank or Aunt Lee may march into your dad's living room and say, "Howdy, Al! Remember me? Do you remember who this is who I dragged along with me?"

This sort of behavior is totally inappropriate and only adds to Dad's burden. The correct thing is for you to advise your parent in a matter-of-fact way who has come to visit. Uncle Frank should have entered your father's room and said, "Hello, Al. This is Frank. I brought along your sister Lee with me today."

Lee might then introduce herself and begin to talk about the old days, mentioning familiar events that might stimulate the elderly relative's memory but not subject him to being tested.

Memory loss can also extend to the automatic connections or associations we make toward the everyday objects of our world. We all know, for example, that when the doorbell rings, it means that someone has come to see us and that we are supposed to open the door. When the telephone rings, we automatically assume that someone wants to speak to us and that we should pick up the receiver and talk into the speaker. When we sit down to dinner, we expect that the plate set in front of us holds food that we may eat. We know that the utensils beside the plate should be used to help us eat the meal.

Our ability to survive requires us to make countless connections of this kind every day. When elderly parents lose their capacity to make such connections, and thus become unable to manage the everyday functions of living, their children's overrash response often is to place them in a nursing home. This happens even when the parents are physically sound in other respects. To move parents under these circumstances is to overlook all the other strengths they may still retain. Drastic as this loss is, there are ways to compensate successfully for it. This rule of thumb often applies to even the most disturbing forms of memory loss. Your father may be unable to recognize that the food set in front of him has any relationship to the hunger pangs he may be feeling. If he is to survive, someone has to feed him. Your mother may complain about strange noises that haunt her all day long. In reality this may just mean that she is unable any longer to associate the wail of a siren with the passing ambulance that produces it. In such a case we have to distinguish between someone who has suffered a particular loss that can be lived with and someone who has slipped into a hopeless state of mental confusion.

Memory loss is also a major contributor to fatal accidents among the elderly. For example, an elderly woman may forget to put out a cigarette she has been smoking or to turn off the burner she has used to prepare her dinner. Perhaps the most upsetting aspect of this deterioration—at least from the point of view of sons and daughters—occurs when a parent forgets to dress properly before going out in public or in some other way shows his or her incapacity.

A loving, thoughtful family will not instantly move a parent into a nursing home if their only concern is memory loss. Instead they will evaluate the resources and the flexibility of their parent's environment. They may try to adapt the environment in a number of ways. For example, they may enlist the help of neighbors, relatives, or paid visitors to ensure that the gas has been turned off, that the parent is properly dressed every morning, and that Mom or Dad takes regular meals each day at home. Sons and daughters may phone at regular intervals every day to make sure the parent is safe and sound. It may require someone to live in and look after your parent, and that might extend, even for a while, his or her continued living at home.

An extended period of hospitalization as a result of some new physical problem is another avenue through which many elderly parents wind up in nursing homes. Their placement is sometimes as automatic as it is premature. Your mother might have suffered from a whole series of ailments before she entered the hospital for much-needed medical attention. Despite such aches and pains, she managed to fend for herself, however marginally. Her stay at the hospital, however, may have negative effects on her. In the past she probably did not have anyone to dress and bathe her, transport her in a wheelchair, or feed her pureed foods three times a day. But hospital personnel are trained and paid to perform such services and are willing to provide them. If your mother feels discouraged by her condition, she may find herself encouraging these efforts. With all the emphasis a hospital staff places upon ailments and weaknesses, a person may suddenly feel that being waited on hand and foot has simply become unavoidable. What neither your mother nor the staff may realize is that she is thereby relinquishing her claims to autonomy and independence. In some cases it amounts to giving up on herself.

Sons and daughters who watch their parents regress to helpless bundles of pain and complaints are usually quite alarmed. Their parents seem to have suddenly and totally collapsed. When it comes time to release the parents, some doctors and staff workers, who may not realize what a move to a nursing home really means, may tell the middle-aged offspring that their parents simply cannot live in the outside world any longer. This medically certified advice often goes unquestioned, but it certainly should be questioned. Only rarely do children have the determination—one might even say the temerity—to disagree with their parents' physician's advice. It would be well for them to point out that since their mother had been able to manage adequately on her own before she entered the hospital, she ought to be able to defer permanent placement in an institution.

At present, middle-aged laymen are in a poor position to evaluate properly modern medical wisdom. It does not occur to most of them that many doctors think of nursing homes as natural extensions of hospitals and that they tend to regard institutional care for the aged as the most beneficial kind available. Nor are most communities able today to meet the needs of disabled persons with halfway houses or temporary residence facilities. Most people are simply overwhelmed when told that the only way their parents can survive in the outside world is by turning their apartments or homes into minihospitals complete with bedpans, beds that crank up and down, wheelchairs, and round-the-clock attention.

Of course if a son or daughter explains to a physician that the mother's sister will move in with her for several months, that a licensed practical nurse has been hired, or that the physical rehabilitation resources of a nursing home will be available to the mother for a limited period of time, the mother's physician will most likely approve of returning her to her home.

Perhaps the most salient point to keep in mind is the need to be conscious of how much dependence is actually created in a parent as a result of exposure to the hospital milieu. In the long run it is to everyone's advantage to insist that a parent struggle to keep as much independence and dignity as possible. It may be "easier" to be wheeled around than to take fifteen minutes to go step by painful step to the bathroom. But for the aged parents, that convenience is a kind of quicksand. Eventually it might lead the parents as well as the children to accept the idea that the end of independence has come for the parents.

An emphasis on self-sufficiency and independence ought to be the basic philosophical concept of any nursing home that you may ultimately select for your parents. A nursing-home operator may show you how bedridden patients are kept in their rooms and fed there three times a day. He or she may point to this as an example of the warm, personal care your parents will receive. The reality is, though, that it is cheaper and more efficient to feed patients this way. It takes more time, effort, and determination to insist that a patient make his or her own way to the dining room and enjoy the dignity of eating with others. Services that foster helplessness and dependence are really nothing more than disservices to an elderly person's sense of self-respect.

If we each had a million dollars, none of our parents would ever set foot inside a nursing home. Money can buy all the substitutes a person needs to live in the outside world. To illustrate this point, we need only follow a day in the life of a fictitious heiress named Flora Dodsworth.

> Flora Dodsworth is an eighty-year-old woman who has suffered a number of serious social, physical, and psychological losses. Her husband and most of her friends have died. She lives in a fashionable high rise in the most exclusive section of a large city, but her neighbors do not know her. Her only child, a son named Thomas, has been living comfortably in Paris for the last twenty years. In other words, no family members or relatives are available to take care of her. Her hearing and eyesight are poor. She cannot handle many ordinary physical tasks, nor can she prepare her meals or keep herself on a regular schedule of medication. She suffers from arthritis, can get about only in a wheelchair, and is occasionally incontinent. Her memory has deteriorated to the point that she can no longer handle her financial affairs.
>
> Mrs. Dodsworth is awakened promptly at eight every

morning by her live-in companion. She is escorted to the bathroom, where her live-in practical nurse bathes and dresses her. She receives her daily injection and morning pills and then is wheeled into the dining room. There her butler serves a light, well-balanced breakfast that was prepared by a live-in cook. Mrs. Dodsworth is fed by her companion, who reads to her the major news stories of the morning and then plans her schedule for the day.

As the butler clears away the dishes, Mrs. Dodsworth and her companion decide to visit a new botanical garden exhibit. The companion bundles her up in a wheelchair and conveys her down an elevator to the building foyer. The doorman escorts them both out to the driveway, where Mrs Dodsworth's chauffeur is waiting with a limousine. The chauffeur helps Mrs. Dodsworth to a specially designed rear seat, folds the wheelchair, and stores the chair in the trunk. After a leisurely, thirty-minute drive Mrs. Dodsworth is taken by her companion to the ladies' room of the garden in order to avoid soiling herself. After seeing the exhibit, they return home, where Mrs. Dodsworth has lunch, receives her afternoon medication from the nurse, and is put to bed for a nap.

Meanwhile, Mrs. Dodsworth's lawyer is placing a call from his office downtown to her accountant. The attorney has spoken recently with the Dodsworth family stockbroker and wants the accountant's advice on how to best avoid taxation from the profits of a recent stock transaction he made on behalf of Mrs. Dodsworth's interests.

At 5:00 P.M. Mrs. Dodsworth is awakened by her nurse. After receiving her evening medication, she is escorted into the dining room for the evening meal. The companion reads a letter to Mrs. Dodsworth that has just arrived from her son. Mrs. Dodsworth nods and indicates in a few phrases what reply to send. Her companion composes it as the dishes are cleared away. The two women then decide to watch television and engage in a game of checkers before bedtime.

After Mrs. Dodsworth has been put to bed, the companion admits a security guard who will provide protection through the night. She then sits down to write Thomas Dodsworth III about his mother's condition. She reminds the nurse that Mrs. Dodsworth's personal physician will call to see her at ten the next morning.

The Dodsworths are fortunate people. Flora Dodsworth is well cared for and enjoys still a dignified way of life. At the same time, her son Thomas's great inherited wealth enables him to insulate himself from the physical and emotional ordeal that forces many middle-aged sons and daughters to move their parents into a nursing home.

When should an aging parent be relocated? There is no set of absolute rules to decide this question for everyone. What often happens is that, for example, a father comes down with a new major malady. This difficulty, in combination with the other health problems he has, makes it impossible for his children and community to care adequately for him any longer. He may have been incontinent and forgetful in the past. But with the help of a visiting nurse, he has been able to live in his home for the last year. Recently, however, his mental faculties have declined to the point that he has been found regularly wandering the streets at night. The stress of this new problem forces his family to provide him with round-the-clock protection and security. Few of us possess the Dodsworth fortune, and we find that the only way to provide such services for our parents is in a nursing home.

Some parents' needs become so great that there is no alternative. Nursing homes are legitimate resources for persons who absolutely require round-the-clock care. It is always a good idea, though, to ask an objective observer—perhaps a social worker from a family service agency—to evaluate your parent's condition before you make this major decision. This expert should be able to tell you about any workable outside resources, and he or she will probably look upon a nursing home as a last resort for your parent—in contrast to the proprietors of the homes, whose livelihood depends upon filling all available beds.

It is not unusual for sons and daughters to feel beset by conflicting emotions once they finally decide to place their parent in a home. Their first reaction may not be articulated, but usually it is a sense of relief. The worry, responsibility, and stress have come to an end. The burden of your parent's care has been shifted to an institution and a group of professionals. Life, at long last, can return to normal.

Some people, though, unconsciously feel ashamed of such a seemingly selfish reaction. They confuse the natural sense of release that comes when any overwhelming burden has been lifted with a suspicion that they are actually satisfied to have gotten rid of their parent. A part in all of us believes that we are expected to take care of our parents under every circumstance. And so without really being aware of it, some children will punish themselves. They do so by feeling that they have failed as offspring; that they are neglectful, unloving people who have turned over their parent's care to outsiders; and that they are abandoning their parent to the equivalent of a death house.

Such energy can be put to more constructive use by evaluating your available options. Your most healthy and realistic goal should be to discern the best possible environment for your mother or father. Your parent doesn't benefit from living in the outside world if this arrangement exacts a tremendous price from those around him or her. When the choice is between placing your parent in a nursing home or sacrificing your daily routine and peace of mind, you do not have *any* pleasant alternatives. You are forced instead to choose the least unpleasant one.

There is no magic formula by which concerned sons and daughters can avoid the emotional upheaval involved in moving a parent into a nursing home. The nature of a home, after all, is institutional. The presence of nursing stations, oxygen tents, personnel in white uniforms, dozens of beds, and so on, is a constant reminder that one is in a hospitallike atmosphere. There *is* something funereal in giving up a parent's apartment and disposing of his or her personal effects, which often follows placement. And although many children as well as parents feel that admission to a nursing home marks the end of the parent's natural life, this extreme reaction is really a form of mourning over the loss of your parent's independence. Concerned, loving families will eventually overcome this period of grief and find that while their parent's lifestyle has been scaled down, their relationship with the parent still exists, and the life of the parent can still hold many gratifications.

This normally takes some effort on a family's part. The last words many sons and daughters hear as they leave their parent for the first day of residence in a home often come from the home's administrator. "Don't worry," he or she may tell them. "Your father is in good hands."

These are consoling and considerate phrases, of course, but they tend to imply that the offspring's responsibilities toward their parent have now officially ended. It is true that fewer than half of all families maintain a regular, ongoing involvement with their elderly parents after they enter a home.

All aged persons, regardless of diagnosis, will suffer some loss in self-confidence, dignity, and self-worth on moving to a nursing home. They will also lose to some degree the ability to interact easily with others and to become wholly involved in the new surroundings. An institution does induce by its very nature some sense of hopelessness. And you may discover that the family's love and devotion and concern are not enough—that the nursing care, rehabilitation service, recreation programs, and constant round-the-clock supervision that a home provides is what your parent now has come to require.

There are some small but important ways in which your family can respond to a parent following admission to a home. Many people, for example, are uncomfortable about making scheduled visits to the home by themselves. Once a month they gather up the entire family and spend a few hours on Sunday with their father. There is nothing wrong with this, but, if at all possible, it would be better to arrange for each member of the family to spend a small period of time with a parent, each on a different day. Instead of one three-hour visit from six people, a parent may then receive the attention and pleasure of six separate hour-long visits in the course of a month.

Observance of special occasions such as birthdays, annversaries, and holidays are also ways in which you can boost your parent's spirits. Almost every nursing home holds mass birthday celebrations for all the residents whose birthdays fall within a particular month. By making a point of bringing your own cake and presents on the actual day of your parent's birthday, you provide your parent with a special warmth he or she would not otherwise experience.

There is no reason that your parent's entrance into a home should mean the severance of all of his or her old and longstanding peer relationships. You might encourage friends to visit your parent occasionally. Your parent's name can also remain on the mailing lists of old clubs and social organizations. A men's club, for example, might well decide to hold a meeting in your father's new home. Its members might also be encouraged to hold one of their card-playing sessions there.

Too often, a family does not take a parent out of a home for dinner in a favorite restaurant because they are afraid that their parent might meet with some sort of accident. Most families, though, can receive instructions from the staff that will permit even the more regressed of patients to enjoy an evening out.

As a general rule, we cannot depend upon our aged parents to register the level of happiness or appreciation we might need to see in order to feel we are doing them some good. We would not expect an infant to ask for his mother's breast and thank her for it after he has finished receiving his nourishment. Just so, we must assume that our efforts enrich our parent's life even if Mother or Dad may be too depressed or withdrawn to tell us so.

Especially if a parent has become dangerous to himself or herself, it is best to simply accept the move as unavoidable. You can then continue to concentrate on the overall goal of providing the most suitable environment for your parent. This involves learning how to inspect and choose the appropriate facility.

There are two major categories of nursing-home ownership: proprietary, that is, profit-making; and ownership by charitable, usually sectarian, groups. The nursing-home industry has boomed into a multibillion-dollar business. Researchers at the Brookings Institution have predicted that in 1988 alone, over 20 billion dollars will be spent for long-term care for the aged—and most of that means nursing homes. Huge profits are made each year from the care of the large numbers of elderly people who now survive into their late seventies, eighties, and beyond. Those who are institutionalized, it goes almost without saying, are a very vulnerable group. They have been subjected to a level of mistreatment and neglect in some private nursing homes that amounts to a national scandal. Not all nursing-home operators, of course, are dishonest or venal people. But the profit motive is, we believe, incompatible with the concept of providing the best medical and social services for the aged. In every area of the country, accounts periodically crop up documenting fraudulent billings of state and federal agencies for services and drugs that were never administered to the patients. There are other disturbing accounts of residents with unexplained bruises, of patients who spend whole days isolated and abandoned in their rooms, of high levels of staff turnover, of thefts by staff members, and of indifference toward and abuse of the aged.

Operators commonly claim that the free-enterprise system through its stiff competition ensures the public of the best possible care. No substandard product, they maintain, can succeed in a free market. But this argument is lame, indeed. After a moment's thought any adult could list a number of shoddy, even lethal, goods that have reaped huge profits for manufacturers who were clever and aggressive enough in their use of advertising and public relations. All nursing homes are regulated by state and federal guidelines. Private operators, however, employ a powerful, influential group of lobbyists that has successfully kept the minimum standards of care artificially low. Representatives of nursing-home associations regularly meet with government officials and licensing agencies to seek higher payments and reduce governmental control. In several states there are state legislators themselves who participate in ownership of nursing homes, and this, too, contributes to the lobby strength. Enforcement of existing standards is generally lax or nonexistent. It would be comforting if there were some sort of self-regulatory body funded by the operators. But the plaque hanging in the lobby proclaiming a home to be a member in good standing of some national association of nursing homes is all but meaningless. It signifies only that the place has paid its dues to an organization that looks after the owner's interests on the local, state, and national levels of government.

A private nursing home's first priority is usually to earn the highest rate of profit for the owner. It requires extra time, labor, and effort to provide the most complete as well as the most compassionate care. From a strictly business standpoint, that means more personnel, better-trained personnel, and more individualized care, and that usually means higher expenses. There are owners who cater exclusively to the wealthy. They can conceivably offer first-rate services and make money at the same time by passing along the added cost to those who can pay out of pocket the thirty thousand dollars a year or more that such care involves.

But the vast majority of nursing-home residents are not wealthy. Few of them enter a home with tens of thousands of dollars to their names. The federal government considers them independent citizens whose children are not legally responsible for their care. Before aged persons are admitted to a home, their net worth is assessed. Arrangements are made to withdraw their savings to pay for services. When they have only a few hundred dollars in their savings accounts, the home applies in their name to the department of public welfare, which then underwrites the costs of future care. This is all a perfectly standard, legally sanctioned operating procedure. But it means several things. One is that placing your parent in a home in almost every instance guarantees that he or she will be pauperized.

For all practical purposes this also means that a home can only maximize profits by offering a minimum of services to its residents. State departments of health set minimum standards of cleanliness, food quality, the numbers of nurses required on duty on every floor, and so on. It is a good bet that if the department requires a minimum of four nurses to a floor, a private home will provide exactly that number. Homes housing five hundred residents are more profitable than those housing only fifty. A social worker, a recreation worker, and a director of nursing will each command a similar salary no matter what size institution they may work for. The larger the institution, though, the more impersonal the care is likely to become. One social worker cannot possibly provide the kind of in-depth care for five hundred clients he or she could for fifty. The result may well be that the social workers must spread themselves so thin that the benefits to a particular client could be practically nonexistent.

Middle-aged sons and daughters should be aggressive and critical in investigating potential homes. It is important to shop around, and to do so some time in advance of the day when your parent might need immediate placement. Simply because a home is well advertised is no guarantee that it offers the kind of treatment your parent deserves. Some owners take advantage of the unsophisticated and those who find the search for a home an overwhelming ordeal. For example, a facility may be called the AAA or the A-1 Nursing Home, which means that its name is listed first in the telephone directory. A certain percentage of the home's business may come from people who phone the first facility they find listed.

Choosing a home for your parent is like choosing a pediatrician for your child. You ask your friends and personal physician for recommendations. When it comes to nursing homes, working up a list can be something of a chore. Some hospitals, for example, will not pass along the names of any homes whatsoever because the quality of service is too unpredictable.

Since private nursing homes are usually eager for your business, there is no reason for you to stay on your best behavior or to be extremely passive and circumspect during an interview. It is a buyer's market. If you were to sit down for the first time with a pediatrician and he were to treat you in an indifferent or belligerent manner, you would not consider allowing him or her to touch your child. Yet many nursing-home personnel treat middle-aged people callously. If this happens, you can be assured that your parent will be treated with similar disdain.

When we enter a doctor's office, most of us take scant notice of the medical diplomas displayed on the walls. They do assure us, though, that our physician is a qualified, licensed practitioner who has been examined and approved by the state medical authority. If we do not see these documents, we are perfectly within our rights to ask that they be produced for our inspection. Any doctor who becomes annoyed at this request or refuses to show his diplomas to us will arouse a quite justifiable suspicion. The equivalent of these documents for a nursing home is the state inspection report, which is provided every year. But a home is not required by law to post this report for visitors' inspection. However, you are legally entitled to examine this report, and you ought to do so. It will alert you to the deficiencies and violations the home may have committed. If the director becomes evasive or puts you off, the nursing home probably has something to hide. In that case you should look elsewhere.

Just as you should never pick a nursing home at random out of the phone book and simply drive your parent up to its door, so, too, you should realize that neither you nor your parent has to pass a test of acceptance. It is the home that must always satisfy you. In many ways the elderly who need institutionalization are helpless and vulnerable. Once admitted, they are not in a good position to press whatever grievances they may have. If they become dissatisfied for legitimate reasons, they would find it difficult if not impossible to pack up and go elsewhere. The stress of moving into a home is great. Your parent may need a few months to become acclimated to the new surroundings, strange faces, and regimentation. The stress of another move, which in some cases becomes necessary, would be terribly hard on your mother or father.

Your aim is to find a home that offers your parent more than mere custodial service. When you first visit a private nursing home, try to see if the staff treats the residents in a warm, respectful way. For instance, do they call all the residents indiscriminately by their first names? This is one small sign of disrespect that may indicate an overall attitude. Do they seem cold, impersonal, or mechanical in the performance of their duties? Ask the person you interview for a list of the specialists on the staff. Get some idea of how many hours each of them spends in the home.

You may be handed a letterhead listing a social worker, an occupational therapist, a recreation worker, an ophthalmologist, and so on. But the social worker may only be under contract for eight hours a month, the ophthalmologist may only make a visit every six months, and the occupational therapist may only work with the institution as a consultant.

The smaller institutions may have a more personal, homelike atmosphere but may lack certain important professional resources. You will have to weigh which of these factors is more important for your parent. Sectarian homes—those built, for example, by Lutheran, Methodist, Catholic, and Jewish charitable organizations—are more likely to prove worthy of trust. Their emphasis has been on care rather than financial gain. The number of these homes was greater years ago than it is today, and most of them are smaller than their private counterparts. Since the payments for care in both kinds of institutions are about the same, the sad fact is that the sectarian homes have simply been unable to maintain their higher level of service without additional financial help. Those that have survived are in such demand that a parent who applies for admission may be put on a waiting list for several years.

An experience at a high-standard sectarian facility in Chicago provides us with an example of how the two philosophies of running nursing homes can differ. As you may know, incontinent elderly people, that is, those unable to control their bowels and bladders, make up a fair percentage of every nursing-home population. Some time ago a worker at the home suggested a project that, she felt, would return a sense of dignity, however fleeting, to the lives of the thirty-five women in her care, more than half of whom were incontinent. She decided to organize for them an afternoon picnic in the park. At first the staff were skeptical of her idea, but they finally gave her the go-ahead signal. It took weeks of planning. Every woman's family was informed of the project and became involved with the planning. On the day of the event, the staff carefully laid out a picnic table that was reasonably close to washroom facilities. Family and staff cars drove to the home, picked up the aged residents, and proceeded to the prepared site. An afternoon of food, sunshine, family and children, games, singing, and fun was enjoyed in a setting most of the women had not visited in years. For a five-hour period, thirty-four out of the thirty-five women had none of the anticipated toileting problems. The only "accident" occurred as one of the cars was pulling up to the front of the home at the end of the day.

This project, of course, required an immense staff effort, and it has not been possible to repeat it. The lesson to be learned was that it is cheaper and more efficient for a nursing home to skip an

event like this one altogether; you simply mop up after your patients. Few nursing homes of any kind have the personnel or interest to undertake such a project. This attitude unquestionably
contributes to the problems already existing in many nursing
homes. As the elderly realize that in the home it does not matter
whether or not they take an interest in their bodies, their own
motivation to do so—simply out of a sense of personal dignity—
may suffer a crushing blow.

Middle-aged people touring nursing homes are often im-
pressed by factors that have only a small bearing on the quality of
care a parent may need. They see a nursing home purely in physical
terms. If it looks spotless and modern, and if it has shiny grab bars
in the bathrooms as well as new furnishings, they believe their
parent will be quite happy. Most private nursing homes have been
built within the last five to ten years and have a modern look.
Owners know that the families of potential residents place a great
deal of emphasis on appearances and accentuate this characteristic
when families visit. You ought to insist on seeing every floor and
work area in the facility. If you meet with any objections, it is
perhaps a sign that there are areas of the home that might not
stand up to public scrutiny.

Sectarian homes constructed thirty to fifty years ago often
appear run-down and weather-beaten from the outside. After several decades of wear and continuous use, the insides may also
suffer in comparison with the facilities of newer institutions.

However, if you ask residents of a home what means the most
to them, they will probably not list modern conveniences or spotless floors. Instead they will probably talk about the warmth of the
personnel, the friends they have made, and the birthday parties and
other social activities.

A brand-new nursing home may also remind middle-aged people of a lovely hotel. But remember that a hotel is not a home.
Anyone who has spent extensive time traveling on business or
vacationing will readily vouch for the estrangement your elderly
parent might feel in such an environment.

Any final decision about a specific home should be made
together with your parent. If your mother knows someone who
already lives in a particular home, that is often helpful. It is a
good idea for a parent to pack a bag and spend a weekend
in any institution under consideration. Good homes will encourage
and even insist that your mother do so. Those that do not

should be avoided, for this indicates that such homes are more interested in their own routines than in the comfort and security of their clients.

There are other steps a good home will take to ensure your parent's peace of mind. For example, the home may encourage your parent to bring along some personal effects and furniture once he or she has decided to move. These objects have a great deal of meaning to an elderly parent. They help preserve the continuity and familiarity so crucial to the aged person. Some facilities, though, will discourage and even forbid this practice. The reason they give may be that the effects will clash with their own well-coordinated decor. If a home is more interested in its color coordination than in an elderly person's comfort, its overall attitude may be just as insensitive.

Nursing homes that show concern for their clients will also try to match your parent, whenever possible, with a roommate he or she will find compatible. Anyone who attended college or served in the army knows how annoying roommate conflicts can be. An aged parent who has developed his or her own life-style over the last eighty years may find it difficult to adapt to a stranger's demands. When two people find after a period of time that they simply cannot live together, a sensitive nursing home will make every effort to help your parent make other arrangements. Again, it takes time and energy to humanize an institution. Places that respond to your parent's requests by stating that "rules are rules," that "we can make no exceptions," or that "it simply cannot be done" are not interested in their clients' peace of mind. Their first priority is preserving their routines with the least amount of inconvenience to themselves.

The location of the home is another factor affecting the choices middle-aged people make, although sometimes for the wrong reasons. Many new private nursing homes have been built in suburban areas. Since they may also be closer to a son's or daughter's home, this factor makes visiting easier. But the location will not enrich your parent's welfare if the home makes no attempt to be a part of its surrounding community. You ought to ask the staff if they welcome volunteers and if neighborhood church choirs or community groups can enter the home on occasion. Is there a family day? Are there religious programs your parent can attend if he or she so chooses? Does the home have grounds in which patients may stroll or sun themselves? If the answer is no to most of these questions, your parent will become a virtual shut-in. The location of the home for all practical purposes has become irrelevant.

Sectarian homes are often situated today in deteriorated neighborhoods. They were built, of course, at a time when the ethnic makeup was different, but members of the original population have now moved away. Even so, in many cases the homes make a real effort to keep your parent in touch with the outside world.

If a nursing home is not open and responsive to the families of residents, the convenience of a nearby location is all but nullified. This can become a serious problem when the family must take a series of complaints about their parent's care to the administration. An occupational hazard of nursing is that it tends to bring out the possessive and protective side of people. Some nurses come to consider an aged person as their own, someone they, and they alone, know how to care for. Sons and daughters begin to be seen as outsiders and meddlesome troublemakers.

To put this problem in the right perspective, you ought to realize that the general public's concept of nursing-home personnel and their relationships with their clients is quite different from what goes on in real life. We tend to think of the staff of a home as altruistic people who have chosen a career of service to the elderly. In fact, the staffs are usually drawn from people trapped in the lowest economic strata of our society. While they may be working in a nursing home today, in the past they may have been waitresses, short-order cooks, maids, or janitors. They are usually undereducated and underpaid. Except for the few professionals in supervisory positions, the staff have as little background in gerontology as the rest of the general population. They perform basically custodial tasks such as changing sheets, serving meals, and mopping floors. While members of the staff do engage in some recreation, counseling, and rehabilitation activity with residents, work in a nursing home more often includes chores almost everyone would find distasteful, distressing, and unpleasant. They may have to empty bedpans, wipe behinds, and clean up after patients who regurgitate or play with their food. Most of the patients, after all, are in nursing homes because their families could no longer cope with the difficult physical and mental deterioration that has occurred.

Since many nursing-home proprietors hire a bare minimum of staff, many of the workers are overburdened. An owner of a home usually promises the middle-aged customers that their parents will receive the best available care. Thus when you visit your parent, you cannot be faulted for expecting that some member of the custodial staff might be in the process of taking your parent for a stroll, leading some patients in a song, or merely chatting informally with the residents. Instead you may find the staff relaxing on a coffee break or sitting in front of a television set. As far as the staff is concerned, they have fulfilled their basic responsibilities. They have accomplished what their superiors expect them to do if all the patients are in their rooms fed and washed and at ease.

The contrast between your expectations and reality can be distressing. After all, you are paying good money for a certain level of care. But most people do not take their complaints to the owner, who made such wonderful promises. Instead they go directly to the staff and demand that they immediately pay closer attention to their parent. A worker may well cut short her coffee break to attend to your mother. But she will most likely resent your criticism and the burden that the extra effort represents to her. The well-intentioned son or daughter may leave the nursing home late that Sunday afternoon satisfied that he or she has done some tangible good for the parent by intervening on the parent's behalf. But unless the children are able to make daily visits, their efforts will often be counterproductive. The staff may well label the children a nuisance and take out their frustration by being less caring and more short-tempered with the parent. The parent, in other words, may now receive the treatment the staff would like to vent on the children.

It is important for you to have some understanding and empathy for the problems of nursing-home personnel. They work under difficult conditions and appreciate expressions of understanding and concern. Often you may find one of the staff who seems to take more of a personal interest in your parent than the other staff members do. Developing a close relationship with this nurse, aide, or recreation worker can allow better communication to occur. She or he may be more receptive to your concerns and will be more effective in interpreting your parent's needs to other staff members than you will be if you march down the hall demanding immediate attention. Sometimes the home may view your concern or request as something beyond their capacity. A discussion with the director of nursing or the home administrator is essential to clarify precisely what the home is required to do. Ultimately these people are re-

212   The Waning of Independence

sponsible for seeing to it that essential services for your parent are performed as required. Many treatments and services in a home must be authorized by the home's attending physician, and you should certainly feel free to contact the doctor to discuss your parent's special needs.

By no means should these words of caution be taken to mean that you will tolerate any form of abuse or neglect of your parents. Too many horror stories have come out of nursing homes, alas, to allow the kind of total trust that we might wish were possible. But the necessary guarding of your parent's welfare after his or her admission to a home must be done with tact, care, and understanding. Of course the careful selection of the right setting in the first place is the best way for you to avoid constant surveillance after your parent's admission to a home.

If you discover that a nursing home simply cannot be trusted, you will have to move your parent. It is a mistake to rid yourself of the strain involved in personally caring for a deteriorated parent only to undergo an equal amount of worry about the care he or she is now receiving at a home. It is far better to place your parent in a home you can trust even if it is an hour and a half away from where you live than to try to depend on a nearby institution you have to check on several times a week.

This chapter concludes with a checklist of things to keep in mind if you come to the point of needing to place your parent or parents in a nursing home.

A NURSING-HOME CHECKLIST

This checklist was prepared by the U.S. Department of Health, Education, and Welfare to help you know what to look for in examining the facilities and services of a nursing home. If your answer is no to any of the first four questions, do not use the home.

In addition, we urge you to inspect the Skilled and Intermediate Nursing Care Facility Survey Reports for information on any nursing home you are seriously considering for a family member. These reports cover about 90 percent of all skilled nursing facilities. They can be obtained from the ten regional offices of the Health Care Financing Administration in Atlanta, Boston, Chicago, Dallas,

Denver, Kansas City, New York, Philadelphia, San Francisco, and Seattle. If there is no regional office near you, contact your local Social Security office or your local welfare or public aid office for information regarding the closest source of these reports.

		Yes	No
1.	Does the home have a current license from the State?	—	—
2.	Does the administrator have a current license from the State?	—	—
3.	If you need and are eligible for financial assistance, is the home certified to participate in Government or other programs that provide it?	—	—
4.	Does the home provide special services such as a specific diet or therapy which the patient needs?	—	—

Physical considerations

5. Location:
   (a) Pleasing to the patient? — —
   (b) Convenient for patient's personal doctor? — —
   (c) Convenient for frequent visits? — —
   (d) Near a hospital? — —
6. Accident prevention:
   (a) Well-lighted inside? — —
   (b) Free of hazards underfoot? — —
   (c) Chairs sturdy and not easily tipped? — —
   (d) Warning signs posted around freshly waxed floors? — —
   (e) Handrails in hallways and grab bars in bathrooms? — —
7. Fire safety:
   (a) Meets Federal and/or State codes? — —
   (b) Exits clearly marked and unobstructed? — —
   (c) Written emergency evacuation plan? — —
   (d) Frequent fire drills? — —
   (e) Exit doors not locked on the inside? — —
   (f) Stairways enclosed and doors to stairways kept closed? — —
8. Bedrooms:
   (a) Open onto hall? — —
   (b) Window? — —

	Yes	No
(c) No more than four beds per room?	___	___
(d) Easy access to each bed?	___	___
(e) Drapery for each bed?	___	___
(f) Nurse call bell by each bed?	___	___
(g) Fresh drinking water at each bed?	___	___
(h) At least one comfortable chair per patient?	___	___
(i) Reading lights?	___	___
(j) Clothes closet and drawers?	___	___
(k) Room for a wheelchair to maneuver?	___	___
(l) Care used in selecting roommates?	___	___

9. Cleanliness:
   (a) Generally clean, even though it may have a lived-in look? ___ ___
   (b) Free of unpleasant odors? ___ ___
   (c) Incontinent patients given prompt attention? ___ ___

10. Lobby:
    (a) Is the atmosphere welcoming? ___ ___
    (b) If also a lounge, is it being used by residents? ___ ___
    (c) Furniture attractive and comfortable? ___ ___
    (d) Plants and flowers? ___ ___
    (e) Certificates and licenses on display? ___ ___

11. Hallways:
    (a) Large enough for two wheelchairs to pass with ease? ___ ___
    (b) Hand-grip railings on the sides? ___ ___

12. Dining room:
    (a) Attractive and inviting? ___ ___
    (b) Comfortable chairs and tables? ___ ___
    (c) Easy to move around in? ___ ___
    (d) Tables convenient for those in wheelchairs? ___ ___
    (e) Food tasty and attractively served? ___ ___
    (f) Meals match posted menu? ___ ___
    (g) Those needing help receiving it? ___ ___

13. Kitchen:
    (a) Food preparation, dishwashing, and garbage areas separated? ___ ___

Yes No

    (b) Food needing refrigeration not standing on counters?   — —

    (c) Kitchen help observe sanitation rules?   — —

14. Activity rooms:

    (a) Rooms available for patients' activities?   — —

    (b) Equipment (such as games, easels, yarn, kiln, etc.) available?   — —

    (c) Residents using equipment?   — —

15. Special purpose rooms:

    (a) Rooms set aside for physical examinations or therapy?   — —

    (b) Rooms being used for stated purpose?   — —

16. Isolation room:

    (a) At least one bed and bathroom available for patients with contagious illness?   — —

17. Toilet facilities:

    (a) Convenient to bedrooms?   — —

    (b) Easy for a wheelchair patient to use?   — —

    (c) Sink?   — —

    (d) Nurse call bell?   — —

    (e) Hand grips on or near toilets?   — —

    (f) Bathtubs and showers with nonslip surfaces?   — —

18. Grounds:

    (a) Residents can get fresh air?   — —

    (b) Ramps to help handicapped?   — —

Services

19. Medical:

    (a) Physician available in emergency?   — —

    (b) Private physician allowed?   — —

    (c) Regular medical attention assured?   — —

    (d) Thorough physical immediately before or upon admission?   — —

    (e) Medical records and plan of care kept?   — —

    (f) Patient involved in developing plans for treatment?   — —

    (g) Other medical services (dentists, optometrists, etc.) available regularly?   — —

Yes   No

    (h) Freedom to purchase medicines outside home?   — —

20. Hospitalization:
    (a) Arrangement with nearby hospital for transfer when necessary?   — —

21. Nursing services:
    (a) RN responsible for nursing staff in a skilled nursing home?   — —
    (b) LPN on duty day and night in a skilled nursing home?   — —
    (c) Trained nurses' aides and orderlies on duty in homes providing some nursing care?   — —

22. Rehabilitation:
    (a) Specialists in various therapies available when needed?   — —

23. Activities program:
    (a) Individual patient preferences observed?   — —
    (b) Group and individual activities?   — —
    (c) Residents encouraged but not forced to participate?   — —
    (d) Outside trips for those who can go?   — —
    (e) Volunteers from the community work with patients?   — —

24. Religious observances:
    (a) Arrangements made for patient to worship as he pleases?   — —
    (b) Religious observances a matter of choice?   — —

25. Social services:
    (a) Social worker available to help residents and families?   — —

26. Food:
    (a) Dietitian plans menus for patients on special diets?   — —
    (b) Variety from meal to meal?   — —
    (c) Meals served at normal times?   — —
    (d) Plenty of time for each meal?   — —
    (e) Snacks?   — —
    (f) Food delivered to patients' rooms?   — —
    (g) Help with eating given when needed?   — —

Yes No

27. Grooming:
    (a) Barbers and beauticians available for men
        and women?   — —

Attitudes and atmosphere
28. General atmosphere friendly and supportive?   — —
29. Residents retain human rights?
    (a) May participate in planning treatment?   — —
    (b) Medical records are held confidential?   — —
    (c) Can veto experimental research?   — —
    (d) Have freedom and privacy to attend to
        personal needs?   — —
    (e) Married couples may share room?   — —
    (f) All have opportunities to socialize?   — —
    (g) May manage own finances if capable or
        obtain accounting if not?   — —
    (h) May decorate their own bedrooms?   — —
    (i) May wear their own clothes?   — —
    (j) May communicate with anyone without
        censorship?   — —
    (k) Are not transferred or discharged arbitrar-
        ily?   — —
30. Administrator and staff available to discuss
    problems?
    (a) Patients and relatives can discuss com-
        plaints without fear of reprisal?   — —
    (b) Staff responds to calls quickly and courte-
        ously?   — —
31. Residents appear alert unless very ill?   — —
32. Visiting hours accommodate residents and
    relatives?   — —
33. Civil rights regulations observed?   — —
34. Visitors and volunteers pleased with home?   — —

When You Have a Complaint
    If you have a complaint about a nursing home, for what-
ever reason, you can tell it to:
1. The nursing home administrator.
2. Your local Social Security office. It functions as a clearing

house for complaints about all nursing homes, whether or not they receive Government funds.

3. The patient's caseworker or the county welfare office if the patient is covered by Medicaid.
4. The State Medicaid Agency if the home is certified for that program.
5. The State Health Department and the State licensing authority.
6. The Nursing Home Ombudsman if such an office has been established in your community or your State or Area Office on Aging which is responsible for Ombudsman activities.
7. The State board responsible for licensing nursing home administrators. (Get address information from the welfare department.)
8. Your Congressman and Senators. (Address Congressmen at House of Representatives, Washington, D.C. 20515; Senators at United States Senate, Washington, D.C. 20510.)
9. Your State and local elected representatives.
10. The Joint Commission on Accreditation of Hospitals (875 North Michigan Avenue, Chicago, Illinois 60611) if the home has a JCAH certificate.
11. The American Health Care Association (1200 15th Street, NW, Washington, D.C. 20005) if the home is a member.
12. The American Association of Homes for the Aging (529 Fourteenth Street, NW, Washington, D.C. 20004) if the home is a member.
13. The American College of Nursing Home Administrators (Suite 409. The Eig Building, 8641 Colesville Road, Silver Spring, Maryland 20910) if the administrator is a member.
14. Your local Better Business Bureau and Chamber of Commerce.
15. Your local hospital association and medical society.
16. A reputable lawyer or legal aid society.

A Healthy Frame of Reference

We believe that it is worthwhile to list briefly the principles of the overall approach toward the aging and their problems followed throughout this book. The approach has been distilled into nine principles that can help you in your relationship with your elderly parents.

I. *The very fact that your parents have survived into their seventies and eighties means that they still have many physical and emotional strengths.*

Living to an old age is more than pure chance. To a great degree it requires a strong physical constitution and the emotional resources to cope with the problems of living. Too often, middle-aged people lose sight of that. They become preoccupied with their parents' arthritis, dizzy spells, or shuffling walk. A father tends to be seen as a handful of vulnerabilities and illnesses. This is partially due to the influence of the medical profession, whose effectiveness requires it to focus upon problems that demand treatment.

But your parents are more than just a list of pathologies. Not only do middle-aged children subject themselves to a good deal of anguish when they see their parents in a bad way, but aging parents also can become demoralized if they are led to accept this view of themselves.

It is most important always to search out and try to build upon the strengths that remain. Most losses are a matter of degree. Arthritis may prevent Dad from going on fishing trips with his buddies as he used to do every summer. But he can still have the pleasure of company and recreation by playing chess or attending public lectures and concerts.

Recall the analogy of probing a slice of Swiss cheese by poking only through the holes and concluding there is no substance at all. The most helpful attitude is one that knows there is material to work with, and that another probe will surely find it.

II. *The new illnesses and weaknesses are continuously brought to your parents' attention.*

Some parents will never admit to their children that they are bothered by physical problems. If pushed, they may still insist that they are not inconvenienced in the least. Others will constantly complain to their children and anyone else who will listen. No matter what public attitude a mother assumes, changes that come about in old age are constant private inner reminders that she is deteriorating and inching closer to death. Although an elderly person can adapt to shortness of breath by taking things slower, it is still a change that makes itself known several times a day. This can be frightening as well as depressing.

III. *Your parents' physical and emotional health is not going to improve in the long run. It is going to deteriorate.*

This is a painful fact of life we would change promptly were it possible. It is mentioned here neither to frighten you nor to prepare you for your parents' imminent death. This concept in no way contradicts the usefulness and importance of searching out your parents' strengths.

Some sons and daughters hold on first to the wish and then to the expectation that their father's memory, hearing, or diabetes will mend and that the health problems will disappear. But these changes are beyond your parents' control. They will feel that they and their bodies have failed a test that could never have been passed if you continuoualy communicate your disappointment, for example, that a parent's hearing "failed" to get better in the last year.

Accepting this principle should free you to set realistic goals. What is best for Dad can then mean helping him function at his current level of ability for as long as possible. It becomes a real and genuine victory for everyone when you can keep your father functioning in his apartment for an extra few days, months, or years. Those of us who have worked professionally with the aged know that *major* improvements in functioning are rarely, if ever, achieved. A significant achievement for elderly people is to be able to say that this week was as good as last week. Slowing down the inevitable decline is a more realistic goal than wishfully striving for unattainable improvement.

IV. *A general understanding of the inevitable changes at work during old age is an essential element in the adult parent-child relationship.*

Some of the ways in which the elderly cope with their physical and emotional needs and fears may appear strange to their children. As parents of a newborn, you made it your business to have some comprehension of the stages of child development. You learned that an infant's crying did not necessarily mean he or she had to be rushed to the hospital. So, too, should you have some idea of why your aging parents behave as they do.

Parents may complain about loneliness and isolation. Usually this problem can be alleviated. Parents may also complain about diminishing eyesight. Ways can be found to compensate for the loss, but on the whole *that* kind of loss must be accepted.

An old myth would have it that old people cannot benefit from psychiatric care. The truth is that elderly women and men with no prior history of psychiatric disorder who suddenly become depressed after the death of a spouse or a move of their children to another part of the country may profit a great deal from therapy. Often, after a few sessions in which they can discuss their feelings, they will dramatically improve. Parents who have successfully handled a lifetime of responsibility and crisis remain pretty well equipped to face the difficulties of aging.

On the other hand, aging parents who have been depressed and bitter throughout their lives are not likely to respond so well. A working knowledge of what aging is can equip you to make the proper distinctions.

V. *Your parents' old habits are not going to change but will probably become more pronounced.*

One of the more curious aspects of the role reversal that can take place when a parent becomes dependent is the temptation the son or daughter may feel to do more than meet the parent's limited needs. A son, throughout most of his life, may have dutifully listened to his father tell him how to dress, what sort of women he ought to date, and what career he ought to pursue. During this time the son probably had to keep his feelings about his father's smelly cigar, dirty room, and drinking habits to himself.

As the elderly man begins to lean on his son, asking for advice and consolation in a way he never did before, the younger man may suddenly become overly self-confident. Unconsciously the son's line of reasoning might run more or less like this: "Now that I am taking care of you, I have the right, and even the responsibility, to mold and shape your character just as you once did mine. Finally I can get you to stop smoking that awful stogie, to clean up your room, and to cut down on your consumption of beer."

The truth is, though, that a father's personal habits are a firm and unyielding part of him. No matter how insistent his son becomes, Dad will not give up his few six-packs of beer a week. No matter how annoying the younger man finds all this, he will simply have to adjust as best he can. He does not have the right to ask his father to modify his life-style and give up some of the few gratifications still available to him. Since the habits came out of a more healthy and prosperous time, they often serve as therapeutic reminders of a life that was satisfying and comfortable. They ought therefore to be preserved.

VI. *The aged suffer a great deal emotionally and physically when they face dramatic changes. Consider those solutions for your parents' infirmities that preserve their daily routines as much as possible.*

This concept is most crucial. We take for granted our own ability to carry out our daily routines. An elderly parent often cannot do that. A mother begins to find she is unable to prepare her own meals or handle housekeeping chores as she has done for the last fifty years. These new limitations undoubtedly cause a great deal of anxiety for many reasons. One of the most pressing is that it pits her in a daily struggle against the total collapse of her capacity to function in the world.

Change, for an elderly parent, has a much different meaning than it does for us. For a seventy- or eighty-year-old, it does not imply novelty or an opportunity for stimulation and growth. It means another piece of one's world and of one's old life has crumbled or been destroyed.

In a less conscious way many middle-aged sons and daughters will connect their own feelings about change with the traditional American belief that "more is better." As a result they will often, with the best of intentions, provide a declining parent with as many services as possible. Instead of hiring a cleaning woman to come into a parent's home once a week, for example, they will relocate a mother in a nursing home. There people will clean up after her and also feed her, clothe her, and supply her with therapies of all sorts. Not only does such a mother not need those extra services, but the strain of the move and the other changes pressed upon her often speeds up her decline and may induce her early death.

To best help your parents and prolong their lives, you must isolate and focus upon their particular problems or hurts. Patching what needs to be patched and leaving the rest alone will minimize the upsetting and frightening effects your parents' difficulties already have upon them.

The most informed social and governmental agencies advocate a concept known as minimal intervention in the normal routines of aged persons. The families of the aged may at first resent this. They feel it is done only because an agency is either not interested in helping the elderly or else trying to serve the largest number of people with the least amount of expenditure. There are solid research findings, however, that back up the wisdom of this approach. Only a small percentage of the aged require massive care. In this instance what is least expensive is also what is least costly to parents, both physically and emotionally.

VII. *Prolong the independent functioning of your parents by whatever combination of means is necessary. Put off the time when they become a burden to you, to themselves, and to society. Familiarize yourself with and make use of all the available community and neighborhood resources.*

At first this principle may appear to be a corollary of the preceding one. It is really a shorthand statement of what your overall strategy should be. There may come a time when you first notice that your mother has become forgetful, that she has trouble getting around on her own, or that her complaints are overwhelming you. Under these circumstances many children are tempted to respond by introducing drastic measures to solve the problem, such as moving a parent to a nursing home. But that step should be considered only as a *last* resort. Nursing homes can mean a new set of problems far more serious than the ones they were supposed to overcome.

Children should not be expected to be nor expect themselves to be the only ones to personally and directly extend their parents' life-style. Your parents' community offers a range of resources that should be investigated and used.

A father may have few friends and come to rely on his son for social outlets. He may retell the younger man the jokes and anecdotes he has been telling for fifty years. It is perfectly reasonable for the son to find this annoying. He can help his father join a group at a neighborhood senior center that will put the father in touch with other elderly people who are unfamiliar with his repertoire. They will probably find him clever, entertaining, and charming.

The point is to search out other people or organizations that can provide emotional support, social contacts, and physical care in as good or in even a better fashion than you can by yourselves.

VIII. *Formulate and set feasible limits to your direct involvement. Learn whether your activities come out of a sincere desire to help or are motivated by feelings of guilt and obligation. Guard against being a martyr.*

Many middle-aged people express their feelings of obligation toward their aging parents as follows: "My parents took care of me when I was a child, and now that they are in need, I must take care of them."

Parental duty is different from filial duty. Aging parents may need assistance, and their children are the first line of resource. But it is essential that the parents continue to be seen as mature adults for their sakes as well as for your own. Equating your duty to them with your duty toward your children cannot help but make your parents childlike in your eyes, and this only increases their need to maintain their sense of competence and independence undiminished. Furthermore, this equation of duty may create multiple resentments between middle-aged children and their own spouses and children, who see such a duty toward the parents as depriving them of their rightful need for attention.

If your desire to help is genuine, by all means respond to it and assist your parents in whatever way you can. But when it comes just from a sense of duty, it comes with a price. You might do your duty better by involving others—friends, relatives, social agencies, neighbors—in creative ways in giving assistance. You can ask, "Who would help my mother if I were not around?" and proceed to enrich and support those whose services are suggested in response to that question.

IX. *There is no right answer or perfect solution to most of these problems. Correctness is a balance between everyone's rightful needs.*

When trying to cope with the problems of aging parents, some children will expect to find solutions that will put their parents on a footing they enjoyed twenty years ago. This simply cannot be accomplished. In dealing with sickness and decline, the available options may all seem unpleasant and unappealing. Often the only choice may be to develop the longest possible list of options and choose among the least unpleasant.

Part of your efforts may well involve asking a neighbor, a coworker, or a friend what he or she has done. But it is important to keep in mind that each parent and each situation is unique. What works for one does not necessarily work for another. Your next-door neighbor may have moved his father into a spare bedroom. He may also have sent his athletic, nonintellectual son to baseball camp for the summer. Your own child may have hated competition and have had only average athletic abilities but may have had a real love for books and the violin. Sending your child to music camp was not for you a defeat or a cause for private feelings of guilt. Deciding that your own parent would be unable to comfortably fit into the routine of your own household and thereby making other arrangements similarly should not create guilt feelings.

Now let's try to draw some conclusions. Keep in mind that a social revolution is slowly and quietly under way in the United States today. The present group of elderly people are the first generation of Americans who can expect to spend fifteen or twenty years of their lives in a stage of life known as old age. Today the aged make up a sizable portion of the general population. Their numbers will be dwarfed, though, in comparison to the percentages of our population that readers of this book and their children will represent when they reach old age. In 1900, people in the United States over sixty-five were a mere 3 million. But the U.S. Bureau of the Census projections indicate that they will number near 30 million by the year 2000. In other words, the needs, hazards, and life-styles that go along with old age are now a permanent element of our society.

Throughout *The Other Generation Gap* we have discussed fresh personal standards and approaches to these problems in terms of your parents. But these guidelines must inevitably be applied on a national scale. That is the surest and perhaps the only way to guarantee for the elderly of today and tomorrow the quality of life to which they are entitled. Every middle-aged person who has struggled with the difficulties an aged parent encounters knows that the United States has a long way to go before it can reasonably claim to have fulfilled its responsibility toward its senior citizens. This means among other things that the days are quickly coming to an end when elderly parents have no choice but to rely solely on their children for survival. The present generation of the middle-aged, in fact, constitutes the most informed and potentially one of the most powerful forces for social betterment in our history. In this concluding chapter we hope to suggest some ways in which you can hasten changes that are urgently needed.

Some of the groundwork has already been laid. Nationally the level of activity is still meager. But even our efforts today were unknown as recently as ten years ago. Some states have organized and funded departments of aging. The elderly themselves have formed groups such as the Gray Panthers and the American Association of Retired Persons to articulate the problems older people encounter in finding housing and jobs. Today there is also a smattering of politicians who realize that the aged might become a valuable part of their constituency. As a result these politicians have proposed and passed legislation designed to meet the needs of their older voters. Some painful aspects of old age such as physical infirmities and the deaths of a spouse and friends cannot be changed. But out-of-date social restrictions can be amended. This includes raising the mandatory retirement age from sixty-five to seventy, increasing Social Security benefits, placing a ceiling on medical fees, instituting discounts on public transportation, and providing incentives for owners of grocery stores, movie houses, and restaurants to offer special discounts to the aged. Politicians prove to be a sensitive group when it comes to keeping themselves in office. You can help refine their sensitivity by following your representatives' stands on such issues as housing and medical care. The elderly need services even more than they need cash. By sending telegrams in support of good programs and by voting against officials who are indifferent to these measures, you can increase your government's general level of effectiveness.

Your goal should be to make sure that your own community and the one where your parents live have a range of services and programs that enable the aged to extend their independence for months and years. This is not going to happen, though, if you merely wait for your senators to take note of local needs and allow them to respond slowly on needed legislation. It is just as self-defeating to wait until your parents can no longer prepare their own meals before you support a community lunch program. Most communities do not offer many or even some of the services that are needed. By phoning your local Area Agency On Aging, you can find out just what is available now. It can be discouraging, at first, to learn that the only day center for senior citizens is on the other side of town. If, for example, there is no legal aid service for the elderly in the area, many people simply shrug their shoulders and feel that they are out of luck.

The best way to get these programs organized and launched is to work through local social service agencies, such as a YMCA, community centers, churches, synagogues, and hospitals. As a rule, these places do not initiate a series of indispensable services on their own. Instead they respond to the requests, efforts, and demands of the citizens in their area. The federal government often provides funds for such projects as the home-delivered meals program. But guidelines must be followed in order to obtain federal grants. They include writing a proposal, staffing a service with volunteers, and supervising the program through an advisory board whose members are drawn from the community.

To become an effective instrument for change, you might begin by sounding out your neighbors and friends to see if they have concerns similar to your own. Getting them together to write a letter, sign a petition, or attend a preliminary meeting at a social agency constitutes a major first step.

There is one agency that might well serve as a model for how services can best be delivered to the elderly. The Council for Jewish Elderly in Chicago has earned national recognition in a short period of time. Professionals in the field of gerontology as well as government officials have traveled from all parts of the country to see firsthand how this agency's approach has succeeded. A summary description of the council's philosophy and programs may serve to illustrate the directions your own efforts might take.

The strategy of the agency differs from that of a private nursing home, which usually supplies all the services an aged person might need under one roof. Such services include food, medical care, shelter, recreation, and opportunities to socialize. But people who want these resources must sell their homes or cancel their leases and relocate into an institution.

The Council, on the other hand, extends its "one roof" over the community in which the elderly at present live. Its board and staff have taken the position that the elderly are entitled to everything they require to ensure their emotional and physical well-being. They have therefore set about to coordinate a range of services flexible enough to handle all but the most serious and specialized problems. The elderly need resources within walking distance of their homes. The Council therefore has established local storefront or neighborhood centers for the elderly. The aged can walk in on an informal basis to enjoy coffee and conversation with friends. They have the opportunity to sit alone and read the paper, make new friends, or, if they wish, to participate in meaningful social activities each morning and afternoon. The staff at the centers is familiar with most of the elderly in the neighborhood. They know where they live and what their quirks, skills, and needs are. Teams of two, composed of a young college graduate and a senior citizen, have gone door to door in an effort to reach out to the aged in the community and explain what the council is, what it has to offer, and what other community services exist for the aged. The team members have also called on local merchants to educate them about the problems and peculiarities of the aged. As a result a local bank permits the Council to set up a table in the lobby in order to explain governmental financial resources to which the elderly may be entitled, a grocery store runs special discounts for the elderly, and a restaurant offers "specials" for meals at certain hours. The local butcher has agreed to notify the Council if he notices that a regular customer has not been seen for some time. In response, a staff member then checks to see if the elderly person is still alive and well.

The Council has several groupings of personnel who provide a variety of evaluation and treatment services. Among these are social workers who provide referral service and advice on day-to-day problems. A lawyer is available for legal service and advice.

An evaluation team that may include a nurse, a doctor, a psychiatrist, and a social worker can provide a comprehensive assessment of an elderly client's emotional and physical health. These professionals can also offer counseling services for personal and family problems.

For elderly people who can still get out and about, the Council offers a lunch program. For the homebound there is a home-delivered meals program. The Council coordinates the efforts of volunteers who deliver meals, assist in personal care, and serve as friendly visitors. In addition, the Council has cars and vans that provide escort service—door to door or along a prearranged route—to medical clinics and doctors' offices, synagogues, and special social programs.

Registered nurses are also employed to make house visits for the purpose of evaluating elderly persons' medical status; to supervise medication; and to aid clients in their getting full service from hospitals, clinics, and physicians. Other staff are available to provide shopping assistance, housekeeping help, bathing help, and other personal services.

Finally, the Council offers a range of living options for persons at various levels of functioning ability. There are several apartment complexes with subsidized apartments at moderate rentals for the fully independent elderly. There are several group living homes where somewhat more dependent people have apartments that, while private, are designed to allow for regular interaction with neighbors. Common recreation areas, jointly prepared communal meals and regularly available staff supervision all enable even those more dependent folks to live in a non-institutional setting. There is even a home-sharing program which works to find suitable matches for elderly clients—other older persons or, often, student-types or others who, with the agency's help, can learn to live together and share both the expense and the daily routines. And, of course, there are those who require 24-hour per day nursing care and the Council has its carefully staffed and equipped nursing home.

It would probably be unrealistic for you to attempt the task of spearheading a drive to create *all* these services in your community. The crucial element, though, is flexibility. This means that you should try to provide as many options to the elderly as possible. A church that runs the proverbial Tuesday evening bingo game, for example, may attract the same two dozen people week after week. Those who attend may say that their social needs have been well met. For thousands of other elderly in the community, though, including perhaps your own parents, bingo is of no interest whatsoever. The general social needs of the population then have been left unfulfilled. The ultimate goal can only be attained gradually. A hospital, for example, may first establish a regular pickup and drop-off service, and later it might be prodded into supplying an information and referral service.

Some middle-aged people are able to channel their concern for the dilemmas of the aging through the wholehearted assistance they give to their own parents. But others—perhaps those whose parents have died or whose relationship with their parents is limited—may find that to improve the conditions of elderly people they may never even meet is an expression of compassion that gives an equal sense of fulfillment.

There is a final way for readers of this book to make constructive use of the experience and insights they may have gained or will gain in dealing with their elderly parents. And that is by rationally preparing for your own old age. Many of the difficulties your parents face and many of the burdens they pose for you are hardly of their own making. Researchers who study the aged have discovered in interviews, especially with persons in their eighties and nineties, a common response: "I never expected to live so long."

As previously stated, the current generation of elderly are the first to survive in large numbers into their seventies and eighties. As a result they have found themselves forced to play what social scientists refer to as "roleless roles." They stepped, in other words, into a cultural limbo as they neared the age of seventy. The societal resources we have discussed or proposed in the last few chapters did not exist then, nor was there in existence an overall understanding of or strategy for the problems of aging.

Middle-aged people in their forties, fifties, and sixties are determined that they are not going to be like their parents when they grow old. Fortunately, our middle-aged readers do not have to find themselves in this position, but it will take hard work and planning to accomplish that objective. A group of social scientists from the University of Chicago published the results of their efforts to project the characteristics and needs of aged people as they are likely to be in the year 2000. Some of these projections are based upon what characterizes today's forty- and fifty-year-olds, since they will be the aged of the year 2000.

As a group, today's middle-aged are inherently different from previous generations in basic ways. They are more socially active and aware, they are more articulate and influential politically, they are better educated, and they have more financial resources than did their parents. This means that they are far more likely to demand and receive new social services that conform to their past life-style. Well-educated aged people are less likely to be satisfied with a daily routine consisting of card games and long chats on park benches. They will want more stimulating activities and more social options because their interests are wider ranging. The University of Chicago researchers predict that this will mean that some people will opt for earlier retirement in pursuit of meaningful leisure activities, while others will return to school or retrain for other careers. Communities will have to create a dignified, useful role for their elderly and find meaningful ways to take advantage of their skills.

The primary responsibility for achieving an enriched old age, however, is still going to fall upon the individual. In the past the efforts most people made toward a planned retirement, if any at all were made, were in relation to financial concerns. That is, they allowed the government to deduct a portion of their salary for Social Security. They may have belonged to a pension plan and perhaps kept up a portfolio of investments. They had a vague awareness that when they no longer worked, they would still receive some sort of income.

Important as financial security is, though, in and of itself it will not equip you to enjoy the rewards of old age. What will do so is an awareness of the concepts we have discussed for coping with your elderly parents' problems.

Old age may seem a long way off, but the time to start preparing for it is now. Just as your parents may have begun to turn to you for help when you were struggling with the problems of middle age, so, too, will your own children have their hands full when *you* begin to decline. (Yes, it is going to happen to you just as it has to your mother and father.) The problems and inner conflicts you face in trying to be a concerned son or daughter may well run through your children's minds one day. We have already indicated how much the problems of growing old have their origins in the increased deterioration of the body, and you have much more knowledge of the destructive effects on life of nicotine, narcotics, cholesterol, pollution, alcohol, and radiation than your parents ever did.

It makes good sense to cut back on cigarettes, alcohol, and other sources of abuse inflicted upon your body. Perhaps your mother did not put herself on a regimen of regular medical examinations and, as a result, contracted an illness that shortened her life. You can avoid that tragedy by choosing a physician today whom you can depend upon long into the future, when your needs will be greater.

As you enter your late sixties and early seventies, many of the physical declines we have discussed may affect you. These changes may be less frightening and disturbing if you realize how normal they are and know that the physical substitutes we urged your parents to employ will also serve you in good stead.

Now is the time to take a hard look at what your present skills and interests are and to think about the ways in which you might use and build upon these strengths in the years to come. We have stressed that in many cases a total dependence upon one's children can be destructive for both parties. An independent life-style is normally the most fullfilling one. Your strategy for your own old age should be to prolong your autonomy in every possible way. If you are able to anticipate the potential and painful losses of a job, friends, income, and spouse, you will be in a much better position to cope through finding substitutes. Just as you may become aware of all your community has to offer your parents, so, too, should you eventually make use of these services yourselves. The senior center you have guided your father toward may one day be a valuable resource for you as well.

The key to successfully coping with aging, whether that of your parents or yourself, is to search out the remaining strengths and build upon them. You know more than you think you do, and in the last analysis it may well be that your generation will be the first to demonstrate to all those that follow it just how broad and solid that foundation truly is.

Appendix

This section is divided into two parts. First is a list of books that have been written especially for the children of aging parents. Included also are other readings that pertain to the elderly in general and may address particular problems which you may be facing. Most of these books have been written with the general public in mind and may most likely be found in your local public library. Many of these books contain additional bibliographies which may give you added information sources. In addition, many contain appendices which contain extensive lists of national, state, and local resources.

The second part of this appendix contains a listing of some of the most important resources available to you to support your involvement with your parents. They are, primarily, useful starting points from which you may be able to learn of a specific, local resource in your own or in your parents' own community. The rapid growth of the aging population has been accompanied by an increase in services to older persons and their families. New programs are constantly being developed and may take a while to become known to those in need. Many of the agencies and organizations listed below have, as one of their main functions, the updating of services and the provision of information on resources. They are in the business of giving information, sending out material, responding to questions, making referrals, etc. Your contacting them to learn if there is a day-care center near your mother's home, or to locate a physician who specializes in care of the elderly, or to locate a support group for caretakers of an Alzheimer's patient will reduce the possibility of aimless searching through telephone directories as well as allow these agencies to give the service they wish to give.

SOME USEFUL READINGS

Bumagin, V. and Hirn, K. *Aging Is a Family Affair.* New York: Crowell Publ., 1979.

Burdman, G.M. *Healthful Aging.* Englewood Cliffs, N.J.: Prentice Hall, 1986.

Circirelli, V. *Helping Elderly Parents: The Role of Adult Children.* Boston: Auburn House, 1981.

Cohler, B. and Grunebaum, H. *Mothers, Grandmothers, and Daughters.* New York: John Wiley & Sons, 1981.

Fischman, J. "The Mystery of Alzheimer's," *Psychology Today* (1984).

Ebersole, P.P. and Hess, P. *Toward Healthy Aging.* St. Louis: C.V. Mosby Co., 1981.

Flax, C.C. and Ubell, E. *Mother, Father, You: The Adult's Guide for Getting Along Great With Parents and In-Laws.* New York: Walden Books, 1980.

Grollman, E.A. *When Your Loved One is Dying.* Boston: Beacon Press, 1980.

Gelfand, D.E. and Olsen, J.K. *The Aging Network: Programs and Services.* New York: Springer, 1980.

Galton, Lawrence. *Don't Give Up On An Aging Parent.* New York: Crown Pub., 1975.

Holmes, M.B. and Homes, D. *Handbook of Human Services for Older Persons.* New York: Human Sciences Press, 1979.

Huttman, E.D. *Social Services for the Elderly.* New York: The Free Press, 1985.

Johnson, E.S. and Williamson, J.B. *The Social Problems of Aging.* New York: Holt, Rinehart and Winston, 1980.

Kart, C.S. *The Realities of Aging.* Boston: Allyn and Bacon, 1985.

Mace, M. and Robins, P. *The 36 Hour Day.* Baltimore: Johns Hopkins Univ. Press, 1981. (Caring for the Alzheimer's Patient)

Maclean, Helene. *Caring for Your Parents: A Sourcebook of Options and Solutions for Both Generations.* Garden City, N.Y.: Doubleday, 1987.

Otten, J. and Shelly, F. *When Your Parents Grow Old.* New York: Funk and Wagnalls, 1976.

Ragan, P. *Aging Parents.* Los Angeles: USC Press, 1979.

Schwartz, A. *Survival Handbook for Children of Aging Parents.* Chicago: Follett, 1977.

Silverstone, B. and Hymen, H.K. *You and Your Aging Parent. The Modern Family's Guide to Emotional, Physical and Financial Problems.* New York: Pantheon Books, 1982.

Finally, there is a new (begun in 1987) monthly newsletter, *The Later Years*, prepared especially for adults with aging parents. It offers information on aging, family relationships, reports on research and advice on dealing with many concerns. To subscribe, you may write:

> *The Later Years*
> Dunn & Hargitt Publ.
> 22 N. Second Street
> Lafayette, Indiana 47902
> (317) 423-2624
>
> Cost (1987) $30.00 per year

SOME USEFUL RESOURCES

Below we have listed only a few of the many organizations, agencies, and programs that offer services to older persons. For a much fuller and complete listing of special programs in virtually all states in the United States, we suggest the following:

> National Association of State Units on Aging, *Family Supports: State Strategies for Enhancement*, Jan., 1987, 139 pages.

> and

> Maclean, Helene. *Caring for your Parents: A Sourcebook of Options and Solutions for Both Generations.* Garden City, N.Y.: Doubleday and Co., 1987.*

*The authors are grateful to Helene Maclean for her effort in developing a most comprehensive list of resources. This appendix is derived in great measure from her work.

For General Information and Referral

In nearly every state, there will be at least 2 governmental agencies responsible for services to the aged which provide information to families about those services.

First there is the State Department on Aging. This is usually a unit within the State's Department of Health, Human Services, or something similar. But they may go by different names, such as:

> Alabama Commission on Aging
> Older Alaskans Commission
> Arizona Aging and Adult Administration
> Arkansas Division of Aging and Adult Services
> California Department of Aging
> Washington D.C. Office on Aging
> Louisiana Office of Elderly Affairs
> Massachusetts Executive Office of Elder Affairs
> Michigan Office of Service to the Aging
> Minnesota Board on Aging
> Mississippi Council on Aging

We can't list them all, but you get the idea. Though each state uses its own name, it's a state government agency and you can reach it in the blue pages of your telephone directory.

The second type of resource which offers information and referral is the Area Agency on Aging. These agencies are mandated and funded under the Older Americans Act by the federal government. The Area Agency may be administered by the state, county, or city and will usually cover a specific limited geographic area. Workers in the agency office are equipped with up-to-date lists of resources for older persons located in the area and they can advise you regarding meals, housing, health care, and the like. If you cannot seem to locate, through your telephone directory, the Area Agency which services your parent's community, you may contact the state agency or write:

> The National Association of Area Agencies on Aging
> 600 Maryland Ave., S.W., Washington D.C. 20024

Remember, your local Area Agency on Aging and your State

Department on Aging (or equivalent) is the best resource for finding services in your local area.

Below we have identified a number of the most frequently needed resources, and provide the name and location of an organization (usually a national center) that specializes in a particular problem.

Finding A Doctor

If you need to locate a physician who specializes in the aged, you can obtain a list of members of the:

American Geriatrics Society
10 Columbus Circle
New York, New York 10019

If you need to locate a geriatric psychiatrist, a list of over 300 arranged according to region of the country is available from:

American Association for Geriatric Psychiatry
230 N. Michigan Avenue
Chicago, Illinois 60601

Help With Alzheimer's

If you wish to obtain information on Alzheimer's Disease, to find out about a support group for caregivers, or to locate the chapter (there are over 125 in 44 states and Washington, D.C.) nearest you, write:

Alzheimer's Disease and Related Disorders Association
360 N. Michigan Avenue, Suite 601
Chicago, Illinois 60601
(312) 853-3060

Note that "Related Disorders" is part of the association's title. Your parent may have a serious mental condition that requires considerable care and effort on your part, and it may not be diagnosed as Alzheimer's. Nevertheless, the association can be of help and some of their services are equally useful for conditions other than Alzheimer's.

Help With Home Care

Many adult children are able to maintain their parent(s) at home with the help of a trained home care specialist. Many communities have developed agencies which train, supervise, and place home health workers, homemakers, and others in the homes of older persons who can manage independently with this sort of assistance. Several pamphlets are available that can inform one of these resources. Write for:

> "Home Care"—free from
> The National Association of Home Care
> 519 C Street, N.E., Staunton Park,
> Washington, D.C. 20202
> (202) 547-7424

> or

> "Information on Home Health Services"—free from
> AARP Fulfillment
> Box 2400
> Long Beach, Calif. 90801

> or

> "All About Home Care: A Consumer's Guide"—$2.00 from
> The National Home Caring Council
> 235 Park Ave. South
> New York, N.Y. 10003

You may wish the services of a Home Health Aide and can obtain information on these services from:

> National Council for Homemakers
> Home Health Aide Service
> 1790 Broadway
> New York, N.Y. 10019

Self Help Groups

You may obtain a list of groups that discuss family issues which meet in your area by writing:

> The National Self-Help Clearing House
> CUNY Graduate Center
> 33 W. 42nd St., Room 1222
> New York, N.Y. 10036

Another organization that helps establish groups and provides referral and reading material is:

> Children of Aging Parents
> 2761 Trenton Road
> Levittown, Pennsylvania 19056
> (215) 946-4012

> or

> The National Support Center for Children of the Aging
> Box 245
> Swarthmore, Pennsylvania 19081
> (215) 544-3605

Help With Bereavement

The AARP sponsors a special service for widowed persons. They have a directory of services as well as a guide entitled "On Being Alone."

To obtain information on programs, write:

> Widowed Persons Services
> American Association of Retired Persons
> 1909 K Street, N.W.
> Washington, D.C. 20049

To get the guide "On Being Alone," write:

> AARP Widowed Persons Service
> Box 199
> Long Beach, Calif. 90801

Index

Gender differences. *See* Men; Women

General practitioner, 85–86

Generation gap: between adult children and aging parents, 7–13, 25–27; defined, 4; midlife crisis and, 25–27

Genontology, 6

Glare, 55, 56

Golden Agers clubs, 145, 155

Grab rails, 77, 208

Grandchildren, 115–16, 137

Grant, Cary, 44, 47

Gray hair, 43–46

Gray Panthers, 226

Grief: and death of a spouse, 149–56; depression and, 100–1; over loss of driver's license, 79; memories and, 108–9; over parents' loss of independence, 201

Group activities, 155

Group living homes, 229

Guardians, 184–85

Guilt: depression and, 100, 102; in children of the elderly, 7, 26, 33, 119, 120, 124, 128, 148, 224; and reminiscence in old age, 106; survivor's, 158; over thoughts of parent's death, 33

Habits, 221–22

Hair, graying, 43–46

Halfway houses, 197

Hallucinations, 97

Handiwork, 144–45

Health Care Financing Administration, 212–13

Health-care system, inadequacy of, 83–84

Hearing aids: adjustment to, 66; fitting for, 66; humming sound from, 65; people who shut off, 67; psychological uneasiness with, 63, 65, 67; stigma attached to, 65; swindles in sales of, 65; unrealistic expectations for, 63, 65; use and limitations of, 63–65

Hearing loss: aging process and, 59–67; autonomy and, 66–67; compensation for, 63–66, 67; emotional responses to, 66–67; gradual nature of, 59–60; identifying, 66; mistaken for mental deterioration, 62–63; not forcing admission of, 66–67; practical problems due to, 60–63, 67; principles behind, 64; reversible, 60; total, 59, 64

Heart, sexual activity and health of, 49

Hobbies and activities, 22

Holidays, 108, 202

Home delivered meals program, 176, 229

Home-sharing program, 229–30

Hostility, 192

House calls, 84

Housing options, 163–64, 180, 229–30. *See also* Institutionalization; Nursing homes; Parents moving in with adult children